THUS SPOKE
ZARATHUSTRA

THUS SPOKE
ZARATHUSTRA

A BOOK FOR ALL AND NONE

FRIEDRICH NIETZSCHE

TRANSLATED AND WITH A PREFACE BY
WALTER KAUFMANN

THE MODERN LIBRARY
NEW YORK

LIBRARY OF CONGRESS CATALOGING-IN-PUBLICATION DATA
Nietzsche, Friedrich Wilhelm, 1844–1900.
[Also sprach Zarathustra. English]
Thus spoke Zarathustra: a book for all and none/translated and with a
preface by Walter Kaufmann.
p.   cm.
ISBN 0-679-60175-9
1. Superman. 2. Philosophy. I. Kaufmann, Walter Arnold. II. Title.
B3313.A43E5   1995
193—dc20   95-15383

Modern Library website address: www.modernlibrary.com

Printed in the United States of America on acid-free paper

12 14 16 18 19 17 15 13 11

FRIEDRICH NIETZSCHE

Friedrich Nietzsche was born in Röcken, a small town in the Prussian province of Saxony, on October 15, 1844, into circumstances that offer a striking contrast to his later thought. Ironically, the philosopher who rejected religion and coined the phrase "God is dead" was descended from a line of respected clergymen. His father, Ludwig, was a Lutheran minister who had tutored the children of Prussian royalty. Following the untimely death of Ludwig Nietzsche in 1849 the family resettled in Naumburg. There Nietzsche grew up as the only male in a household comprising his mother, sister, maternal grandmother, and two maiden aunts. Nicknamed "the little pastor," he was a pious, fearfully well-behaved child who walked home from the local gymnasium at a measured pace, even in a sudden downpour, because school rules called for decorous conduct in the streets. Nietzsche completed his secondary education at the exacting boarding school of Pforta. A brilliant student, he received rigorous training in Latin, Greek, and German. In 1864 the young man entered the University of Bonn to study theology and classical philology. A year later, however, he abandoned theology and transferred to the University of Leipzig to pursue a doctorate in philology. At Leipzig Nietzsche became an ardent admirer of philosopher Arthur Schopenhauer, whose work he accidentally discovered in a secondhand bookstore, and the composer Richard Wagner, whom he met in 1868 and came to regard as a second father.

In 1869, at the age of twenty-four, Nietzsche was appointed professor of classical philology at the University of Basel, where he taught for the next ten years. The publication in 1872 of his first major book, *The Birth of Tragedy*, brought him immediate notoriety. Dedicated to Wagner, it exploded the nineteenth-century conception of Greek culture and sounded themes later developed by twentieth-century philosophers, psychoanalysts, and novelists. Nietzsche's next work, four essays collectively titled *Untimely Meditations* (1873–76), focused on contemporary issues and criticism. Two attacked German "cultural philistinism" and challenged the value of historical knowledge, while tributes to Schopenhauer and Wagner were at once reflections on philosophy and art.

"[I am] a man who wishes nothing more than daily to lose some reassuring belief, who seeks and finds his happiness in this daily greater liberation of the mind," wrote Nietzsche during this period. "It may be that I want to be even more of a freethinker than I can be." Indeed, *Human All-too-Human* (1878) represented an entirely new direction in his thought. Written in an aphoristic style perfectly suited to Nietzsche's multifaceted, iconoclastic beliefs, the work contains piercing observations that lay bare the hidden motivations underlying many aspects of human behavior. (Freud remarked that Nietzsche's "premonitions and insights often agree in the most amazing manner with the laborious results of psychoanalysis.") Subtitled "A Book for Free Spirits," *Human All-too-Human* also signaled the beginning of Nietzsche's break with Wagner. Two sequels, *Mixed Opinions and Maxims* (1879) and *The Wanderer and His Shadow* (1880), presented further investigations of psychological phenomena.

Nietzsche resigned from his professorship in 1879 owing to chronic ill health; he had long suffered from paralyzing migraine headaches, and brief military service in the Franco-Prussian War left him shattered. Afterward he existed on a university pension as an unassuming gentleman lodger at resorts in Italy, France, and Switzerland. Yet his intellectual revolt continued unabated over the next decade. Though almost constantly in pain he produced, to quote Thomas Mann, "stylistically dazzling books—works sparkling with audacious insults to his age, venturing into more and more radical psychology, radiating a more and more glaring white light." In *The Dawn* (1881), another collection of aphorisms, he exposed the prejudices of European morality. *The Gay Science* (1882), which Nietzsche regarded as his most personal book, includes sustained discussions of truth, art, and knowledge.

Then, in 1883 and 1884, Nietzsche published the first three sections of *Thus Spoke Zarathustra;* the fourth part, completed in 1885, did not appear until 1892. Cast as a series of parables about a prophet who proclaims the death of God and challenges mankind to face its destiny, *Zarathustra* is a mine of ideas and perhaps Nietzsche's most popular work. "*Zarathustra* is in a way a document of our time, and it surely has much to do with our own psychological condition," noted Jung. "It is like a dream in its representation of events. It expresses renewal and self-destruction, the death of a god and the birth of a god, the end of an epoch and the beginning of a new one. . . . It is so paradoxical that without the help of the whole equipment of our modern psychology of the unconscious, I would not know how to deal with it."

In his last productive years Nietzsche turned out a number of landmark works. *Beyond Good and Evil,* subtitled "Prelude to a Philosophy of the Future," appeared in 1886. The epitome of his prophetic, independent thought, it remains "one of the great books of the nineteenth century, indeed of any century," according to Walter Kaufmann. Nietzsche's sober, single-minded study on ethics, *On the Genealogy of Morals* (1887), was followed by *The Case of*

Wagner (1888), a brilliantly sarcastic polemic that endures as one of his wittiest books. In 1888 he wrote *The Antichrist*, a final assault on institutional Christianity, and compiled *Nietzsche contra Wagner*, a brief selection of passages from earlier works. (Both were brought out in 1895.) *Twilight of the Idols* (1889), a grand declaration of war on many ideas of the age, is a final formulation of Nietzsche's opinions that underscores his inherent optimism.

In January 1889 Nietzsche collapsed on a street in Turin, Italy, and from that moment he rapidly descended into insanity. It is generally agreed that madness was brought on by syphilis, although it is not known when or where he caught the disease. Cared for by his mother and sister, he remained in a condition of mental and physical paralysis until his death in Weimar on August 25, 1900. The following year Nietzsche's sister published *The Will to Power*, which he had abandoned in 1888. *Ecce Homo*, the philosopher's exuberant, passionate analysis of his life and work, came out in 1908.

To Edith Kaufmann

Wenn's etwas gibt, gewalt'ger als das Schicksal,
So ist's der Mut, der's unerschüttert trägt.
—GEIBEL

I am greatly indebted to Hazel and Felix Kaufmann, my wife and my brother, for helpful criticism of my translation.

—W. K.

Contents

Zarathustra is by far Nietzsche's most popular book, but Nietzsche himself never witnessed its success. The first three parts, each composed in about ten days, were at first published separately, and scarcely sold at all. Of Part Four, Nietzsche had only a few copies printed privately; and the first public edition was held up at the last moment in 1891 when his family feared that it would be confiscated on a charge of blasphemy. By then Nietzsche was insane and unaware of what was happening. Part Four appeared in 1892, and it was not confiscated. The first edition of the whole work followed not long after.

Zarathustra is as different from its reputation as its author is different from the widely reproduced busts and pictures commissioned by his sister. Her grandiose conception of the heroic strikes us as childish and has provoked the reaction, understandably enough, that Nietzsche was really a mere *petit rentier*. But perhaps there are more kinds of valor than are dreamed of by most of Nietzsche's admirers and detractors. And the most important single clue to *Zarathustra* is that it is the work of an utterly lonely man.

He is shy, about five-foot-eight, but a little stooped, almost blind, reserved, unaffected, and especially polite; he lives in modest boarding houses in Sils Maria, Nizza, Mentone, Rome, Turin. This is how Stefan Zweig brings him to life for us: "Carefully the myopic man sits down to a table; carefully, the man with the sensitive stomach considers every item on the menu: whether the tea is not too strong, the food not spiced too much, for every mistake in his diet upsets his sensitive digestion, and every transgression in his nourishment wreaks havoc with his quivering nerves for days. No glass of wine, no glass of beer, no alcohol, no coffee at his place, no cigar and no cigarette after his meal, nothing that stimulates, refreshes, or rests him: only the short meager meal and a little urbane, unprofound conversation in a soft voice with an occasional neighbor (as a man speaks who for years has been unused to talking and is afraid of being asked too much).

"And up again into the small, narrow, modest, coldly furnished *chambre garnie*, where innumerable notes, pages, writings, and proofs are piled up on the table, but no flower, no decoration, scarcely a book and rarely a letter. Back in a corner, a heavy and graceless wooden trunk, his only possession, with the two shirts and the other worn suit. Otherwise only books and manuscripts, and on a tray innumerable bottles and jars and potions: against the migraines, which often render him all but senseless for hours, against his stomach cramps, against spasmodic vomiting, against the slothful intestines, and above all the dreadful sedatives against his insomnia, chloral hydrate and Veronal. A frightful arsenal of poisons and drugs, yet the only helpers in the empty silence of this strange room in which he never rests except in brief and artificially conquered sleep. Wrapped in his overcoat and a woolen scarf (for the wretched stove smokes only and does not give warmth), his fingers freezing, his double glasses pressed close to the paper, his hurried hand writes for hours—words the dim eyes can hardly decipher. For hours he sits like this and writes until his eyes burn."

That is the framework, which changes little wherever he is. But his letters seem to reveal another dimension, for at times they are shrill and strange and remind us of his vitriolic remark about Jesus: it is regrettable that no Dostoevski lived near him. Who else could do justice to this weird, paradoxical personality? Yet the clue to these letters, as also to *Zarathustra* and some of the last books, is that they are the work of a thoroughly lonely man. Sometimes they are really less letters than fantastic fragments out of the soul's dialogue with itself. Now pleasant and polite, now such that arrogance is far too mild a word—and yet his feeling of his own importance, painfully pronounced even in some very early letters, was of course not as insane as it must have appeared at times to those to whom he wrote. Resigned that those surrounding him had no idea who he was, and invariably kind to his social and intellectual inferiors, he sometimes felt doubly hurt that those who ought to have understood him really had less respect for him than his most casual acquaintances. Book after book—and either no response, or some kind words, which were far more unkind than any serious criticism, or even good advice, or pity, worst of all. Is it surprising that on rare occasions, when he was sufficiently provoked, we find appeals to his old-fashioned sense of honor, even his brief military service, and at one point the idea that he must challenge a man to a duel with pistols? For that matter, he once wrote a close friend: "The barrel of a pistol is for me at the moment a source of relatively agreeable thoughts."

Then there are his several hasty proposals of marriage, apparently followed by a real sense of relief when the suggestion was refused politely. The proposals may seem quite fantastic, the more so because, except in the case of Lou Salomé, no really deep feelings were involved. But a few times he was desperate enough to grasp at any possibility at all of rescue from the sea of his solitude.

In his letters these dramatic outbursts are relatively exceptional. But the histrionics of *Zarathustra* should be seen in the same light. For impulses that others vent upon their wives or friends, or at a party, perhaps over drinks, Nietzsche had no other outlet. In Nizza, where he wrote Part Three of *Zarathustra,* he met a young man, Dr. Paneth, who had read the published portion and was eager to talk with the author. On December 26, 1883, Paneth wrote home: "There is not a trace of false pathos or the prophet's pose in him, as I had rather feared after his last work. Instead his manner is completely inoffensive and natural. We began a very banal conversation about the climate, living accommodations, and the like. Then he told me, but without the least affectation or conceit, that he always felt himself to have a task and that now, as far as his eyes would permit it, he wanted to get out of himself and work up whatever might be in him."

We might wish that he had taken out his histrionics on Paneth and spared us some of the melodrama in *Zarathustra.* In places, of course, the writing is superb and only a pedant could prefer a drabber style. But often painfully adolescent emotions distract our attention from ideas that we cannot dismiss as immature at all. For that matter, adolescence is not simply immaturity; it also marks a breakdown of communication, a failure in human relations, and generally the first deep taste of solitude. And what we find again and again in *Zarathustra* are the typical emotions with which a boy tries to compensate himself.

Nietzsche's apparent blindness to these faults and his extravagant praise of the book in some of his last works are understandable. His condition had become even more unbearable as time went on; and we should also keep in mind not only the complete failure of the book to elicit any adequate response or understanding, but also the frantic sense of inspiration which had marked the rapid writing of the first three parts. Moreover, others find far lesser obstacles sufficient excuse for creating nothing. Nietzsche had every reason for not writing anything—the doctors, for example, told him not to use his eyes for any length of time, and he often wrote for ten hours at a time—and fashioned work on work, making his suffering and his torments the occasion for new insights.

After all has been said, *Zarathustra* still cries out to be blue-penciled; and if it were more compact, it would be more lucid too. Even so, there are few works to match its wealth of ideas, the abundance of profound suggestions, the epigrams, the wit. What distinguishes *Zarathustra* is the profusion of "sapphires in the mud." But what the book loses artistically and philosophically by never having been critically edited by its author, it gains as a uniquely personal record.

In a passage that is quoted again as the motto of Part Three, Zarathustra asks: "Who among you can laugh and be elevated at the same time?" The fusion of seriousness and satire, pathos and pun, is as characteristic of the message as it is of the style of the book. This modern blend of the sublime and the ridiculous places the work somewhere between the Second Part of *Faust* and Joyce's *Ulysses*—both of which, after all, might also have profited from further editing—and it helps to account for Nietzsche's admiration for Heine.

This overflowing sense of humor, which prefers even a poor joke to no joke at all, runs counter to the popular images of Nietzsche—not only to the grim creation of his sister, but also to the piteous portrait of Stefan Zweig, who was, in this respect, still too much under the influence of Bertram's *Nietzsche: Attempt at a Mythol-*

ogy. Nietzsche had the sense of humor which Stefan George and his minions, very much including Bertram, lacked; and if Zarathustra occasionally excels George's austere prophetic affectation, he soon laughs at his own failings and punctures his pathos, like Heine, whom George hated. The puncture, however, does not give the impression of diffident self-consciousness and a morbid fear of self-betrayal, but rather of that Dionysian exuberance which *Zarathustra* celebrates.

Nietzsche's fate in the English-speaking world has been rather unkind, in spite of, or perhaps even in some measure because of, the ebullient enthusiasm of some of the early English and American Nietzscheans. He has rarely been accorded that perceptive understanding which is relatively common among the French. And when we look back today, one of the main reasons must be sought in the inadequacies of some of the early translations, particularly of *Zarathustra*. For one thing, they completely misrepresent the mood of the original—beginning, but unfortunately not ending, with their many unjustified archaisms, their "thou" and "ye" with the clumsy attendant verb forms, and their whole misguided effort to approximate the King James Bible. As if Zarathustra's attacks on the spirit of gravity and his praise of "light feet" were not among the leitmotifs of the book! In fact, this alone makes the work bearable.

To be sure, *Zarathustra* abounds in allusions to the Bible, most of them highly irreverent, but just these have been missed for the most part by Thomas Common. His version, nevertheless, was considered a sufficient improvement over Alexander Tille's earlier attempt to merit inclusion in the "Authorized English Translation of the Complete Works"; and while some of Common's other efforts were supplanted by slightly better translations, his *Zarathustra* survived, *faute de mieux*. For that matter, the book comes close to being untranslatable. What is one to do with Nietzsche's constant plays on words? Say, *in der rechten Wissen-Gewissenschaft gibt es nichts grosses und nichts kleines*. This can probably be salvaged only for the eye, not for the ear, with "the conscience of science." But then almost anything would be better than Common's "true knowing-knowledge." Such passages, and there are many, make us wonder whether he had little German and less English. More often than not, he either overlooks a play on words or misunderstands it, and in both cases makes nonsense of Nietzsche. What is the point, to give a final example, of Nietzsche's derision of German writing, once "plain language" is substituted for "German"? One can sympathize with the translator, but one cannot understand or discuss Nietzsche on the basis of the versions hitherto available.

The problems encountered in translating *Zarathustra* are tremendous. Where Nietzsche does not deliberately bypass idioms in favor of coinages, he makes fun of them —now by taking them literally, then again by varying them slightly. Here too he is a dedicated enemy of all convention, intent on exposing the stupidity and arbitrariness of custom. This linguistic iconoclasm greatly impressed Christian Morgenstern and helped to inspire his celebrated *Galgenlieder*, in which similar aims are pursued more systematically.

Nietzsche, like Morgenstern a generation later, even creates a new animal when he speaks of *Pöbel-Schwindhunde*. *Windhund* means greyhound but, more to the point, is often used to designate a person without brains or character. Yet *Wind*, the wind, is celebrated in this passage, and so the first part of the animal's name had to be varied to underline the opprobrium. What kind of animal should the translator create? A weathercock is the same sort of person as a *Windhund* (he turns with the wind) and permits the coinage of blether-cock. Hardly a major triumph, but few works of world literature can rival *Zarathustra* in its abundance of coinages, some of them clearly prompted by the feeling that the worst coinage is still better than the best cliché. And this lightheartedness is an essential aspect of Nietzsche.

Many of Nietzsche's plays on words are, of course, extremely suggestive. To give one example among scores, there is his play on *Eheschliessen, Ehebrechen, Ehebiegen, Ehe-lügen,* in section 24 of "Old and New Tablets." Here the old translations did not even try, and it is surely scant compensation when Common gratuitously introduces, elsewhere in the book, "sumpter asses and assesses" or coins "baddest" in a passage in which Nietzsche says "most evil." In fact, Nietzsche devoted one-third of his *Genealogy of Morals* to his distinction between "bad" and "evil."

The poems in *Zarathustra* present a weird blend of passion and whimsy, but the difference between "Oh, everything human is strange" and "O human hubbub, thou wonderful thing!" in the hitherto standard translation is still considerable. Or consider the fate of two perfectly straightforward lines at the end of "The Song of Melancholy": "That I should banned be/From all the trueness!" And two chapters later Common gives us these lines:

> How it, to a dance-girl, like,
> Doth bow and bend and on its haunches bob,
> —One doth it too, when one view'th it long!—

In fact, Common still doth it in the next chapter: "How it bobbeth, the blessed one, the home-returning one, in its purple saddles!"

It may be ungracious, though hardly un-Nietzschean,

to ridicule such faults. But in the English-speaking world, *Zarathrustra* has been read, written about, and discussed for decades on the basis of such travesties, and most criticisms of the style have no relevance whatever to the original. A few thrusts at those who exposed Nietzsche to so many thrusts may therefore be defensible —in defense of Nietzsche.

For that matter, the new translation here offered certainly does not do justice to him either. Probably no translation could; and perhaps the faults of his predecessors are really a comfort to the translator who can ask to have his work compared with theirs as well as with the original. Or is the spirit of *Zarathustra* with its celebration of laughter contagious? After all, most of the plays on words have no ulterior motive whatever. Must we have a justification for laughing?

Much of what is most untranslatable is an expression of that *Übermut* which Nietzsche associates with the *Übermensch:* a lightness of mind, a prankish exuberance —though the term can also designate that overbearing which the Greeks called *hubris.* In any case, such plays on words must be kept in translation: how else is the reader to know which remarks are inspired primarily by the possibility of a pun or a daring rhyme? And robbed of its rapidly shifting style, clothed in archaic solemnity, *Zarathustra* would become a different work—like Faulkner done into the King's English. Nietzsche's writing, too, is occasionally downright bad, but at its best— superb.

The often elusive ideas of the book cannot be explained briefly, apart from the text. The editor's notes, however, which introduce each of the four parts, may facilitate a preliminary orientation, aid the reader in finding passages for which he may be looking, and provide a miniature commentary.

Only one of Zarathustra's notions shall be mentioned here: the eternal recurrence of the same events. In the plot this thought becomes more and more central as the work progresses, yet it is not an afterthought. Nietzsche himself, in *Ecce Homo*, called it "the basic conception of the work" which had struck him in August 1881; and, as a matter of fact, he first formulated it in *The Gay Science*, the book immediately preceding *Zarathustra*. As long as Nietzsche was misunderstood as a Darwinist who expected the improvement of the human race in the course of evolution, this conception was considered a stumbling block, and Nietzsche was gratuitously charged with gross self-contradiction. But Nietzsche himself rejected the evolutionary misinterpretation as the fabrication of "scholarly oxen." And while he was mistaken in believing that the eternal recurrence must be accepted as an ineluctable implication of impartial science, its personal meaning for him is expressed very well in *Ecce Homo*, in the sentence already cited, where he calls it the "highest formula of affirmation which is at all attainable." The eternal recurrence of his solitude and despair and of all the agonies of his tormented body! And yet it was not his own recurrence that he found hardest to accept, but that of the small man too. For the existence of paltriness and pettiness seemed meaningless even after he had succeeded in giving meaning to his own inherently meaningless suffering. Were not his work and his love of his work and his joy in it inseparable from his tortures? And man is capable of standing superhuman suffering if only he feels sure that there is some point and purpose to it, while much less pain will seem intolerable if devoid of meaning.

Zarathustra is not only a mine of ideas but also a major work of literature and a personal triumph.

—WALTER KAUFMANN

THUS SPOKE

ZARATHUSTRA

Thus Spoke Zarathustra: First Part

Prologue: Zarathustra speaks of the death of God and pro-claims the overman. Faith in God is dead as a matter of cultural fact, and any "meaning" of life in the sense of a supernatural purpose is gone. Now it is up to man to give his life meaning by raising himself above the animals and the all-too-human. What else is human nature but a euphemism for inertia, cultural conditioning, and what we are before we make something of ourselves? Our so-called human nature is precisely what we should do well to overcome; and the man who has overcome it Zarathustra calls the overman.

Shaw has popularized the ironic word "superman," which has since become associated with Nietzsche and the comics without ever losing its sarcastic tinge. In the present trans-lation the older term, "overman," has been reinstated: it may help to bring out the close relation between Nietzsche's conceptions of the overman and self-overcoming, and to recapture something of his rhapsodical play on the words "over" and "under," particularly marked throughout the Prologue. Of the many "under" words, the German *unter-gehen* poses the greatest problem of translation: it is the ordinary word for the setting of the sun, and it also means "to perish"; but Nietzsche almost always uses it with the accent on "under"—either by way of echoing another "under" in the same sentence or, more often, by way of contrast with an "over" word, usually overman. Again and again, a smooth idiomatic translation would make nonsense of such passages, and "go under" seemed the least evil. After all, Zarathustra has no compunctions about worse linguistic sins.

"Over" words, some of them coinages, are common in this work, and *Übermensch* has to be understood in its context. *Mensch* means human being as opposed to animal, and what is called for is not a super-brute but a human being who has created for himself that unique

3

position in the cosmos which the Bible considered his divine birthright. The meaning of life is thus found on earth, in *this* life, not as the inevitable outcome of evolution, which might well give us the "last man" instead, but in the few human beings who raise themselves above the all-too-human mass. In the first edition the Prologue had the title "On the Overman and the Last Man." The latter invites comparison with Huxley's *Brave New World* and with Heidegger's famous discussion of *Das Man* in *Sein und Zeit*.

1. *On the Three Metamorphoses:* To become more than an all-too-human animal man must become a creator. But this involves a break with previous norms. Beethoven, for example, creates new norms with his works. Yet this break is constructive only when accomplished not by one who wants to make things easy for himself, but by one who has previously subjected himself to the discipline of tradition. First comes the beast of burden, then the defiant lion, then creation. "Parting from our cause when it triumphs"—as Nietzsche did when Wagner triumphed in Bayreuth.

2. *On the Teachers of Virtue:* Sunny sarcasm. Our traditional virtues consecrate stereotyped mediocrity and make for sound sleep. But where sleep is the goal, life lacks meaning. To bring out the full meaning of the blasphemous final sentence, it may be well to quote from Stefan Zweig's essay, "Friedrich Nietzsche," which is unsurpassed in its brief sketch of Nietzsche's way of life: "No devilish torture is lacking in this dreadful pandemonium of sickness: headaches, deafening, hammering headaches, which knock out the reeling Nietzsche for days and prostrate him on sofa and bed, stomach cramps with bloody vomiting, migraines, fevers, lack of appetite, weariness, hemorrhoids, constipation, chills, night sweat—a gruesome circle. In addition, there are his 'three-quarters blind eyes,' which, at the least exertion, begin immediately to swell and fill with tears and grant the intellectual worker only 'an hour and a half of vision a day.' But Nietzsche despises this hygiene

of his body and works at his desk for ten hours, and for this excess his overheated brain takes revenge with raging headaches and a nervous overcharge; at night, when the body has long become weary, it does not permit itself to be turned off suddenly, but continues to burrow in visions and ideas until it is forcibly knocked out by opiates. But ever greater quantities are needed (in two months Nietzsche uses up fifty grams of chloral hydrate to purchase this handful of sleep); then the stomach refuses to pay so high a price and rebels. And now—vicious circle—spasmodic vomiting, new headaches which require new medicines, an inexorable, insatiable, passionate conflict of the infuriated organs, which throw the thorny ball of suffering to each other as in a mad game. Never a point of rest in this up and down, never an even stretch of contentment or a short month full of comfort and self-forgetfulness." For Nietzsche, sleep was clearly not the end of life. Yet he could well say, "Blessed are the sleepy ones: for they shall soon drop off."

3. *On the Afterworldly:* A literal translation of "metaphysicians"; but Zarathustra takes issue with all who deprecate this world for the greater glory of another world. The passage about the "leap" may seem to be aimed at Kierkegaard—of whom Nietzsche, however, heard only in 1888, too late to acquaint himself with the ideas of the Dane.

4. *On the Despisers of the Body:* The psychological analysis begun in the previous chapter is here carried further. The use of the term "ego" influenced Freud, via Georg Groddeck.

5. *On Enjoying and Suffering the Passions (Von den Freuden- und Leidenschaften):* The passions, called evil because they are potentially destructive, can also be creatively employed and enjoyed. Unlike Kant, who had taught that "a collision of duties is unthinkable," Nietzsche knows that a passion for justice or honesty may frequently conflict with other virtues. But even if Rembrandt was torn between his dedication to his art and his devotion to his

family, who would wish that he had been less passionate a painter or poorer in compassion?

6. *On the Pale Criminal:* Too abstract to make sense to Nietzsche's first readers, including even his once close friend Rohde, much of this chapter now seems like reflections on Dostoevski's Raskolnikov. But Nietzsche had not yet discovered Dostoevski. And some of the psychological insights offered here go beyond Dostoevski.

7. *On Reading and Writing:* Compulsory education for all has lowered cultural standards; thinkers and writers have come to think and write for the masses. References to novelists and artists who end up in Hollywood are lacking because Nietzsche died in 1900. The dance is to Nietzsche a symbol of joy and levity, and the antithesis of gravity. He associates it with Dionysus; but the Hindus too have a dancing god, Shiva Nataraja—no less a contrast to the three great monotheistic religions.

8. *On the Tree on the Mountainside:* Advice for adolescents.

9. *On the Preachers of Death:* An encounter with a sick man, an old man, and a corpse is said to have prompted the Buddha's departure from his father's palace. But relentless work, too, can be sought as a narcotic and a living death.

10. *On War and Warriors:* The "saints of knowledge" are above "hatred and envy"; but those still seeking knowledge must fight, must wage war, for their thoughts. Vanquished in this contest, they may yet find cause for triumph in the victory of truth. They must be like warriors: brave and without consideration for the feelings of others. In this context, "You should love peace as a means to new wars—and the short peace more than the long," is surely far from fascism; but the epigram invites quotation out of context. The same applies to "the good war that hallows any cause"; we revere Plato's *Republic* not for its cause (which many of us believe to have been, at least in part, totalitarianism), but because few men, if any, have ever waged a more brilliant war for any cause.

Being able to coin better slogans for positions he detested than the men believing in them—and then using such phrases in an entirely different sense—seems to have given Nietzsche uncommon satisfaction. He felt that he was hitting right and left, and he was horrified when he found that the rightist parties began brazenly to use him. (For a more detailed discussion of this chapter, see my *Nietzsche,* Chapter 12, section VII.)

11. *On the New Idol:* A vehement denunciation of the state and of war in the literal sense. Straight anti-fascism, but not in the name of any rival political creed. In Nietzsche's own phrase: anti-political.

12. *On the Flies of the Market Place:* Against the mass and its idols. Inspired by the contrast of Bayreuth and Sils Maria, Wagner and Nietzsche. But today we are more apt to think of Hitler than of Wagner.

13. *On Chastity:* One man's virtue is another man's poison.

14. *On the Friend:* Nietzsche's extreme individualism is tempered by his development of the Greek conception of friendship.

15. *On the Thousand and One Goals:* Except for private notes, published much later, this chapter contains the first mention of the will to power. What is meant in this context is clearly power over self, and the phrase is taken up again in the chapter "On Self-Overcoming" in Part Two. The four historical examples are: Greeks, Persians, Jews, Germans. (For an analysis, see my *Nietzsche,* 6, III; for a discussion of "The Discovery of the Will to Power," the whole of Chapter 6.)

16. *On Love of the Neighbor:* Jesus said: "Ye have heard that it hath been said, Thou shalt love thy neighbor, and hate thine enemy. But I say unto you: Love your enemies." He took issue not with the old Mosaic commandment to love thy neighbor—that had never been coupled with any commandment to hate the enemy but had even been pointedly extended to include him—but with that comfortable state of mind which makes things easy for itself while

hiding behind a façade of virtue. In this respect Nietzsche's polemic is profoundly similar to Jesus'. But, in the words of Zarathustra, he remains "faithful to the earth" and deprecates the shortcomings of mutual indulgence, while celebrating friendship between those who spur each other on toward man's perfection. (See my *Nietzsche*, 12, IV.)

17. *On the Way of the Creator:* Zarathustra does not preach universal anarchy: only the creator must break with ancient norms.

18. *On Little Old and Young Women:* The affectionate diminutive in the title (*Weiblein*) suggests at once what is the main difference between this chapter and its vitriolic prototype, Schopenhauer's essay *Von den Weibern:* a touch of humor. In Part Three, moreover, in "The Other Dancing Song," Nietzsche makes fun of the little old woman's dictum that concludes the present chapter. A photograph taken less than a year before he wrote Part One also supplies an amusing perspective. It shows Nietzsche and his friend Paul Rée (author of *Der Ursprung der moralischen Empfindungen*) pretending to pull a little cart on which Lou Salomé, then their mutual friend, is enthroned with a tiny whip. We have it on her authority that the picture was posed under Nietzsche's direction, and that he decorated the whip with flowers. But although Nietzsche should be defended against witless admirers and detractors, his remarks about women are surely, more often than not, second-hand and third-rate.

19. *On the Adder's Bite:* One might wish that the following lines were better known than the preceding chapter: "But if you have an enemy, do not requite him evil with good, for that would put him to shame. Rather prove that he did you some good. And rather be angry than put to shame. And if you are cursed, I do not like it that you want to bless. Rather join a little in the cursing." This should be compared with Paul's Epistle to the Romans, 12:14 ff.: "Bless them which persecute you: bless, and curse not. . . . Avenge not yourselves, but give place unto wrath: for it is written, Vengeance is mine: I will repay,

saith the Lord. Therefore, if thine enemy hunger, feed him; if he thirst, give him drink: for in so doing thou shalt heap coals of fire on his head." Nietzsche's whole chapter is an attack on what he later called *ressentiment*. (See my *Nietzsche*, 12, V.)

20. *On Child and Marriage:* It may require careful reading to see that Nietzsche repudiates only certain kinds of pity and love of the neighbor, but in this chapter he makes a clear distinction indeed between the kind of marriage he opposes and the kind he would applaud.

21. *On Free Death:* A celebration of Socrates' way of dying as opposed to Jesus'. Nietzsche's own creeping death was to take eleven years to destroy his body after it had destroyed his mind.

22. *On the Gift-Giving Virtue:* The egoism of the powerful, whose happiness consists in giving, is contrasted with that of the weak. The core of the last section is quoted again in the Preface to *Ecce Homo,* late in 1888: Nietzsche wants no believers but, like Socrates, aims to help others to find themselves and surpass him.

Zarathustra's Prologue

1

When Zarathustra was thirty years old he left his home and the lake of his home and went into the mountains. Here he enjoyed his spirit and his solitude, and for ten years did not tire of it. But at last a change came over his heart, and one morning he rose with the dawn, stepped before the sun, and spoke to it thus:

"You great star, what would your happiness be had you not those for whom you shine?

"For ten years you have climbed to my cave: you would have tired of your light and of the journey had it not been for me and my eagle and my serpent.

"But we waited for you every morning, took your overflow from you, and blessed you for it.

"Behold, I am weary of my wisdom, like a bee that has gathered too much honey; I need hands outstretched to receive it.

"I would give away and distribute, until the wise among men find joy once again in their folly, and the poor in their riches.

"For that I must descend to the depths, as you do in the evening when you go behind the sea and still bring light to the underworld, you overrich star.

"Like you, I must *go under*—go down, as is said by man, to whom I want to descend.

"So bless me then, you quiet eye that can look even upon an all-too-great happiness without envy!

"Bless the cup that wants to overflow, that the water may flow from it golden and carry everywhere the reflection of your delight.

"Behold, this cup wants to become empty again, and Zarathustra wants to become man again."

Thus Zarathustra began to go under.

2

Zarathustra descended alone from the mountains, encountering no one. But when he came into the forest, all at once there stood before him an old man who had left his holy cottage to look for roots in the woods. And thus spoke the old man to Zarathustra:

"No stranger to me is this wanderer: many years ago he passed this way. Zarathustra he was called, but he has changed. At that time you carried your ashes to the mountains; would you now carry your fire into the valleys? Do you not fear to be punished as an arsonist?

"Yes, I recognize Zarathustra. His eyes are pure, and

around his mouth there hides no disgust. Does he not walk like a dancer?

"Zarathustra has changed, Zarathustra has become a child, Zarathustra is an awakened one; what do you now want among the sleepers? You lived in your solitude as in the sea, and the sea carried you. Alas, would you now climb ashore? Alas, would you again drag your own body?"

Zarathustra answered: "I love man."

"Why," asked the saint, "did I go into the forest and the desert? Was it not because I loved man all-too-much? Now I love God; man I love not. Man is for me too imperfect a thing. Love of man would kill me."

Zarathustra answered: "Did I speak of love? I bring men a gift."

"Give them nothing!" said the saint. "Rather, take part of their load and help them to bear it—that will be best for them, if only it does you good! And if you want to give them something, give no more than alms, and let them beg for that!"

"No," answered Zarathustra. "I give no alms. For that I am not poor enough."

The saint laughed at Zarathustra and spoke thus: "Then see to it that they accept your treasures. They are suspicious of hermits and do not believe that we come with gifts. Our steps sound too lonely through the streets. And what if at night, in their beds, they hear a man walk by long before the sun has risen—they probably ask themselves, Where is the thief going?

"Do not go to man. Stay in the forest! Go rather even to the animals! Why do you not want to be as I am—a bear among bears, a bird among birds?"

"And what is the saint doing in the forest?" asked Zarathustra.

The saint answered: "I make songs and sing them; and when I make songs, I laugh, cry, and hum: thus I praise God. With singing, crying, laughing, and humming, I praise the god who is my god. But what do you bring us as a gift?"

When Zarathustra had heard these words he bade the saint farewell and said: "What could I have to give you? But let me go quickly lest I take something from you!" And thus they separated, the old one and the man, laughing as two boys laugh.

But when Zarathustra was alone he spoke thus to his heart: "Could it be possible? This old saint in the forest has not yet heard anything of this, that *God is dead!*"

3

When Zarathustra came into the next town, which lies on the edge of the forest, he found many people gathered together in the market place; for it had been promised that there would be a tightrope walker. And Zarathustra spoke thus to the people:

"*I teach you the overman.* Man is something that shall be overcome. What have you done to overcome him?

"All beings so far have created something beyond themselves; and do you want to be the ebb of this great flood and even go back to the beasts rather than overcome man? What is the ape to man? A laughingstock or a painful embarrassment. And man shall be just that for the overman: a laughingstock or a painful embarrassment. You have made your way from worm to man, and much in you is still worm. Once you were apes, and even now, too, man is more ape than any ape.

"Whoever is the wisest among you is also a mere

conflict and cross between plant and ghost. But do I bid you become ghosts or plants?

"Behold, I teach you the overman. The overman is the meaning of the earth. Let your will say: the overman *shall be* the meaning of the earth! I beseech you, my brothers, *remain faithful to the earth,* and do not believe those who speak to you of otherworldly hopes! Poison-mixers are they, whether they know it or not. Despisers of life are they, decaying and poisoned themselves, of whom the earth is weary: so let them go.

"Once the sin against God was the greatest sin; but God died, and these sinners died with him. To sin against the earth is now the most dreadful thing, and to esteem the entrails of the unknowable higher than the meaning of the earth.

"Once the soul looked contemptuously upon the body, and then this contempt was the highest: she wanted the body meager, ghastly, and starved. Thus she hoped to escape it and the earth. Oh, this soul herself was still meager, ghastly, and starved: and cruelty was the lust of this soul. But you, too, my brothers, tell me: what does your body proclaim of your soul? Is not your soul poverty and filth and wretched contentment?

"Verily, a polluted stream is man. One must be a sea to be able to receive a polluted stream without becoming unclean. Behold, I teach you the overman: he is this sea; in him your great contempt can go under.

"What is the greatest experience you can have? It is the hour of the great contempt. The hour in which your happiness, too, arouses your disgust, and even your reason and your virtue.

"The hour when you say, 'What matters my happiness? It is poverty and filth and wretched contentment. But my happiness ought to justify existence itself.'

"The hour when you say, 'What matters my reason?

Does it crave knowledge as the lion his fooar It is poverty and filth and wretched contentment.'

"The hour when you say, 'What matters my virtue? As yet it has not made me rage. How weary I am of my good and my evil! All that is poverty and filth and wretched contentment.'

"The hour when you say, 'What matters my justice? I do not see that I am flames and fuel. But the just are flames and fuel.'

"The hour when you say, 'What matters my pity? Is not pity the cross on which he is nailed who loves man? But my pity is no crucifixion.'

"Have you yet spoken thus? Have you yet cried thus? Oh, that I might have heard you cry thus!

"Not your sin but your thrift cries to heaven; your meanness even in your sin cries to heaven.

"Where is the lightning to lick you with its tongue? Where is the frenzy with which you should be inoculated?

"Behold, I teach you the overman: he is this lightning, he is this frenzy."

When Zarathustra had spoken thus, one of the people cried: "Now we have heard enough about the tightrope walker; now let us see him too!" And all the people laughed at Zarathustra. But the tightrope walker, believing that the word concerned him, began his performance.

4

Zarathustra, however, beheld the people and was amazed. Then he spoke thus:

"Man is a rope, tied between beast and overman—a rope over an abyss. A dangerous across, a dangerous on-the-way, a dangerous looking-back, a dangerous shuddering and stopping.

"What is great in man is that he is a bridge and not an end: what can be loved in man is that he is an *overture* and a *going under*.

"I love those who do not know how to live, except by going under, for they are those who cross over.

"I love the great despisers because they are the great reverers and arrows of longing for the other shore.

"I love those who do not first seek behind the stars for a reason to go under and be a sacrifice, but who sacrifice themselves for the earth, that the earth may some day become the overman's.

"I love him who lives to know, and who wants to know so that the overman may live some day. And thus he wants to go under.

"I love him who works and invents to build a house for the overman and to prepare earth, animal, and plant for him: for thus he wants to go under.

"I love him who loves his virtue, for virtue is the will to go under and an arrow of longing.

"I love him who does not hold back one drop of spirit for himself, but wants to be entirely the spirit of his virtue: thus he strides over the bridge as spirit.

"I love him who makes his virtue his addiction and his catastrophe: for his virtue's sake he wants to live on and to live no longer.

"I love him who does not want to have too many virtues. One virtue is more virtue than two, because it is more of a noose on which his catastrophe may hang.

"I love him whose soul squanders itself, who wants no thanks and returns none: for he always gives away and does not want to preserve himself.

"I love him who is abashed when the dice fall to make his fortune, and asks, 'Am I then a crooked gambler?' For he wants to perish.

"I love him who casts golden words before his deeds

and always does even more than he promises: for he wants to go under.

"I love him who justifies future and redeems past generations: for he wants to perish of the present.

"I love him who chastens his god because he loves his god: for he must perish of the wrath of his god.

"I love him whose soul is deep, even in being wounded, and who can perish of a small experience: thus he goes gladly over the bridge.

"I love him whose soul is overfull so that he forgets himself, and all things are in him: thus all things spell his going under.

"I love him who has a free spirit and a free heart: thus his head is only the entrails of his heart, but his heart drives him to go under.

"I love all those who are as heavy drops, falling one by one out of the dark cloud that hangs over men: they herald the advent of lightning, and, as heralds, they perish.

"Behold, I am a herald of the lightning and a heavy drop from the cloud; but this lightning is called *overman*."

5

When Zarathustra had spoken these words he beheld the people again and was silent. "There they stand," he said to his heart; "there they laugh. They do not understand me; I am not the mouth for these ears. Must one smash their ears before they learn to listen with their eyes? Must one clatter like kettledrums and preachers of repentance? Or do they believe only the stammerer?

"They have something of which they are proud. What do they call that which makes them proud? Education they call it; it distinguishes them from goatherds.

That is why they do not like to hear the word 'contempt' applied to them. Let me then address their pride. Let me speak to them of what is most contemptible: but that is the *last man*."

And thus spoke Zarathustra to the people: "The time has come for man to set himself a goal. The time has come for man to plant the seed of his highest hope. His soil is still rich enough. But one day this soil will be poor and domesticated, and no tall tree will be able to grow in it. Alas, the time is coming when man will no longer shoot the arrow of his longing beyond man, and the string of his bow will have forgotten how to whir!

"I say unto you: one must still have chaos in oneself to be able to give birth to a dancing star. I say unto you: you still have chaos in yourselves.

"Alas, the time is coming when man will no longer give birth to a star. Alas, the time of the most despicable man is coming, he that is no longer able to despise himself. Behold, I show you the *last man*.

" 'What is love? What is creation? What is longing? What is a star?' thus asks the last man, and he blinks.

"The earth has become small, and on it hops the last man, who makes everything small. His race is as ineradicable as the flea-beetle; the last man lives longest.

" 'We have invented happiness,' say the last men, and they blink. They have left the regions where it was hard to live, for one needs warmth. One still loves one's neighbor and rubs against him, for one needs warmth.

"Becoming sick and harboring suspicion are sinful to them: one proceeds carefully. A fool, whoever still stumbles over stones or human beings! A little poison now and then: that makes for agreeable dreams. And much poison in the end, for an agreeable death.

"One still works, for work is a form of entertainment. But one is careful lest the entertainment be too harrowing. One no longer becomes poor or rich: both require too much exertion. Who still wants to rule? Who obey? Both require too much exertion.

"No shepherd and one herd! Everybody wants the same, everybody is the same: whoever feels different goes voluntarily into a madhouse.

" 'Formerly, all the world was mad,' say the most refined, and they blink.

"One is clever and knows everything that has ever happened: so there is no end of derision. One still quarrels, but one is soon reconciled—else it might spoil the digestion.

"One has one's little pleasure for the day and one's little pleasure for the night: but one has a regard for health.

" 'We have invented happiness,' say the last men, and they blink."

And here ended Zarathustra's first speech, which is also called "the Prologue"; for at this point he was interrupted by the clamor and delight of the crowd. "Give us this last man, O Zarathustra," they shouted. "Turn us into these last men! Then we shall make you a gift of the overman!" And all the people jubilated and clucked with their tongues.

But Zarathustra became sad and said to his heart: "They do not understand me: I am not the mouth for these ears. I seem to have lived too long in the mountains; I listened too much to brooks and trees: now I talk to them as to goatherds. My soul is unmoved and bright as the mountains in the morning. But they think I am cold and I jeer and make dreadful jests. And now they look at me and laugh: and as they laugh they even hate me. There is ice in their laughter."

6

Then something happened that made every mouth dumb and every eye rigid. For meanwhile the tight-rope walker had begun his performance: he had stepped out of a small door and was walking over the rope, stretched between two towers and suspended over the market place and the people. When he had reached the exact middle of his course the small door opened once more and a fellow in motley clothes, looking like a jester, jumped out and followed the first one with quick steps.

"Forward, lamefoot!" he shouted in an awe-inspiring voice. "Forward, lazybones, smuggler, pale-face, or I shall tickle you with my heel! What are you doing here between towers? The tower is where you belong. You ought to be locked up; you block the way for one better than yourself." And with every word he came closer and closer; but when he was but one step behind, the dreadful thing happened which made every mouth dumb and every eye rigid: he uttered a devilish cry and jumped over the man who stood in his way. This man, however, seeing his rival win, lost his head and the rope, tossed away his pole, and plunged into the depth even faster, a whirlpool of arms and legs. The market place became as the sea when a tempest pierces it: the people rushed apart and over one another, especially at the place where the body must hit the ground.

Zarathustra, however, did not move; and it was right next to him that the body fell, badly maimed and disfigured, but not yet dead. After a while the shattered man recovered consciousness and saw Zarathustra kneeling beside him. "What are you doing here?" he asked at last. "I have long known that the devil would trip me. Now he will drag me to hell. Would you prevent him?"

"By my honor, friend," answered Zarathustra, "all that of which you speak does not exist: there is no devil and no hell. Your soul will be dead even before your body: fear nothing further."

The man looked up suspiciously. "If you speak the truth," he said, "I lose nothing when I lose my life. I am not much more than a beast that has been taught to dance by blows and a few meager morsels."

"By no means," said Zarathustra. "You have made danger your vocation; there is nothing contemptible in that. Now you perish of your vocation: for that I will bury you with my own hands."

When Zarathustra had said this, the dying man answered no more; but he moved his hand as if he sought Zarathustra's hand in thanks.

7

Meanwhile the evening came, and the market place hid in darkness. Then the people scattered, for even curiosity and terror grow weary. But Zarathustra sat on the ground near the dead man, and he was lost in thought, forgetting the time. At last night came, and a cold wind blew over the lonely one.

Then Zarathustra rose and said to his heart: "Verily, it is a beautiful catch of fish that Zarathustra has brought in today! Not a man has he caught but a corpse. Human existence is uncanny and still without meaning: a jester can become man's fatality. I will teach men the meaning of their existence—the overman, the lightning out of the dark cloud of man. But I am still far from them, and my sense does not speak to their senses. To men I am still the mean between a fool and a corpse.

"Dark is the night, dark are Zarathustra's ways. Come, cold, stiff companion! I shall carry you where I may bury you with my own hands."

8

When Zarathustra had said this to his heart he hoisted the corpse on his back and started on his way. And he had not taken a hundred steps when a man sneaked up to him and whispered in his ear—and behold, it was the jester from the tower. "Go away from this town, Zarathustra," said he; "there are too many here who hate you. You are hated by the good and the just, and they call you their enemy and despiser; you are hated by the believers in the true faith, and they call you the danger of the multitude. It was your good fortune that you were laughed at; and verily, you talked like a jester. It was your good fortune that you stooped to the dead dog; when you lowered yourself so far, you saved your own life for today. But go away from this town, or tomorrow I shall leap over you, one living over one dead." And when he had said this the man vanished; but Zarathustra went on through the dark lanes.

At the gate of the town he met the gravediggers; they shone their torches in his face, recognized Zarathustra, and mocked him. "Zarathustra carries off the dead dog: how nice that Zarathustra has become a gravedigger! For our hands are too clean for this roast. Would Zarathustra steal this bite from the devil? Well then, we wish you a good meal. If only the devil were not a better thief than Zarathustra: he will steal them both, he will gobble up both." And they laughed and put their heads together.

Zarathustra never said a word and went his way. When he had walked two hours, past forests and swamps, he heard so much of the hungry howling of the wolves that he himself felt hungry. So he stopped at a lonely house in which a light was burning.

"Like a robber, hunger overtakes me," said Zarathustra. "In forests and swamps my hunger overtakes me, and in the deep of night. My hunger is certainly capricious: often it comes to me only after a meal, and today it did not come all day; where could it have been?"

And at that Zarathustra knocked at the door of the house. An old man appeared, carrying the light, and asked: "Who is it that comes to me and to my bad sleep?"

"A living and a dead man," said Zarathustra. "Give me something to eat and to drink; I forgot about it during the day. He who feeds the hungry refreshes his own soul: thus speaks wisdom."

The old man went away, but returned shortly and offered Zarathustra bread and wine. "This is an evil region for the hungry," he said; "that is why I live here. Beast and man come to me, the hermit. But bid your companion, too, eat and drink; he is wearier than you are."

Zarathustra replied: "My companion is dead; I should hardly be able to persuade him."

"I don't care," said the old man peevishly. "Whoever knocks at my door must also take what I offer. Eat and be off!"

Thereupon Zarathustra walked another two hours, trusting the path and the light of the stars; for he was used to walking at night and he liked to look in the face of all that slept. But when the dawn came Zarathustra found himself in a deep forest, and he did not see a path anywhere. So he laid the dead man into a hollow tree—for he wanted to protect him from the wolves—and he himself lay down on the ground and the moss, his head under the tree. And soon he fell asleep, his body weary but his soul unmoved.

9

For a long time Zarathustra slept, and not only dawn passed over his face but the morning too. At last, however, his eyes opened: amazed, Zarathustra looked into the woods and the silence; amazed, he looked into himself. Then he rose quickly, like a seafarer who suddenly sees land, and jubilated, for he saw a new truth. And thus he spoke to his heart:

"An insight has come to me: companions I need, living ones—not dead companions and corpses whom I carry with myself wherever I want to. Living companions I need, who follow me because they want to follow themselves—wherever I want.

"An insight has come to me: let Zarathustra speak not to the people but to companions. Zarathustra shall not become the shepherd and dog of a herd.

"To lure many away from the herd, for that I have come. The people and the herd shall be angry with me: Zarathustra wants to be called a robber by the shepherds.

"Shepherds, I say; but they call themselves the good and the just. Shepherds, I say; but they call themselves believers in the true faith.

"Behold the good and the just! Whom do they hate most? The man who breaks their tables of values, the breaker, the lawbreaker; yet he is the creator.

"Behold the believers of all faiths! Whom do they

hate most? The man who breaks their tables of values, the breaker, the lawbreaker; yet he is the creator.

"Companions, the creator seeks, not corpses, not herds and believers. Fellow creators, the creator seeks —those who write new values on new tablets. Companions, the creator seeks, and fellow harvesters; for everything about him is ripe for the harvest. But he lacks a hundred sickles: so he plucks ears and is annoyed. Companions, the creator seeks, and such as know how to whet their sickles. Destroyers they will be called, and despisers of good and evil. But they are the harvesters and those who celebrate. Fellow creators, Zarathustra seeks, fellow harvesters and fellow celebrants: what are herds and shepherds and corpses to him?

"And you, my first companion, farewell! I buried you well in your hollow tree; I have hidden you well from the wolves. But I part from you; the time is up. Between dawn and dawn a new truth has come to me. No shepherd shall I be, nor gravedigger. Never again shall I speak to the people: for the last time have I spoken to the dead.

"I shall join the creators, the harvesters, the celebrants: I shall show them the rainbow and all the steps to the overman. To the hermits I shall sing my song, to the lonesome and the twosome; and whoever still has ears for the unheard-of—his heart shall become heavy with my happiness.

"To my goal I will go—on my own way; over those who hesitate and lag behind I shall leap. Thus let my going be their going under."

10

This is what Zarathustra had told his heart when the sun stood high at noon; then he looked into the air, questioning, for overhead he heard the sharp call of a bird. And behold! An eagle soared through the sky in wide circles, and on him there hung a serpent, not like prey but like a friend: for she kept herself wound around his neck.

"These are my animals," said Zarathustra and was happy in his heart. "The proudest animal under the sun and the wisest animal under the sun—they have gone out on a search. They want to determine whether Zarathustra is still alive. Verily, do I still live? I found life more dangerous among men than among animals; on dangerous paths walks Zarathustra. May my animals lead me!"

When Zarathustra had said this he recalled the words of the saint in the forest, sighed, and spoke thus to his heart: "That I might be wiser! That I might be wise through and through like my serpent! But there I ask the impossible: so I ask my pride that it always go along with my wisdom. And when my wisdom leaves me one day—alas, it loves to fly away—let my pride then fly with my folly."

Thus Zarathustra began to go under.

Zarathustra's Speeches

ON THE THREE METAMORPHOSES

Of three metamorphoses of the spirit I tell you: how the spirit becomes a camel; and the camel, a lion; and the lion, finally, a child.

There is much that is difficult for the spirit, the strong reverent spirit that would bear much: but the difficult and the most difficult are what its strength demands.

What is difficult? asks the spirit that would bear much, and kneels down like a camel wanting to be well loaded. What is most difficult, O heroes, asks the spirit that would bear much, that I may take it upon myself and exult in my strength? Is it not humbling oneself to wound one's haughtiness? Letting one's folly shine to mock one's wisdom?

Or is it this: parting from our cause when it triumphs? Climbing high mountains to tempt the tempter?

Or is it this: feeding on the acorns and grass of knowledge and, for the sake of the truth, suffering hunger in one's soul?

Or is it this: being sick and sending home the comforters and making friends with the deaf, who never hear what you want?

Or is it this: stepping into filthy waters when they are the waters of truth, and not repulsing cold frogs and hot toads?

Or is it this: loving those who despise us and offering a hand to the ghost that would frighten us?

All these most difficult things the spirit that would bear much takes upon itself: like the camel that, burdened, speeds into the desert, thus the spirit speeds into its desert.

In the loneliest desert, however, the second metamorphosis occurs: here the spirit becomes a lion who would conquer his freedom and be master in his own desert. Here he seeks out his last master: he wants to fight him and his last god; for ultimate victory he wants to fight with the great dragon.

Who is the great dragon whom the spirit will no longer call lord and god? "Thou shalt" is the name of the great dragon. But the spirit of the lion says, "I will." "Thou shalt" lies in his way, sparkling like gold, an animal covered with scales; and on every scale shines a golden "thou shalt."

Values, thousands of years old, shine on these scales; and thus speaks the mightiest of all dragons: "All value of all things shines on me. All value has long been created, and I am all created value. Verily, there shall be no more 'I will.'" Thus speaks the dragon.

My brothers, why is there a need in the spirit for the lion? Why is not the beast of burden, which renounces and is reverent, enough?

To create new values—that even the lion cannot do; but the creation of freedom for oneself for new creation—that is within the power of the lion. The creation of freedom for oneself and a sacred "No" even to duty—for that, my brothers, the lion is needed. To assume the right to new values—that is the most terrifying assumption for a reverent spirit that would bear much. Verily, to him it is preying, and a matter for a beast of prey. He once loved "thou shalt" as most sacred: now he must find illusion and caprice even in the most sacred, that freedom from his love may become his prey: the lion is needed for such prey.

But say, my brothers, what can the child do that even the lion could not do? Why must the preying lion still become a child? The child is innocence and forgetting, a new beginning, a game, a self-propelled wheel, a first movement, a sacred "Yes." For the game of creation, my brothers, a sacred "Yes" is needed: the spirit now wills his own will, and he who had been lost to the world now conquers his own world.

Of three metamorphoses of the spirit I have told you: how the spirit became a camel; and the camel, a lion; and the lion, finally, a child.

Thus spoke Zarathustra. And at that time he sojourned in the town that is called The Motley Cow.

ON THE TEACHERS OF VIRTUE

A sage was praised to Zarathustra for knowing how to speak well of sleep and of virtue: he was said to be honored and rewarded highly for this, and all the youths were said to be sitting at his feet. To him Zarathustra went, and he sat at his feet with all the youths. And thus spoke the sage:

"Honor sleep and be bashful before it—that first of all. And avoid all who sleep badly and stay awake at night. Even the thief is bashful before sleep: he always steals silently through the night. Shameless, however, is the watchman of the night; shamelessly he carries his horn.

"Sleeping is no mean art: for its sake one must stay awake all day. Ten times a day you must overcome yourself: that makes you good and tired and is opium for the soul. Ten times you must reconcile yourself again with yourself; for, overcoming is bitterness, and the unreconciled sleep badly. Ten truths a day you must find; else you will still be seeking truth by night, and your soul will remain hungry. Ten times a day you must laugh and be cheerful; else you will be disturbed at night by your stomach, this father of gloom.

"Few know it, but one must have all the virtues to sleep well. Shall I bear false witness? Shall I commit adultery? Shall I covet my neighbor's maid? All that would go ill with good sleep.

"And even if one has all the virtues, there is one further thing one must know: to send even the virtues to sleep at the right time. Lest they quarrel with each other, the fair little women, about you, child of misfortune. Peace with God and the neighbor: that is what good sleep demands. And peace even with the neighbor's devil—else he will haunt you at night.

"Honor the magistrates and obey them—even the crooked magistrates. Good sleep demands it. Is it my fault that power likes to walk on crooked legs?

"I shall call him the best shepherd who leads his sheep to the greenest pasture: that goes well with good sleep.

"I do not want many honors, or great jewels: that inflames the spleen. But one sleeps badly without a good name and a little jewel.

"A little company is more welcome to me than evil company: but they must go and come at the right time. That goes well with good sleep.

"Much, too, do I like the poor in spirit: they promote sleep. Blessed are they, especially if one always tells them that they are right.

"Thus passes the day of the virtuous. And when night comes I guard well against calling sleep. For sleep, who is the master of the virtues, does not want to be called. Instead, I think about what I have done and thought during the day. Chewing the cud, I ask myself, patient as a cow, Well, what were your ten overcomings? and what were your ten reconciliations and the ten truths and the ten laughters with which your heart edified itself? Weighing such matters and rocked by forty thoughts, I am suddenly overcome by sleep, the uncalled, the master of the virtues. Sleep knocks at my eyes: they become heavy. Sleep touches my mouth: it stays open. Verily, on soft soles he comes to me, the dearest of thieves, and steals my thoughts: stupid I stand, like this chair here. But not for long do I stand like this: soon I lie."

When Zarathustra heard the sage speak thus he

laughed in his heart, for an insight had come to him. And thus he spoke to his heart:

"This sage with his forty thoughts is a fool; but I believe that he knows well how to sleep. Happy is he that even lives near this sage! Such sleep is contagious—contagious even through a thick wall. There is magic even in his chair; and it is not in vain that the youths sit before this preacher of virtue. His wisdom is: to wake in order to sleep well. And verily, if life had no sense and I had to choose nonsense, then I too should consider this the most sensible nonsense.

"Now I understand clearly what was once sought above all when teachers of virtue were sought. Good sleep was sought. and opiate virtues for it. For all these much praised sages who were teachers of virtue, wisdom was the sleep without dreams: they knew no better meaning of life.

"Today too there may still be a few like this preacher of virtue, and not all so honest; but their time is up. And not for long will they stand like this: soon they will lie.

"Blessed are the sleepy ones: for they shall soon drop off."

Thus spoke Zarathustra.

ON THE AFTERWORLDLY

At one time Zarathustra too cast his delusion beyond man, like all the afterworldly. The work of a suffering and tortured god, the world then seemed to me. A dream the world then seemed to me, and the fiction of a god: colored smoke before the eyes of a dissatisfied deity. Good and evil and joy and pain and I and you—colored smoke this seemed to me before creative eyes. The creator wanted to look away from himself; so he created the world.

Drunken joy it is for the sufferer to look away from his suffering and to lose himself. Drunken joy and loss of self the world once seemed to me. This world, eternally imperfect, the image of an eternal contradiction, an imperfect image—a drunken joy for its imperfect creator: thus the world once appeared to me.

Thus I too once cast my delusion beyond man, like all the afterworldly. Beyond man indeed?

Alas, my brothers, this god whom I created was man-made and madness, like all gods! Man he was, and only a poor specimen of man and ego: out of my own ashes and fire this ghost came to me, and, verily, it did not come to me from beyond. What happened, my brothers? I overcame myself, the sufferer; I carried my own ashes to the mountains; I invented a brighter flame for myself. And behold, then this ghost *fled* from me. Now it would be suffering for me and agony for the recovered to believe in such ghosts: now it would be suffering for me and humiliation. Thus I speak to the afterworldly.

It was suffering and incapacity that created all afterworlds—this and that brief madness of bliss which is experienced only by those who suffer most deeply.

Weariness that wants to reach the ultimate with one leap, with one fatal leap, a poor ignorant weariness that does not want to want any more: this created all gods and afterworlds.

Believe me, my brothers: it was the body that despaired of the body and touched the ultimate walls with the fingers of a deluded spirit. Believe me, my brothers: it was the body that despaired of the earth and heard the belly of being speak to it. It wanted to crash through these ultimate walls with its head, and not only with its head—over there to "that world." But "that world" is well concealed from humans—that de-humanized inhuman world which is a heavenly noth-ing; and the belly of being does not speak to humans at all, except as a human.

Verily, all being is hard to prove and hard to induce to speak. Tell me, my brothers, is not the strangest of all things proved most nearly?

Indeed, this ego and the ego's contradiction and con-fusion still speak most honestly of its being—this creat-ing, willing, valuing ego, which is the measure and value of things. And this most honest being, the ego, speaks of the body and still wants the body, even when it poetizes and raves and flutters with broken wings. It learns to speak ever more honestly, this ego: and the more it learns, the more words and honors it finds for body and earth.

A new pride my ego taught me, and this I teach men: no longer to bury one's head in the sand of heavenly things, but to bear it freely, an earthly head, which creates a meaning for the earth.

A new will I teach men: to *will* this way which man has walked blindly, and to affirm it, and no longer to sneak away from it like the sick and decaying.

It was the sick and decaying who despised body and earth and invented the heavenly realm and the re-demptive drops of blood: but they took even these sweet and gloomy poisons from body and earth. They wanted to escape their own misery, and the stars were too far for them. So they sighed: "Would that there were heavenly ways to sneak into another state of be-ing and happiness!" Thus they invented their sneaky ruses and bloody potions. Ungrateful, these people deemed themselves transported from their bodies and this earth. But to whom did they owe the convulsions and raptures of their transport? To their bodies and this earth.

Zarathustra is gentle with the sick. Verily, he is not angry with their kinds of comfort and ingratitude. May they become convalescents, men of overcoming, and create a higher body for themselves! Nor is Zarathustra angry with the convalescent who eyes his delusion tenderly and, at midnight, sneaks around the grave of his god: but even so his tears still betray sickness and a sick body to me.

Many sick people have always been among the poetizers and God-cravers; furiously they hate the lover of knowledge and that youngest among the virtues, which is called "honesty." They always look backward toward dark ages; then, indeed, delusion and faith were another matter: the rage of reason was godlikeness, and doubt was sin.

I know these godlike men all too well: they want one to have faith in them, and doubt to be sin. All too well I also know what it is in which they have most faith. Verily, it is not in afterworlds and redemptive drops of blood, but in the body, that they too have most faith; and their body is to them their thing-in-itself. But a sick thing it is to them, and gladly would they shed their skins. Therefore they listen to the preachers of death and themselves preach afterworlds.

Listen rather, my brothers, to the voice of the healthy body: that is a more honest and purer voice. More honestly and purely speaks the healthy body that is perfect and perpendicular: and it speaks of the meaning of the earth.

Thus spoke Zarathustra.

ON THE DESPISERS OF THE BODY

I want to speak to the despisers of the body. I would not have them learn and teach differently, but merely say farewell to their own bodies—and thus become silent.

"Body am I, and soul"—thus speaks the child. And why should one not speak like children?

But the awakened and knowing say: body am I entirely, and nothing else; and soul is only a word for something about the body.

The body is a great reason, a plurality with one sense, a war and a peace, a herd and a shepherd. An instrument of your body is also your little reason, my brother, which you call "spirit"—a little instrument and toy of your great reason.

"I," you say, and are proud of the word. But greater is that in which you do not wish to have faith—your body and its great reason: that does not say "I," but does "I."

What the sense feels, what the spirit knows, never has its end in itself. But sense and spirit would persuade you that they are the end of all things: that is how vain they are. Instruments and toys are sense and spirit: behind them still lies the self. The self also seeks with the eyes of the senses; it also listens with the ears of the spirit. Always the self listens and seeks: it compares, overpowers, conquers, destroys. It controls, and it is in control of the ego too.

Behind your thoughts and feelings, my brother, there stands a mighty ruler, an unknown sage—whose name is self. In your body he dwells; he is your body.

There is more reason in your body than in your best

wisdom. And who knows why your body needs precisely your best wisdom?

Your self laughs at your ego and at its bold leaps. "What are these leaps and flights of thought to me?" it says to itself. "A detour to my end. I am the leading strings of the ego and the prompter of its concepts."

The self says to the ego, "Feel pain here!" Then the ego suffers and thinks how it might suffer no more—and that is why it is *made* to think.

The self says to the ego, "Feel pleasure here!" Then the ego is pleased and thinks how it might often be pleased again—and that is why it is *made* to think.

I want to speak to the despisers of the body. It is their respect that begets their contempt. What is it that created respect and contempt and worth and will? The creative self created respect and contempt; it created pleasure and pain. The creative body created the spirit as a hand for its will.

Even in your folly and contempt, you despisers of the body, you serve your self. I say unto you: your self itself wants to die and turns away from life. It is no longer capable of what it would do above all else: to create beyond itself. That is what it would do above all else, that is its fervent wish.

But now it is too late for it to do this: so your self wants to go under, O despisers of the body. Your self wants to go under, and that is why you have become despisers of the body! For you are no longer able to create beyond yourselves.

And that is why you are angry with life and the earth. An unconscious envy speaks out of the squint-eyed glance of your contempt.

I shall not go your way, O despisers of the body! You are no bridge to the overman!

Thus spoke Zarathustra.

ON ENJOYING AND SUFFERING THE PASSIONS

My brother, if you have a virtue and she is your virtue, then you have her in common with nobody. To be sure, you want to call her by name and pet her; you want to pull her ear and have fun with her. And behold, now you have her name in common with the people and have become one of the people and herd with your virtue.

You would do better to say, "Inexpressible and nameless is that which gives my soul agony and sweetness and is even the hunger of my entrails."

May your virtue be too exalted for the familiarity of names: and if you must speak of her, then do not be ashamed to stammer of her. Then speak and stammer, "This is *my* good; this I love; it pleases me wholly; thus alone do *I* want the good. I do not want it as divine law; I do not want it as human statute and need: it shall not be a signpost for me to overearths and paradises. It is an earthly virtue that I love: there is little prudence in it, and least of all the reason of all men. But this bird built its nest with me: therefore I love and caress it; now it dwells with me, siting on its golden eggs." Thus you shall stammer and praise your virtue.

Once you suffered passions and called them evil. But now you have only your virtues left: they grew out of your passions. You commended your highest goal to the heart of these passions: then they become your virtues and passions you enjoyed.

And whether you came from the tribe of the choleric or of the voluptuous or of the fanatic or of the vengeful, in the end all your passions became virtues and all your devils, angels. Once you had wild dogs in your cellar, but in the end they turned into birds and lovely singers. Out of your poisons you brewed your balsam. You milked your cow, melancholy; now you drink the sweet milk of her udder.

And nothing evil grows out of you henceforth, unless it be the evil that grows out of the fight among your virtues. My brother, if you are fortunate you have only one virtue and no more: then you will pass over the bridge more easily. It is a distinction to have many virtues, but a hard lot; and many have gone into the desert and taken their lives because they had wearied of being the battle and battlefield of virtues.

My brother, are war and battle evil? But this evil is necessary; necessary are the envy and mistrust and calumny among your virtues. Behold how each of your virtues covets what is highest: each wants your whole spirit that it might become *her* herald; each wants your whole strength in wrath, hatred, and love. Each virtue is jealous of the others, and jealousy is a terrible thing. Virtues too can perish of jealousy. Surrounded by the flame of jealousy, one will in the end, like the scorpion, turn one's poisonous sting against oneself. Alas, my brother, have you never yet seen a virtue deny and stab herself?

Man is something that must be overcome; and therefore you shall love your virtues, for you will perish of them.

Thus spoke Zarathustra.

ON THE PALE CRIMINAL

You do not want to kill, O judges and sacrificers, until the animal has nodded? Behold, the pale criminal has nodded: out of his eyes speaks the great contempt.

"My ego is something that shall be overcome: my

ego is to me the great contempt of man," that is what his eyes say.

That he judged himself, that was his highest moment; do not let the sublime return to his baseness! There is no redemption for one who suffers so of himself, except a quick death.

Your killing, O judges, shall be pity and not revenge. And as you kill, be sure that you yourselves justify life! It is not enough to make your peace with the man you kill. Your sadness shall be love of the overman: thus you shall justify your living on.

"Enemy" you shall say, but not "villain"; "sick" you shall say, but not "scoundrel"; "fool" you shall say, but not "sinner."

And you, red judge, if you were to tell out loud all that you have already done in thought, everyone would cry, "Away with this filth and this poisonous worm!"

But thought is one thing, the deed is another, and the image of the deed still another: the wheel of causality does not roll between them.

An image made this pale man pale. He was equal to his deed when he did it; but he could not bear its image after it was done. Now he always saw himself as the doer of one deed. Madness I call this: the exception now became the essence for him. A chalk streak stops a hen; the stroke that he himself struck stopped his poor reason: madness *after* the deed I call this.

Listen, O judges: there is yet another madness, and that comes *before* the deed. Alas, you have not yet crept deep enough into this soul.

Thus speaks the red judge, "Why did this criminal murder? He wanted to rob." But I say unto you: his soul wanted blood, not robbery; he thirsted after the bliss of the knife. His poor reason, however, did not comprehend this madness and persuaded him: "What matters blood?" it asked; "don't you want at least to commit a robbery with it? To take revenge?" And he listened to his poor reason: its speech lay upon him like lead; so he robbed when he murdered. He did not want to be ashamed of his madness.

And now the lead of his guilt lies upon him, and again his poor reason is so stiff, so paralyzed, so heavy. If only he could shake his head, then his burden would roll off: but who could shake this head?

What is this man? A heap of diseases, which, through his spirit, reach out into the world: there they want to catch their prey.

What is this man? A ball of wild snakes, which rarely enjoy rest from each other: so they go forth singly and seek prey in the world.

Behold this poor body! What it suffered and coveted this poor soul interpreted for itself: it interpreted it as murderous lust and greed for the bliss of the knife.

Those who become sick today are overcome by that evil which is evil today: they want to hurt with that which hurts them. But there have been other ages and another evil and good. Once doubt was evil and the will to self. Then the sick became heretics or witches: as heretics or witches they suffered and wanted to inflict suffering.

But your ears do not want to accept this: it harms your good people, you say to me. But what matter your good people to me? Much about your good people nauseates me; and verily, it is not their evil. Indeed, I wish they had a madness of which they might perish like this pale criminal.

Verily, I wish their madness were called truth or

loyalty or justice: but they have their virtue in order to live long and in wretched contentment.

I am a railing by the torrent: let those who can, grasp me! Your crutch, however, I am not.

Thus spoke Zarathustra.

ON READING AND WRITING

Of all that is written I love only what a man has written with his blood. Write with blood, and you will experience that blood is spirit.

It is not easily possible to understand the blood of another: I hate reading idlers. Whoever knows the reader will henceforth do nothing for the reader. Another century of readers—and the spirit itself will stink.

That everyone may learn to read, in the long run corrupts not only writing but also thinking. Once the spirit was God, then he became man, and now he even becomes rabble.

Whoever writes in blood and aphorisms does not want to be read but to be learned by heart. In the mountains the shortest way is from peak to peak: but for that one must have long legs. Aphorisms should be peaks—and those who are addressed, tall and lofty. The air thin and pure, danger near, and the spirit full of gay sarcasm: these go well together. I want to have goblins around me, for I am courageous. Courage that puts ghosts to flight creates goblins for itself: courage wants to laugh.

I no longer feel as you do: this cloud which I see beneath me, this blackness and gravity at which I laugh—this is your thundercloud.

You look up when you feel the need for elevation. And I look down because I am elevated. Who among you can laugh and be elevated at the same time? Whoever climbs the highest mountains laughs at all tragic plays and tragic seriousness.

Brave, unconcerned, mocking, violent—thus wisdom wants us: she is a woman and always loves only a warrior.

You say to me, "Life is hard to bear." But why would you have your pride in the morning and your resignation in the evening? Life is hard to bear; but do not act so tenderly! We are all of us fair beasts of burden, male and female asses. What do we have in common with the rosebud, which trembles because a drop of dew lies on it?

True, we love life, not because we are used to living but because we are used to loving. There is always some madness in love. But there is also always some reason in madness.

And to me too, as I am well disposed toward life, butterflies and soap bubbles and whatever among men is of their kind seem to know most about happiness. Seeing these light, foolish, delicate, mobile little souls flutter—that seduces Zarathustra to tears and songs.

I would believe only in a god who could dance. And when I saw my devil I found him serious, thorough, profound, and solemn: it was the spirit of gravity—through him all things fall.

Not by wrath does one kill but by laughter. Come, let us kill the spirit of gravity!

I have learned to walk: ever since, I let myself run. I have learned to fly: ever since, I do not want to be pushed before moving along.

Now I am light, now I fly, now I see myself beneath myself, now a god dances through me.

Thus spoke Zarathustra.

ON THE TREE ON THE MOUNTAINSIDE

Zarathustra's eye had noted that a youth avoided him. And one evening as he walked alone through the mountains surrounding the town which is called The Motley Cow—behold, on his walk he found this youth as he sat leaning against a tree, looking wearily into the valley. Zarathustra gripped the tree under which the youth was sitting and spoke thus:

"If I wanted to shake this tree with my hands I should not be able to do it. But the wind, which we do not see, tortures and bends it in whatever direction it pleases. It is by invisible hands that we are bent and tortured worst."

Then the youth got up in consternation and said: "I hear Zarathustra, and just now I was thinking of him."

Zarathustra replied: "Why should that frighten you? But it is with man as it is with the tree. The more he aspires to the height and light, the more strongly do his roots strive earthward, downward, into the dark, the deep—into evil."

"Yes, into evil!" cried the youth. "How is it possible that you discovered my soul?"

Zarathustra smiled and said: "Some souls one will never discover, unless one invents them first."

"Yes, into evil!" the youth cried once more. "You have spoken the truth, Zarathustra. I no longer trust myself since I aspire to the height, and nobody trusts me any more; how did this happen? I change too fast: my today refutes my yesterday. I often skip steps when I climb: no step forgives me that. When I am at the top I always find myself alone. Nobody speaks to me; the frost of loneliness makes me shiver. What do I want up high? My contempt and my longing grow at the same time; the higher I climb, the more I despise the climber. What does he want up high? How ashamed I am of my climbing and stumbling! How I mock at my violent panting! How I hate the flier! How weary I am up high!"

Here the youth stopped. And Zarathustra contemplated the tree beside which they stood and spoke thus: "This tree stands lonely here in the mountains; it grew high above man and beast. And if it wanted to speak it would have nobody who could understand it, so high has it grown. Now it waits and waits—for what is it waiting? It dwells too near the seat of the clouds: surely, it waits for the first lightning."

When Zarathustra had said this the youth cried with violent gestures: "Yes, Zarathustra, you are speaking the truth. I longed to go under when I aspired to the height, and you are the lightning for which I waited. Behold, what am I, now that you have appeared among us? It is the *envy* of you that has destroyed me." Thus spoke the youth, and he wept bitterly. But Zarathustra put his arm around him and led him away.

And when they had walked together for a while, Zarathustra began to speak thus: "It tears my heart. Better than your words tell it, your eyes tell me of all your dangers. You are not yet free, you still *search* for freedom. You are worn from your search and over-awake. You aspire to the free heights, your soul thirsts for the stars. But your wicked instincts, too, thirst for freedom. Your wild dogs want freedom; they bark with joy in their cellar when your spirit plans to open all prisons. To me you are still a prisoner who is plotting his freedom: alas, in such prisoners the soul becomes clever, but also deceitful and bad. And even the liberated spirit must still purify himself. Much prison and mustiness still remain in him: his eyes must still become pure.

"Indeed, I know your danger. But by my love and hope I beseech you: do not throw away your love and hope.

"You still feel noble, and the others too feel your nobility, though they bear you a grudge and send you evil glances. Know that the noble man stands in everybody's way. The noble man stands in the way of the good too: and even if they call him one of the good, they thus want to do away with him. The noble man wants to create something new and a new virtue. The good want the old, and that the old be preserved. But this is not the danger of the noble man, that he might become one of the good, but a churl, a mocker, a destroyer.

"Alas, I knew noble men who lost their highest hope. Then they slandered all high hopes. Then they lived impudently in brief pleasures and barely cast their goals beyond the day. Spirit too is lust, so they said. Then the wings of their spirit broke: and now their spirit crawls about and soils what it gnaws. Once they thought of becoming heroes: now they are voluptuaries. The hero is for them an offense and a fright.

"But by my love and hope I beseech you: do not throw away the hero in your soul! Hold holy your highest hope!"

Thus spoke Zarathustra.

ON THE PREACHERS OF DEATH

There are preachers of death; and the earth is full of those to whom one must preach renunciation of life. The earth is full of the superfluous; life is spoiled by the all-too-many. May they be lured from this life with the "eternal life"! Yellow the preachers of death wear, or black. But I want to show them to you in still other colors.

There are the terrible ones who carry around within themselves the beast of prey and have no choice but lust or self-laceration. And even their lust is still self-laceration. They have not even become human beings yet, these terrible ones: let them preach renunciation of life and pass away themselves!

There are those with consumption of the soul: hardly are they born when they begin to die and to long for doctrines of weariness and renunciation. They would like to be dead, and we should welcome their wish. Let us beware of waking the dead and disturbing these living coffins!

They encounter a sick man or an old man or a corpse, and immediately they say, "Life is refuted." But only they themselves are refuted, and their eyes, which see only this one face of existence. Shrouded in thick melancholy and eager for the little accidents that bring death, thus they wait with clenched teeth. Or they reach for sweets while mocking their own childishness; they clutch the straw of their life and mock that they still clutch a straw. Their wisdom says, "A fool who stays alive—but such fools are we. And this is surely the most foolish thing about life."

"Life is only suffering," others say, and do not lie: see to it, then, that *you* cease! See to it, then, that the life which is only suffering ceases!

And let this be the doctrine of your virtue: "Thou shalt kill thyself! Thou shalt steal away!"

"Lust is sin," says one group that preaches death; "let us step aside and beget no children."

"Giving birth is troublesome," says another group; "why go on giving birth? One bears only unfortunates!"

And they too are preachers of death.

"Pity is needed," says the third group. "Take from me what I have! Take from me what I am! Life will bind me that much less!"

If they were full of pity through and through, they would make life insufferable for their neighbors. To be evil, that would be their real goodness. But they want to get out of life: what do they care that with their chains and presents they bind others still more tightly?

And you, too, for whom life is furious work and unrest—are you not very weary of life? Are you not very ripe for the preaching of death? All of you to whom furious work is dear, and whatever is fast, new, and strange—you find it hard to bear yourselves; your industry is escape and the will to forget yourselves. If you believed more in life you would fling yourselves less to the moment. But you do not have contents enough in yourselves for waiting—and not even for idleness.

Everywhere the voice of those who preach death is heard; and the earth is full of those to whom one must preach death. Or "eternal life"—that is the same to me, if only they pass away quickly.

Thus spoke Zarathustra.

ON WAR AND WARRIORS

We do not want to be spared by our best enemies, nor by those whom we love thoroughly. So let me tell you the truth!

My brothers in war, I love you thoroughly; I am and I was of your kind. And I am also your best enemy. So let me tell you the truth!

I know of the hatred and envy of your hearts. You

are not great enough not to know hatred and envy. Be great enough, then, not to be ashamed of them.

And if you cannot be saints of knowledge, at least be its warriors. They are the companions and fore-runners of such sainthood.

I see many soldiers: would that I saw many warriors! "Uniform" one calls what they wear: would that what it conceals were not uniform!

You should have eyes that always seek an enemy—*your* enemy. And some of you hate at first sight. Your enemy you shall seek, your war you shall wage—for your thoughts. And if your thought be vanquished, then your honesty should still find cause for triumph in that. You should love peace as a means to new wars—and the short peace more than the long. To you I do not recommend work but struggle. To you I do not recom-mend peace but victory. Let your work be a struggle. Let your peace be a victory! One can be silent and sit still only when one has bow and arrow: else one chatters and quarrels. Let your peace be a victory!

You say it is the good cause that hallows even war? I say unto you: it is the good war that hallows any cause. War and courage have accomplished more great things than love of the neighbor. Not your pity but your courage has so far saved the unfortunate.

"What is good?" you ask. To be brave is good. Let the little girls say, "To be good is what is at the same time pretty and touching."

They call you heartless: but you have a heart, and I love you for being ashamed to show it. You are ashamed of your flood, while others are ashamed of their ebb.

You are ugly? Well then, my brothers, wrap the sublime around you, the cloak of the ugly. And when your soul becomes great, then it becomes prankish; and in your sublimity there is sarcasm. I know you.

In sarcasm the prankster and the weakling meet. But they misunderstand each other. I know you.

You may have only enemies whom you can hate, not enemies you despise. You must be proud of your enemy: then the successes of your enemy are your successes too.

Recalcitrance—that is the nobility of slaves. Your nobility should be obedience. Your very commanding should be an obeying. To a good warrior "thou shalt" sounds more agreeable than "I will." And everything you like you should first let yourself be commanded to do.

Your love of life shall be love of your highest hope; and your highest hope shall be the highest thought of life. Your highest thought, however, you should receive as a command from me—and it is: man is something that shall be overcome.

Thus live your life of obedience and war. What matters long life? What warrior wants to be spared?

I do not spare you; I love you thoroughly, my brothers in war!

Thus spoke Zarathustra.

ON THE NEW IDOL

Somewhere there are still peoples and herds, but not where we live, my brothers: here there are states. State? What is that? Well then, open your ears to me, for now I shall speak to you about the death of peoples.

State is the name of the coldest of all cold monsters. Coldly it tells lies too; and this lie crawls out of its mouth: "I, the state, am the people." That is a lie! It was creators who created peoples and hung a faith and a love over them: thus they served life.

It is annihilators who set traps for the many and call them "state": they hang a sword and a hundred appetites over them.

Where there is still a people, it does not understand the state and hates it as the evil eye and the sin against customs and rights.

This sign I give you: every people speaks its tongue of good and evil, which the neighbor does not understand. It has invented its own language of customs and rights. But the state tells lies in all the tongues of good and evil; and whatever it says it lies—and whatever it has it has stolen. Everything about it is false; it bites with stolen teeth, and bites easily. Even its entrails are false. Confusion of tongues of good and evil: this sign I give you as the sign of the state. Verily, this sign signifies the will to death. Verily, it beckons to the preachers of death.

All-too-many are born: for the superfluous the state was invented.

Behold, how it lures them, the all-too-many—and how it devours them, chews them, and ruminates!

"On earth there is nothing greater than I: the ordering finger of God am I"—thus roars the monster. And it is not only the long-eared and shortsighted who sink to their knees. Alas, to you too, you great souls, it whispers its dark lies. Alas, it detects the rich hearts which like to squander themselves. Indeed, it detects you too, you vanquishers of the old god. You have grown weary with fighting, and now your weariness still serves the new idol. With heroes and honorable men it would surround itself, the new idol! It likes to bask in the sunshine of good consciences—the cold monster!

It will give you everything if you will adore it, this

new idol: thus it buys the splendor of your virtues and the look of your proud eyes. It would use you as bait for the all-too-many.

Indeed, a hellish artifice was invented there, a horse of death, clattering in the finery of divine honors. Indeed, a dying for many was invented there, which praises itself as life: verily, a great service to all preachers of death!

State I call it where all drink poison, the good and the wicked; state, where all lose themselves, the good and the wicked; state, where the slow suicide of all is called "life."

Behold the superfluous! They steal the works of the inventors and the treasures of the sages for themselves; "education" they call their theft—and everything turns to sickness and misfortune for them.

Behold the superfluous! They are always sick; they vomit their gall and call it a newspaper. They devour each other and cannot even digest themselves.

Behold the superfluous! They gather riches and become poorer with them. They want power and first the lever of power, much money—the impotent paupers!

Watch them clamber, these swift monkeys! They clamber over one another and thus drag one another into the mud and the depth. They all want to get to the throne: that is their madness—as if happiness sat on the throne. Often mud sits on the throne—and often also the throne on mud. Mad they all appear to me, clambering monkeys and overardent. Foul smells their idol, the cold monster: foul they smell to me altogether, these idolators.

My brothers, do you want to suffocate in the fumes of their snouts and appetites? Rather break the windows and leap to freedom.

Escape from the bad smell! Escape from the idolatry of the superfluous!

Escape from the bad smell! Escape from the steam of these human sacrifices!

The earth is free even now for great souls. There are still many empty seats for the lonesome and the twosome, fanned by the fragrance of silent seas.

A free life is still free for great souls. Verily, whoever possesses little is possessed that much less: praised be a little poverty!

Only where the state ends, there begins the human being who is not superfluous: there begins the song of necessity, the unique and inimitable tune.

Where the state *ends*—look there, my brothers! Do you not see it, the rainbow and the bridges of the overman?

Thus spoke Zarathustra.

ON THE FLIES OF THE MARKET PLACE

Flee, my friend, into your solitude! I see you dazed by the noise of the great men and stung all over by the stings of the little men. Woods and crags know how to keep a dignified silence with you. Be like the tree that you love with its wide branches: silently listening, it hangs over the sea.

Where solitude ceases the market place begins; and where the market place begins the noise of the great actors and the buzzing of the poisonous flies begins too.

In the world even the best things amount to nothing without someone to make a show of them: great men the people call these showmen.

Little do the people comprehend the great—that is, the creating. But they have a mind for all showmen and actors of great things.

Around the inventors of new values the world revolves: invisibly it revolves. But around the actors
revolve the people and fame: that is "the way of the
world."

The actor has spirit but little conscience of the
spirit. Always he has faith in that with which he inspires the most faith—faith in himself. Tomorrow he
has a new faith, and the day after tomorrow a newer
one. He has quick senses, like the people, and capricious moods. To overthrow—that means to him: to
prove. To drive to frenzy—that means to him: to persuade. And blood is to him the best of all reasons. A
truth that slips into delicate ears alone he calls a lie
and nothing. Verily, he believes only in gods who make
a big noise in the world!

Full of solemn jesters is the market place—and the
people pride themselves on their great men, their masters of the hour. But the hour presses them; so they
press you. And from you too they want a Yes or No.
Alas, do you want to place your chair between pro and
con?

Do not be jealous of these unconditional, pressing
men, you lover of truth! Never yet has truth hung on
the arm of the unconditional. On account of these
sudden men, go back to your security: it is only in
the market place that one is assaulted with Yes? or No?
Slow is the experience of all deep wells: long must
they wait before they know *what* fell into their depth.

Far from the market place and from fame happens
all that is great: far from the market place and from
fame the inventors of new values have always dwelt.

Flee, my friend, into your solitude: I see you stung
all over by poisonous flies. Flee where the air is raw
and strong.

Flee into your solitude! You have lived too close to

the small and the miserable. Flee their invisible revenge! Against you they are nothing but revenge.

No longer raise up your arm against them. Numberless are they, and it is not your lot to shoo flies. Numberless are these small and miserable creatures; and many a proud building has perished of raindrops and weeds. You are no stone, but you have already become hollow from many drops. You will yet burst from many drops. I see you wearied by poisonous flies, bloody in a hundred places; and your pride refuses even to be angry. Blood is what they want from you in all innocence. Their bloodless souls crave blood, and so they sting in all innocence. But you, you deep one, suffer too deeply even from small wounds; and even before you have healed, the same poisonous worm crawls over your hand. You are too proud to kill these greedy creatures. But beware lest it become your downfall that you suffer all their poisonous injustice.

They hum around you with their praise too: obtrusiveness is their praise. They want the proximity of your skin and your blood. They flatter you as a god or devil; they whine before you as before a god or devil. What does it matter? They are flatterers and whiners and nothing more.

Often they affect charm. But that has always been the cleverness of cowards. Indeed, cowards are clever! They think a lot about you with their petty souls— you always seem problematic to them. Everything that one thinks about a lot becomes problematic.

They punish you for all your virtues. They forgive you entirely—your mistakes.

Because you are gentle and just in disposition you say, "They are guiltless in their small existence." But their petty souls think, "Guilt is every great existence."

Even when you are gentle to them they still feel

despised by you: and they return your benefaction with
hidden malefactions. Your silent pride always runs
counter to their taste; they are jubilant if for once you
are modest enough to be vain. That which we recognize in a person we also inflame in him: therefore, beware of the small creatures. Before you they feel small,
and their baseness glimmers and glows in invisible revenge. Have you not noticed how often they became
mute when you stepped among them, and how their
strength went from them like smoke from a dying fire?

Indeed, my friend, you are the bad conscience of
your neighbors: for they are unworthy of you. They
hate you, therefore, and would like to suck your blood.
Your neighbors will always be poisonous flies; that
which is great in you, just that must make them more
poisonous and more like flies.

Flee, my friend, into your solitude and where the
air is raw and strong! It is not your lot to shoo flies.

Thus spoke Zarathustra.

ON CHASTITY

I love the forest. It is bad to live in cities: there too
many are in heat. Is it not better to fall into the hands
of a murderer than into the dreams of a woman in heat?
And behold these men: their eyes say it—they know
of nothing better on earth than to lie with a woman.
Mud is at the bottom of their souls; and woe if their
mud also has spirit!

Would that you were as perfect as animals at least!
But animals have innocence.

Do I counsel you to slay your senses? I counsel the
innocence of the senses.

Do I counsel you to chastity? Chastity is a virtue in
some, but almost a vice in many. They abstain, but

the bitch, sensuality, leers enviously out of every-thing they do. Even to the heights of their virtue and to the cold regions of the spirit this beast follows them with her lack of peace. And how nicely the bitch, sensuality, knows how to beg for a piece of spirit when denied a piece of meat.

Do you love tragedies and everything that breaks the heart? But I mistrust your bitch. Your eyes are too cruel and you search lustfully for sufferers. Is it not merely your lust that has disguised itself and now calls itself pity?

And this parable too I offer you: not a few who wanted to drive out their devil have themselves entered into swine.

Those for whom chastity is difficult should be coun-seled against it, lest it become their road to hell—the mud and heat of their souls.

Do I speak of dirty things? That is not the worst that could happen. It is not when truth is dirty, but when it is shallow, that the lover of knowledge is re-luctant to step into its waters. Verily, some are chaste through and through: they are gentler of heart, fonder of laughter, and laugh more than you. They laugh at chastity too and ask, "What is chastity? Is chastity not folly? Yet this folly came to us, not we to it. We offered this guest hostel and heart: now it dwells with us—may it stay as long as it will!"

Thus spoke Zarathustra.

ON THE FRIEND

"There is always one too many around me"—thus thinks the hermit. "Always one times one—eventually that makes two."

I and me are always too deep in conversation: how

could one stand that if there were no friend? For the hermit the friend is always the third person: the third is the cork that prevents the conversation of the two from sinking into the depths. Alas, there are too many depths for all hermits; therefore they long so for a friend and his height.

Our faith in others betrays in what respect we would like to have faith in ourselves. Our longing for a friend is our betrayer. And often love is only a device to overcome envy. And often one attacks and makes an enemy in order to conceal that one is open to attack. "At least be my enemy!"—thus speaks true reverence, which does not dare ask for friendship.

If one wants to have a friend one must also want to wage war for him: and to wage war, one must be *capable* of being an enemy.

In a friend one should still honor the enemy. Can you go close to your friend without going over to him?

In a friend one should have one's best enemy. You should be closest to him with your heart when you resist him.

You do not want to put on anything for your friend? Should it be an honor for your friend that you give yourself to him as you are? But he sends you to the devil for that. He who makes no secret of himself, enrages: so much reason have you for fearing nakedness. Indeed, if you were gods, then you might be ashamed of your clothes. You cannot groom yourself too beautifully for your friend: for you shall be to him an arrow and a longing for the overman.

Have you ever seen your friend asleep—and found out how he looks? What is the face of your friend anyway? It is your own face in a rough and imperfect mirror.

Have you ever seen your friend asleep? Were you not shocked that your friend looks like that? O my friend, man is something that must be overcome.

A friend should be a master at guessing and keeping still: you must not want to see everything. Your dream should betray to you what your friend does while awake.

Your compassion should be a guess—to know first whether your friend wants compassion. Perhaps what he loves in you is the unbroken eye and the glance of eternity. Compassion for the friend should conceal itself under a hard shell, and you should break a tooth on it. That way it will have delicacy and sweetness.

Are you pure air and solitude and bread and medicine for your friend? Some cannot loosen their own chains and can nevertheless redeem their friends.

Are you a slave? Then you cannot be a friend. Are you a tyrant? Then you cannot have friends. All-too-long have a slave and a tyrant been concealed in woman. Therefore woman is not yet capable of friendship: she knows only love.

Woman's love involves injustice and blindness against everything that she does not love. And even in the knowing love of a woman there are still assault and lightning and night alongside light.

Woman is not yet capable of friendship: women are still cats and birds. Or at best, cows.

Woman is not yet capable of friendship. But tell me, you men, who among you is capable of friendship?

Alas, behold your poverty, you men, and the meanness of your souls! As much as you give the friend, I will give even my enemy, and I shall not be any the poorer for it. There is comradeship: let there be friendship!

Thus spoke Zarathustra.

ON THE THOUSAND AND ONE GOALS

Zarathustra saw many lands and many peoples: thus he discovered the good and evil of many peoples. And Zarathustra found no greater power on earth than good and evil.

No people could live without first esteeming; but if they want to preserve themselves, then they must not esteem as the neighbor esteems. Much that was good to one people was scorn and infamy to another: thus I found it. Much I found called evil here, and decked out with purple honors there. Never did one neighbor understand the other: ever was his soul amazed at the neighbor's delusion and wickedness.

A tablet of the good hangs over every people. Behold, it is the tablet of their overcomings; behold, it is the voice of their will to power.

Praiseworthy is whatever seems difficult to a people; whatever seems indispensable and difficult is called good; and whatever liberates even out of the deepest need, the rarest, the most difficult—that they call holy.

Whatever makes them rule and triumph and shine, to the awe and envy of their neighbors, that is to them the high, the first, the measure, the meaning of all things.

Verily, my brother, once you have recognized the need and land and sky and neighbor of a people, you may also guess the law of their overcomings, and why they climb to their hope on this ladder.

"You shall always be the first and excel all others: your jealous soul shall love no one, unless it be the friend"—that made the soul of the Greek quiver: thus he walked the path of his greatness.

"To speak the truth and to handle bow and arrow well"—that seemed both dear and difficult to the people who gave me my name—the name which is both dear and difficult to me.

"To honor father and mother and to follow their will to the root of one's soul"— this was the tablet of overcoming that another people hung up over themselves and became powerful and eternal thereby.

"To practice loyalty and, for the sake of loyalty, to risk honor and blood even for evil and dangerous things"—with this teaching another people conquered themselves; and through this self-conquest they became pregnant and heavy with great hopes.

Verily, men gave themselves all their good and evil. Verily, they did not take it, they did not find it, nor did it come to them as a voice from heaven. Only man placed values in things to preserve himself—he alone created a meaning for things, a human meaning. Therefore he calls himself "man," which means: the esteemer.

To esteem is to create: hear this, you creators! Esteeming itself is of all esteemed things the most estimable treasure. Through esteeming alone is there value: and without esteeming, the nut of existence would be hollow. Hear this, you creators!

Change of values—that is a change of creators. Whoever must be a creator always annihilates.

First, peoples were creators; and only in later times, individuals. Verily, the individual himself is still the most recent creation.

Once peoples hung a tablet of the good over themselves. Love which would rule and love which would obey have together created such tablets.

The delight in the herd is more ancient than the

delight in the ego; and as long as the good conscience is identified with the herd, only the bad conscience says: I.

Verily, the clever ego, the loveless ego that desires its own profit in the profit of the many—that is not the origin of the herd, but its going under.

Good and evil have always been created by lovers and creators. The fire of love glows in the names of all the virtues, and the fire of wrath.

Zarathustra saw many lands and many peoples. No greater power did Zarathustra find on earth than the works of the lovers: "good" and "evil" are their names.

Verily, a monster is the power of this praising and censuring. Tell me, who will conquer it, O brothers? Tell me, who will throw a yoke over the thousand necks of this beast?

A thousand goals have there been so far, for there have been a thousand peoples. Only the yoke for the thousand necks is still lacking: the one goal is lacking. Humanity still has no goal.

But tell me, my brothers, if humanity still lacks a goal—is humanity itself not still lacking too?

Thus spoke Zarathustra.

ON LOVE OF THE NEIGHBOR

You crowd around your neighbor and have fine words for it. But I say unto you: your love of the neighbor is your bad love of yourselves. You flee to your neighbor from yourselves and would like to make a virtue out of that: but I see through your "selflessness."

The *you* is older than the *I*; the *you* has been pronounced holy, but not yet the *I*: so man crowds toward his neighbor.

Do I recommend love of the neighbor to you? Sooner I should even recommend flight from the neighbor and love of the farthest. Higher than love of the neighbor is love of the farthest and the future; higher yet than the love of human beings I esteem the love of things and ghosts. This ghost that runs after you, my brother, is more beautiful than you; why do you not give him your flesh and your bones? But you are afraid and run to your neighbor.

You cannot endure yourselves and do not love yourselves enough: now you want to seduce your neighbor to love, and then gild yourselves with his error. Would that you could not endure all sorts of neighbors and their neighbors; then you would have to create your friend and his overflowing heart out of yourselves.

You invite a witness when you want to speak well of yourselves; and when you have seduced him to think well of you, then you think well of yourselves.

Not only are they liars who speak when they know better, but even more those who speak when they know nothing. And thus you speak of yourselves to others and deceive the neighbor with yourselves.

Thus speaks the fool: "Association with other people corrupts one's character—especially if one has none."

One man goes to his neighbor because he seeks himself; another because he would lose himself. Your bad love of yourselves turns your solitude into a prison. It is those farther away who must pay for your love of your neighbor; and even if five of you are together, there is always a sixth who must die.

I do not love your festivals either: I found too many actors there, and the spectators, too, often behaved like actors.

I teach you not the neighbor, but the friend. The friend should be the festival of the earth to you and an anticipation of the overman. I teach you the friend and his overflowing heart. But one must learn to be a sponge if one wants to be loved by hearts that overflow. I teach you the friend in whom the world stands completed, a bowl of goodness—the creating friend who always has a completed world to give away. And as the world rolled apart for him, it rolls together again in circles for him, as the becoming of the good through evil, as the becoming of purpose out of accident.

Let the future and the farthest be for you the cause of your today: in your friend you shall love the overman as your cause.

My brothers, love of the neighbor I do not recommend to you: I recommend to you love of the farthest.

Thus spoke Zarathustra.

ON THE WAY OF THE CREATOR

Is it your wish, my brother, to go into solitude? Is it your wish to seek the way to yourself? Then linger a moment, and listen to me.

"He who seeks, easily gets lost. All loneliness is guilt"—thus speaks the herd. And you have long belonged to the herd. The voice of the herd will still be audible in you. And when you will say, "I no longer have a common conscience with you," it will be a lament and an agony. Behold, this agony itself was born of the common conscience, and the last glimmer of that conscience still glows on your affliction.

But do you want to go the way of your affliction, which is the way to yourself? Then show me your right and your strength to do so. Are you a new strength and a new right? A first movement? A self-propelled wheel? Can you compel the very stars to revolve around you?

Alas, there is so much lusting for the heights! There are so many convulsions of the ambitious. Show me that you are not one of the lustful and ambitious.

Alas, there are so many great thoughts which do no more than a bellows: they puff up and make emptier.

You call yourself free? Your dominant thought I want to hear, and not that you have escaped from a yoke. Are you one of those who had the *right* to escape from a yoke? There are some who threw away their last value when they threw away their servitude.

Free *from* what? As if that mattered to Zarathustra! But your eyes should tell me brightly: free *for* what?

Can you give yourself your own evil and your own good and hang your own will over yourself as a law? Can you be your own judge and avenger of your law? Terrible it is to be alone with the judge and avenger of one's own law. Thus is a star thrown out into the void and into the icy breath of solitude. Today you are still suffering from the many, being one: today your courage and your hopes are still whole. But the time will come when solitude will make you weary, when your pride will double up, and your courage gnash its teeth. And you will cry, "I am alone!" The time will come when that which seems high to you will no longer be in sight, and that which seems low will be all-too-near; even what seems sublime to you will frighten you like a ghost. And you will cry, "All is false!"

There are feelings which want to kill the lonely; and if they do not succeed, well, then they themselves must die. But are you capable of this—to be a murderer?

My brother, do you know the word "contempt" yet? And the agony of your justice—being just to those who despise you? You force many to relearn about you; they charge it bitterly against you. You came close to them and yet passed by: that they will never forgive. You pass over and beyond them: but the higher you ascend, the smaller you appear to the eye of envy. But most of all they hate those who fly.

"How would you be just to me?" you must say. "I choose your injustice as my proper lot." Injustice and filth they throw after the lonely one: but, my brother, if you would be a star, you must not shine less for them because of that.

And beware of the good and the just! They like to crucify those who invent their own virtue for themselves—they hate the lonely one. Beware also of holy simplicity! Everything that is not simple it considers unholy; it also likes to play with fire—the stake. And beware also of the attacks of your love! The lonely one offers his hand too quickly to whomever he encounters. To some people you may not give your hand, only a paw: and I desire that your paw should also have claws.

But the worst enemy you can encounter will always be you, yourself; you lie in wait for yourself in caves and woods.

Lonely one, you are going the way to yourself. And your way leads past yourself and your seven devils. You will be a heretic to yourself and a witch and soothsayer and fool and doubter and unholy one and a villain. You must wish to consume yourself in your own flame: how could you wish to become new unless you had first become ashes!

Lonely one, you are going the way of the creator:

you would create a god for yourself out of your seven devils.

Lonely one, you are going the way of the lover: yourself you love, and therefore you despise yourself, as only lovers despise. The lover would create because he despises. What does he know of love who did not have to despise precisely what he loved!

Go into your loneliness with your love and with your creation, my brother; and only much later will justice limp after you.

With my tears go into your loneliness, my brother. I love him who wants to create over and beyond himself and thus perishes.

Thus spoke Zarathustra.

ON LITTLE OLD AND YOUNG WOMEN

"Why do you steal so cautiously through the twilight, Zarathustra? And what do you conceal so carefully under your coat? Is it a treasure you have been given? or a child born to you? Or do you yourself now follow the ways of thieves, you friend of those who are evil?"

"Verily, my brother," said Zarathustra, "it is a treasure I have been given: it is a little truth that I carry. But it is troublesome like a young child, and if I don't hold my hand over its mouth, it will cry overloudly.

"When I went on my way today, alone, at the hour when the sun goes down, I met a little old woman who spoke thus to my soul: 'Much has Zarathustra spoken to us women too; but never did he speak to us about woman.' And I answered her: 'About woman one should speak only to men.' Then she said: 'Speak to me too of woman; I am old enough to forget it immediately.' And I obliged the little old woman and I spoke to her thus:

"Everything about woman is a riddle, and everything about woman has one solution: that is pregnancy. Man is for woman a means: the end is always the child. But what is woman for man?

"A real man wants two things: danger and play. Therefore he wants woman as the most dangerous plaything. Man should be educated for war, and woman for the recreation of the warrior; all else is folly. The warrior does not like all-too-sweet fruit; therefore he likes woman: even the sweetest woman is bitter. Woman understands children better than man does, but man is more childlike than woman.

"In a real man a child is hidden—and wants to play. Go to it, women, discover the child in man! Let woman be a plaything, pure and fine, like a gem, irradiated by the virtues of a world that has not yet arrived. Let the radiance of a star shine through your love! Let your hope be: May I give birth to the overman!

"Let there be courage in your love! With your love you should proceed toward him who arouses fear in you. Let your honor be in your love! Little does woman understand of honor otherwise. But let this be your honor: always to love more than you are loved, and never to be second.

"Let man fear woman when she loves: then she makes any sacrifice, and everything else seems without value to her. Let man fear woman when she hates: for deep down in his soul man is merely evil, while woman is bad. Whom does woman hate most? Thus spoke the iron to the magnet: 'I hate you most because you attract, but are not strong enough to pull me to you.'

"The happiness of man is: I will. The happiness of woman is: he wills. 'Behold, just now the world became perfect!'—thus thinks every woman when she obeys out of entire love. And woman must obey and find a depth for her surface. Surface is the disposition of woman: a mobile, stormy film over shallow water. Man's disposition, however, is deep; his river roars in subterranean caves: woman feels his strength but does not comprehend it.

"Then the little old woman answered me: 'Many fine things has Zarathustra said, especially for those who are young enough for them. It is strange: Zarathustra knows women little, and yet he is right about them. Is this because nothing is impossible with woman? And now, as a token of gratitude, accept a little truth. After all, I am old enough for it. Wrap it up and hold your hand over its mouth: else it will cry overloudly, this little truth.'

"Then I said: 'Woman, give me your little truth.' And thus spoke the little old woman:

"'You are going to women? Do not forget the whip!'"

Thus spoke Zarathustra.

ON THE ADDER'S BITE

One day Zarathustra had fallen asleep under a fig tree, for it was hot, and had put his arms over his face. And an adder came and bit him in the neck, so that Zarathustra cried out in pain. When he had taken his arm from his face, he looked at the snake, and it recognized the eyes of Zarathustra, writhed awkwardly, and wanted to get away. "Oh no," said Zarathustra, "as yet you have not accepted my thanks. You waked me in time, my way is still long." "Your way is short," the adder said sadly; "my poison kills." Zarathustra smiled. "When has a dragon ever died of the poison of a snake?" he said. "But take back your poison. You are not rich enough to give it to me." Then the adder fell around his neck a second time and licked his wound.

When Zarathustra once related this to his disciples they asked: "And what, O Zarathustra, is the moral of your story?" Then Zarathustra answered thus:

The annihilator of morals, the good and just call me: my story is immoral.

But if you have an enemy, do not requite him evil with good, for that would put him to shame. Rather prove that he did you some good.

And rather be angry than put to shame. And if you are cursed, I do not like it that you want to bless. Rather join a little in the cursing.

And if you have been done a great wrong, then quickly add five little ones: a gruesome sight is a person single-mindedly obsessed by a wrong.

Did you already know this? A wrong shared is half right. And he who is able to bear it should take the wrong upon himself.

A little revenge is more human than no revenge. And if punishment is not also a right and an honor for the transgressor, then I do not like your punishments either.

It is nobler to declare oneself wrong than to insist on being right—especially when one is right. Only one must be rich enough for that.

I do not like your cold justice; and out of the eyes of your judges there always looks the executioner and his cold steel. Tell me, where is that justice which is love with open eyes? Would that you might invent for me the love that bears not only all punishment but also all guilt! Would that you might invent for me the justice that acquits everyone, except him that judges!

Do you still want to hear this too? In him who would be just through and through even lies become kindness to others. But how could I think of being just through and through? How can I give each his own? Let this be sufficient for me: I give each my own.

Finally, my brothers, beware of doing wrong to any hermit. How could a hermit forget? How could he repay? Like a deep well is a hermit. It is easy to throw in a stone; but if the stone sank to the bottom, tell me, who would get it out again? Beware of insulting the hermit. But if you have done so—well, then kill him too.

Thus spoke Zarathustra.

ON CHILD AND MARRIAGE

I have a question for you alone, my brother: like a sounding lead, I cast this question into your soul that I might know how deep it is.

You are young and wish for a child and marriage. But I ask you: Are you a man *entitled* to wish for a child? Are you the victorious one, the self-conqueror, the commander of your senses, the master of your virtues? This I ask you. Or is it the animal and need that speak out of your wish? Or loneliness? Or lack of peace with yourself?

Let your victory and your freedom long for a child. You shall build living monuments to your victory and your liberation. You shall build over and beyond yourself, but first you must be built yourself, perpendicular in body and soul. You shall not only reproduce yourself, but produce something higher. May the garden of marriage help you in that!

You shall create a higher body, a first movement, a self-propelled wheel—you shall create a creator.

Marriage: thus I name the will of two to create the one that is more than those who created it. Reverence for each other, as for those willing with such a will, is what I name marriage. Let this be the meaning and truth of your marriage. But that which the all-too-many, the superfluous, call marriage—alas, what shall I name that? Alas, this poverty of the soul in pair! Alas, this filth of the soul in pair! Alas, this wretched contentment in pair! Marriage they call this; and they say that their marriages are made in heaven. Well, I do not like it, this heaven of the superfluous. No, I do not like them—these animals entangled in the heavenly net. And let the god who limps near to bless what he never joined keep his distance from me! Do not laugh at such marriages! What child would not have cause to weep over its parents?

Worthy I deemed this man, and ripe for the sense of the earth; but when I saw his wife, the earth seemed to me a house for the senseless. Indeed, I wished that the earth might tremble in convulsions when a saint mates with a goose.

This one went out like a hero in quest of truths, and eventually he conquered a little dressed-up lie. His marriage he calls it.

That one was reserved and chose choosily. But all at once he spoiled his company forever: his marriage he calls it.

That one sought a maid with the virtues of an angel. But all at once he became the maid of a woman; and now he must turn himself into an angel.

Careful I have found all buyers now, and all of them have cunning eyes. But even the most cunning still buys his wife in a poke.

Many brief follies—that is what you call love. And your marriage concludes many brief follies, as a long stupidity. Your love of woman, and woman's love of man—oh, that it were compassion for suffering and shrouded gods! But, for the most part, two beasts find each other.

But even your best love is merely an ecstatic parable and a painful ardor. It is a torch that should light up higher paths for you. Over and beyond yourselves you shall love one day. Thus *learn* first to love. And for that you had to drain the bitter cup of your love. Bitterness lies in the cup of even the best love: thus it arouses longing for the overman; thus it arouses your thirst, creator. Thirst for the creator, an arrow and longing for the overman: tell me, my brother, is this your will to marriage? Holy I call such a will and such a marriage.

Thus spoke Zarathustra.

ON FREE DEATH

Many die too late, and a few die too early. The doctrine still sounds strange: "Die at the right time!" Die at the right time—thus teaches Zarathustra. Of course, how could those who never live at the right time die at the right time? Would that they had never been born! Thus I counsel the superfluous. But even the superfluous still make a fuss about their dying; and even the hollowest nut still wants to be cracked. Everybody considers dying important; but as yet death is no festival. As yet men have not learned how one hallows the most beautiful festivals.

I show you the death that consummates—a spur and a promise to the survivors. He that consummates his life dies his death victoriously, surrounded by those who hope and promise. Thus should one learn to die; and there should be no festival where one dying thus does not hallow the oaths of the living.

To die thus is best; second to this, however, is to die fighting and to squander a great soul. But equally hateful to the fighter and the victor is your grinning death, which creeps up like a thief—and yet comes as the master.

My death I praise to you, the free death which comes to me because *I* want it. And when shall I want it? He who has a goal and an heir will want death at the right time for his goal and heir. And from reverence for his goal and heir he will hang no more dry wreaths in the sanctuary of life. Verily, I do not want to be like the ropemakers: they drag out their threads and always walk backwards.

Some become too old even for their truths and victories: a toothless mouth no longer has the right to every truth. And everybody who wants fame must take leave of honor betimes and practice the difficult art of leaving at the right time.

One must cease letting oneself be eaten when one tastes best: that is known to those who want to be loved long. There are sour apples, to be sure, whose lot requires that they wait till the last day of autumn: and they become ripe, yellow, and wrinkled all at once. In some, the heart grows old first; in others, the spirit. And some are old in their youth: but late youth preserves long youth.

For some, life turns out badly: a poisonous worm eats its way to their heart. Let them see to it that their dying turns out that much better. Some never become sweet; they rot already in the summer. It is cowardice that keeps them on their branch.

All-too-many live, and all-too-long they hang on their

branches. Would that a storm came to shake all this worm-eaten rot from the tree!

Would that there came preachers of *quick* death! I would like them as the true storms and shakers of the trees of life. But I hear only slow death preached, and patience with everything "earthly."

Alas, do you preach patience with the earthly? It is the earthly that has too much patience with you, blasphemers!

Verily, that Hebrew died too early whom the preachers of slow death honor; and for many it has become a calamity that he died too early. As yet he knew only tears and the melancholy of the Hebrew, and hatred of the good and the just—the Hebrew Jesus: then the longing for death overcame him. Would that he had remained in the wilderness and far from the good and the just! Perhaps he would have learned to live and to love the earth—and laughter too.

Believe me, my brothers! He died too early; he himself would have recanted his teaching, had he reached my age. Noble enough was he to recant. But he was not yet mature. Immature is the love of the youth, and immature his hatred of man and earth. His mind and the wings of his spirit are still tied down and heavy.

But in the man there is more of the child than in the youth, and less melancholy: he knows better how to die and to live. Free to die and free in death, able to say a holy No when the time for Yes has passed: thus he knows how to die and to live.

That your dying be no blasphemy against man and earth, my friends, that I ask of the honey of your soul. In your dying, your spirit and virtue should still glow like a sunset around the earth: else your dying has turned out badly.

Thus I want to die myself that you, my friends, may

love the earth more for my sake; and to earth I want to return that I may find rest in her who gave birth to me.

Verily, Zarathustra had a goal; he threw his ball: now you, my friends, are the heirs of my goal; to you I throw my golden ball. More than anything, I like to see you, my friends, throwing the golden ball. And so I still linger a little on the earth: forgive me for that.

Thus spoke Zarathustra.

ON THE GIFT-GIVING VIRTUE

1

When Zarathustra had said farewell to the town to which his heart was attached, and which was named The Motley Cow, many who called themselves his disciples followed him and escorted him. Thus they came to a crossroads; then Zarathustra told them that he now wanted to walk alone, for he liked to walk alone. His disciples gave him as a farewell present a staff with a golden handle on which a serpent coiled around the sun. Zarathustra was delighted with the staff and leaned on it; then he spoke thus to his disciples:

Tell me: how did gold attain the highest value? Because it is uncommon and useless and gleaming and gentle in its splendor; it always gives itself. Only as the image of the highest virtue did gold attain the highest value. Goldlike gleam the eyes of the giver. Golden splendor makes peace between moon and sun. Uncommon is the highest virtue and useless; it is gleaming and gentle in its splendor: a gift-giving virtue is the highest virtue.

Verily, I have found you out, my disciples: you strive, as I do, for the gift-giving virtue. What would you have in common with cats and wolves? This is your thirst: to become sacrifices and gifts yourselves; and that is why you thirst to pile up all the riches in your soul. Insatiably your soul strives for treasures and gems, because your virtue is insatiable in wanting to give. You force all things to and into yourself that they may flow back out of your well as the gifts of your love. Verily, such a gift-giving love must approach all values as a robber; but whole and holy I call this selfishness.

There is also another selfishness, an all-too-poor and hungry one that always wants to steal—the selfishness of the sick: sick selfishness. With the eyes of a thief it looks at everything splendid; with the greed of hunger it sizes up those who have much to eat; and always it sneaks around the table of those who give. Sickness speaks out of such craving and invisible degeneration; the thievish greed of this selfishness speaks of a diseased body.

Tell me, my brothers: what do we consider bad and worst of all? Is it not *degeneration*? And it is degeneration that we always infer where the gift-giving soul is lacking. Upward goes our way, from genus to over-genus. But we shudder at the degenerate sense which says, "Everything for me." Upward flies our sense: thus it is a parable of our body, a parable of elevation. Parables of such elevations are the names of the virtues.

Thus the body goes through history, becoming and fighting. And the spirit—what is that to the body? The herald of its fights and victories, companion and echo.

All names of good and evil are parables: they do not define, they merely hint. A fool is he who wants knowledge of them!

Watch for every hour, my brothers, in which your spirit wants to speak in parables: there lies the origin of your virtue. There your body is elevated and resurrected; with its rapture it delights the spirit so that it turns creator and esteemer and lover and benefactor of all things.

When your heart flows broad and full like a river, a blessing and a danger to those living near: there is the origin of your virtue.

When you are above praise and blame, and your will wants to command all things, like a lover's will: there is the origin of your virtue.

When you despise the agreeable and the soft bed and cannot bed yourself far enough from the soft: there is the origin of your virtue.

When you will with a single will and you call this cessation of all need "necessity": there is the origin of your virtue.

Verily, a new good and evil is she. Verily, a new deep murmur and the voice of a new well!

Power is she, this new virtue; a dominant thought is she, and around her a wise soul: a golden sun, and around it the serpent of knowledge.

2

Here Zarathustra fell silent for a while and looked lovingly at his disciples. Then he continued to speak thus, and the tone of his voice had changed:

Remain faithful to the earth, my brothers, with the power of your virtue. Let your gift-giving love and your knowledge serve the meaning of the earth. Thus I beg and beseech you. Do not let them fly away from earthly things and beat with their wings against eternal walls. Alas, there has always been so much virtue that has flown away. Lead back to the earth the virtue that flew away, as I do—back to the body, back to life, that it may give the earth a meaning, a human meaning.

In a hundred ways, thus far, have spirit as well as virtue flown away and made mistakes. Alas, all this delusion and all these mistakes still dwell in our body: they have there become body and will.

In a hundred ways, thus far, spirit as well as virtue has tried and erred. Indeed, an experiment was man. Alas, much ignorance and error have become body within us.

Not only the reason of millennia, but their madness too, breaks out in us. It is dangerous to be an heir. Still we fight step by step with the giant, accident; and over the whole of humanity there has ruled so far only nonsense—no sense.

Let your spirit and your virtue serve the sense of the earth, my brothers; and let the value of all things be posited newly by you. For that shall you be fighters! For that shall you be creators!

With knowledge, the body purifies itself; making experiments with knowledge, it elevates itself; in the lover of knowledge all instincts become holy; in the elevated, the soul becomes gay.

Physician, help yourself: thus you help your patient too. Let this be his best help that he may behold with his eyes the man who heals himself.

There are a thousand paths that have never yet been trodden—a thousand healths and hidden isles of life. Even now, man and man's earth are unexhausted and undiscovered.

Wake and listen, you that are lonely! From the future come winds with secret wing-beats; and good tidings are proclaimed to delicate ears. You that are lonely today, you that are withdrawing, you shall one day be the people: out of you, who have chosen yourselves, there shall grow a chosen people—and out of them, the overman. Verily, the earth shall yet become a site of recovery. And even now a new fragrance surrounds it, bringing salvation—and a new hope.

3

When Zarathustra had said these words he became silent, like one who has not yet said his last word; long he weighed his staff in his hand, doubtfully. At last he spoke thus, and the tone of his voice had changed.

Now I go alone, my disciples. You too go now, alone. Thus I want it. Verily, I counsel you: go away from me and resist Zarathustra! And even better: be ashamed of him! Perhaps he deceived you.

The man of knowledge must not only love his enemies, he must also be able to hate his friends.

One repays a teacher badly if one always remains nothing but a pupil. And why do you not want to pluck at my wreath?

You revere me; but what if your reverence tumbles one day? Beware lest a statue slay you.

You say you believe in Zarathustra? But what matters Zarathustra? You are my believers—but what matter all believers? You had not yet sought yourselves: and you found me. Thus do all believers; therefore all faith amounts to so little.

Now I bid you lose me and find yourselves; and only when you have all denied me will I return to you.

Verily, my brothers, with different eyes shall I then seek my lost ones; with a different love shall I then love you.

And once again you shall become my friends and the children of a single hope—and then shall I be with you the third time, that I may celebrate the great noon with you.

And that is the great noon when man stands in the middle of his way between beast and overman and celebrates his way to the evening as his highest hope: for it is the way to a new morning.

Then will he who goes under bless himself for being
one who goes over and beyond; and the sun of his
knowledge will stand at high noon for him.

*"Dead are all gods: now we want the overman to
live"*—on that great noon, let this be our last will.

Thus spoke Zarathustra.

Thus Spoke Zarathustra: Second Part

*. . . and only when you have all denied me will
I return to you.*

*Verily, my brothers, with different eyes shall I
then seek my lost ones; with a different love shall
I then love you.* (Zarathustra, "On the Gift-Giving Virtue." I, p. 78)

TRANSLATOR'S NOTES

1. *The Child with the Mirror:* Transition to Part Two with
its partly new style: "A new speech comes to me. . . .
My spirit no longer wants to walk on worn soles."

2. *Upon the Blessed Isles:* The creative life versus belief
in God: "God is a conjecture." The polemic against the
opening lines of the final chorus in Goethe's *Faust* is taken
up again in the chapter "On Poets" (see comments, p. 81).
But the lines immediately following in praise of impermanence and creation are thoroughly in the spirit of Goethe.

3. *On the Pitying:* A return to the style of Part One and
a major statement of Nietzsche's ideas on pity, *ressentiment,*
and repression.

4. *On Priests:* Relatively mild, compared to the portrait
of the priest in *The Antichrist* five years later.

5. *On the Virtuous:* A typology of different conceptions of
virtue, with vivisectional intent. Nietzsche denounces "the
filth of the words: revenge, punishment, reward, retribution," which he associates with Christianity; but also

that rigorism for which "virtue is the spasm under the scourge" and those who "call it virtue when their vices grow lazy." The pun on "I am just" is, in German: *wenn sie sagen: "ich bin gerecht," so klingt es immer gleich wie: "ich bin gerächt!"*

6. *On the Rabble:* The theme of Zarathustra's nausea is developed *ad nauseam* in later chapters. *La Nausée*—to speak in Sartre's terms—is one of his chief trials, and its eventual conquest is his greatest triumph. "I often grew weary of the spirit when I found that even the rabble had *esprit*" may help to account for some of Nietzsche's remarks elsewhere. Generally he celebrates the spirit—not in opposition to the body but as *mens sana in corpore sano.*

7. *On the Tarantulas:* One of the central motifs of Nietzsche's philosophy is stated in italics: "that man be delivered from revenge." In this chapter, the claim of human equality is criticized as an expression of the *ressentiment* of the subequal.

8. *On the Famous Wise Men:* One cannot serve two masters: the people and the truth. The philosophers of the past have too often rationalized popular prejudices. But the service of truth is a passion and martyrdom, for "spirit is the life that itself cuts into life: with its agony it increases its own knowledge." The song of songs on the spirit in this chapter may seem to contradict Nietzsche's insistence, in the chapter "On the Despisers of the Body," that the spirit is a mere instrument. Both themes are central in Nietzsche's thought, and their apparent contradiction is partly due to the fact that both are stated metaphorically. For, in truth, Nietzsche denies any crude dualism of body and spirit as a popular prejudice. The life of the spirit and the life of the body are aspects of a single life. But up to a point the contradiction can also be resolved metaphorically: life uses the spirit against its present form to attain a higher perfection. Man's enhancement is inseparable from the spirit; but Nietzsche denounces the occasional efforts of the spirit to destroy life instead of pruning it.

9. *The Night Song:* "Light am I; ah, that I were night!"

10. *The Dancing Song:* Life and wisdom as jealous women.

11. *The Tomb Song:* "Invulnerable am I only in the heel."

12. *On Self-Overcoming:* The first long discussion of the will to power marks, together with the chapters "On the Pitying" and "On the Tarantulas," one of the high points of Part Two. Philosophically, however, it raises many difficulties. (See my *Nietzsche*, 6, III.)

13. *On Those Who Are Sublime:* The doctrine of self-overcoming is here guarded against misunderstandings: far from favoring austere heroics, Nietzsche praises humor (and practices it: witness the whole of *Zarathustra*, especially Part Four) and, no less, gracefulness and graciousness. The three sentences near the end, beginning "And there is nobody . . . ," represent a wonderfully concise statement of much of his philosophy.

14. *On the Land of Education:* Against modern eclecticism and lack of style. "Rather would I be a day laborer in Hades . . .": in the *Odyssey*, the shade of Achilles would rather be a day laborer on the smallest field than king of all the dead in Hades. *Zarathustra* abounds in similar allusions. "Everything deserves to perish," for example, is an abbreviation of a dictum of Goethe's Mephistopheles.

15. *On Immaculate Perception:* Labored sexual imagery, already notable in "The Dancing Song," keeps this critique of detachment from becoming incisive. Not arid but, judged by high standards, a mismatch of message and metaphor. Or put positively: something of a personal document. Therefore the German references to the sun as feminine have been retained in translation. "Loving and perishing (*Lieben und Untergehn*)" do not rhyme in German either.

16. *On Scholars:* Nietzsche's, not Zarathustra's, autobiography.

17. *On Poets:* This chapter is full of allusions to the final chorus in Goethe's *Faust*, which might be translated thus:

> What is destructible
> Is but a parable;

What fails ineluctably
The undeclarable,
Here it was seen,
Here it was action;
The Eternal-Feminine
Lures to perfection.

18. *On Great Events:* How successful Nietzsche's attempts at narrative are is at least debatable. Here the story distracts from his statement of his anti-political attitude. But the curious mixture of the solemn and frivolous, myth, epigram, and "bow-wow," is of course entirely intentional. Even the similarity between the ghost's cry and the words of the white rabbit in *Alice in Wonderland* probably would not have dismayed Nietzsche in the least.

19. *The Soothsayer:* In the chapter "On the Adder's Bite" a brief parable introduces some of Zarathustra's finest sayings; but here the parable is offered for its own sake, and we feel closer to Rimbaud than to Proverbs. The soothsayer reappears in Part Four.

20. *On Redemption:* In the conception of inverse cripples and the remarks on revenge and punishment Zarathustra's moral pathos reappears to some extent; but the mood of the preceding chapter figures in his subsequent reflections, which lead up to, but stop short of, Nietzsche's notion of the eternal recurrence of the same events.

21. *On Human Prudence:* First: better to be deceived occasionally than always to watch out for deceivers. Second: vanity versus pride. Third: men today (1883) are too concerned about petty evil, but great things are possible only where great evil is harnessed.

22. *The Stillest Hour:* Zarathustra cannot yet get himself to proclaim the eternal recurrence and hence he must leave in order to "ripen."

THE CHILD WITH THE MIRROR

Then Zarathustra returned again to the mountains and to the solitude of his cave and withdrew from men, waiting like a sower who has scattered his seed. But his soul grew full of impatience and desire for those whom he loved, because he still had much to give them. For this is what is hardest: to close the open hand because one loves, and to keep a sense of shame as a giver.

Thus months and years passed for the solitary; but his wisdom grew and caused him pain with its fullness. One morning, however, he woke even before the dawn, reflected long, lying on his bed, and at last spoke to his heart:

Why was I so startled in my dream that I awoke? Did not a child step up to me, carrying a mirror? "O Zarathustra," the child said to me, "look at yourself in the mirror." But when I looked into the mirror I cried out, and my heart was shaken: for it was not myself I saw, but a devil's grimace and scornful laughter. Verily, all-too-well do I understand the sign and admonition of the dream: my *teaching* is in danger; weeds pose as wheat. My enemies have grown powerful and have distorted my teaching till those dearest to me must be ashamed of the gifts I gave them. I have lost my friends; the hour has come to seek my lost ones."

With these words Zarathustra leaped up, not like a frightened man seeking air but rather as a seer and singer who is moved by the spirit. Amazed, his eagle and his serpent looked at him: for, like dawn, a coming happiness lay reflected in his face.

What has happened to me, my animals? said Zarathustra. Have I not changed? Has not bliss come to me as a storm? My happiness is foolish and will say foolish things: it is still young, so be patient with it. I am wounded by my happiness: let all who suffer be my physicians. I may go down again to my friends, and to my enemies too. Zarathustra may speak again and give and do what is dearest to those dear to him. My impatient love overflows in rivers, downward, toward sunrise and sunset. From silent mountains and thunderstorms of suffering my soul rushes into the valleys.

Too long have I longed and looked into the distance. Too long have I belonged to loneliness; thus I have forgotten how to be silent. Mouth have I become through and through, and the roaring of a stream from towering cliffs: I want to plunge my speech down into the valleys. Let the river of my love plunge where there is no way! How could a river fail to find its way to the sea? Indeed, a lake is within me, solitary and self-sufficient; but the river of my love carries it along, down to the sea.

New ways I go, a new speech comes to me; weary I grow, like all creators, of the old tongues. My spirit no longer wants to walk on worn soles.

Too slowly runs all speech for me: into your chariot I leap, storm! And even you I want to whip with my sarcasm. Like a cry and a shout of joy I want to sweep over wide seas, till I find the blessed isles where my friends are dwelling. And my enemies among them! How I now love all to whom I may speak! My enemies too are part of my bliss.

And when I want to mount my wildest horse, it is always my spear that helps me up best, as the ever-ready servant of my foot: the spear that I hurl against my enemies. How grateful I am to my enemies that I may finally hurl it!

The tension of my cloud was too great: between the laughter of lightning bolts I want to throw showers of hail into the depths. Violently my chest will expand, violently will it blow its storm over the mountains and thus find relief. Verily, like a storm come my happiness and my freedom. But let my enemies believe that *the evil one* rages over their heads.

Indeed, you too will be frightened, my friends, by my wild wisdom; and perhaps you will flee from it, together with my enemies. Would that I knew how to lure you back with shepherds' flutes! Would that my lioness, wisdom, might learn how to roar tenderly! And many things have we already learned together.

My wild wisdom became pregnant on lonely mountains; on rough stones she gave birth to her young, her youngest. Now she runs foolishly through the harsh desert and seeks and seeks gentle turf—my old wild wisdom. Upon your hearts' gentle turf, my friends, upon your love she would bed her most dearly beloved.

Thus spoke Zarathustra.

UPON THE BLESSED ISLES

The figs are falling from the trees; they are good and sweet; and, as they fall, their red skin bursts. I am a north wind to ripe figs.

Thus, like figs, these teachings fall to you, my friends; now consume their juice and their sweet meat. It is autumn about us, and pure sky and afternoon. Behold what fullness there is about us! And out of such overflow it is beautiful to look out upon distant seas. Once one said God when one looked upon distant seas; but now I have taught you to say: overman.

God is a conjecture; but I desire that your conjectures should not reach beyond your creative will. Could you *create* a god? Then do not speak to me of any gods. But you could well create the overman. Perhaps not you yourselves, my brothers. But into fathers and forefathers of the overman you could re-create yourselves: and let this be your best creation.

God is a conjecture; but I desire that your conjectures should be limited by what is thinkable. Could you *think* a god? But this is what the will to truth should mean to you: that everything be changed into what is thinkable for man, visible for man, feelable by man. You should think through your own senses to their consequences.

And what you have called world, that shall be created only by you: your reason, your image, your will, your love shall thus be realized. And verily, for your own bliss, you lovers of knowledge.

And how would you bear life without this hope, you lovers of knowledge? You could not have been born either into the incomprehensible or into the irrational.

But let me reveal my heart to you entirely, my friends: *if* there were gods, how could I endure not to be a god! *Hence* there are no gods. Though I drew this conclusion, now it draws me.

God is a conjecture; but who could drain all the agony of this conjecture without dying? Shall his faith be taken away from the creator, and from the eagle, his soaring to eagle heights?

God is a thought that makes crooked all that is straight, and makes turn whatever stands. How? Should time be gone, and all that is impermanent a mere lie? To think this is a dizzy whirl for human bones, and a vomit for the stomach; verily, I call it the turning sickness to conjecture thus. Evil I call it, and misanthropic —all this teaching of the One and the Plenum and the Unmoved and the Sated and the Permanent. All the permanent—that is only a parable. And the poets lie too much.

It is of time and becoming that the best parables

should speak: let them be a praise and a justification of all impermanence.

Creation—that is the great redemption from suffering, and life's growing light. But that the creator may be, suffering is needed and much change. Indeed, there must be much bitter dying in your life, you creators. Thus are you advocates and justifiers of all impermanence. To be the child who is newly born, the creator must also want to be the mother who gives birth and the pangs of the birth-giver.

Verily, through a hundred souls I have already passed on my way, and through a hundred cradles and birth pangs. Many a farewell have I taken; I know the heart-rending last hours. But thus my creative will, my destiny, wills it. Or, to say it more honestly: this very destiny—my will wills.

Whatever in me has feeling, suffers and is in prison; but my will always comes to me as my liberator and joy-bringer. Willing liberates: that is the true teaching of will and liberty—thus Zarathustra teaches it. Willing no more and esteeming no more and creating no more—oh, that this great weariness might always remain far from me! In knowledge too I feel only my will's joy in begetting and becoming; and if there is innocence in my knowledge, it is because the will to beget is in it. Away from God and gods this will has lured me; what could one create if gods existed?

But my fervent will to create impels me ever again toward man; thus is the hammer impelled toward the stone. O men, in the stone there sleeps an image, the image of my images. Alas, that it must sleep in the hardest, the ugliest stone! Now my hammer rages cruelly against its prison. Pieces of rock rain from the stone: what is that to me? I want to perfect it; for a shadow came to me—the stillest and lightest of all things once came to me. The beauty of the overman came to me as a shadow. O my brothers, what are the gods to me now?

Thus spoke Zarathustra.

ON THE PITYING

My friends, a gibe was related to your friend: "Look at Zarathustra! Does he not walk among us as if we were animals?"

But it were better said: "He who has knowledge walks among men *as* among animals."

To him who has knowledge, man himself is "the animal with red cheeks." How did this come about? Is it not because man has had to be ashamed too often? O my friends! Thus speaks he who has knowledge: shame, shame, shame—that is the history of man. And that is why he who is noble bids himself not to shame: shame he imposes on himself before all who suffer.

Verily, I do not like them, the merciful who feel blessed in their pity: they are lacking too much in shame. If I must pity, at least I do not want it known; and if I do pity, it is preferably from a distance.

I should also like to shroud my face and flee before I am recognized; and thus I bid you do, my friends. Would that my destiny led those like you, who do not suffer, across my way, and those with whom I *may* share hope and meal and honey. Verily, I may have done this and that for sufferers; but always I seemed to have done better when I learned to feel better joys. As long as there have been men, man has felt too little joy: that alone, my brothers, is our original sin. And learning better to feel joy, we learn best not to hurt others or to plan hurts for them.

Therefore I wash my hand when it has helped the

sufferer; therefore I wipe even my soul. Having seen the sufferer suffer, I was ashamed for the sake of his shame; and when I helped him, I transgressed grievously against his pride.

Great indebtedness does not make men grateful, but vengeful; and if a little charity is not forgotten, it turns into a gnawing worm.

"Be reserved in accepting! Distinguish by accepting!" Thus I advise those who have nothing to give.

But I am a giver of gifts: I like to give, as a friend to friends. Strangers, however, and the poor may themselves pluck the fruit from my tree: that will cause them less shame.

But beggars should be abolished entirely! Verily, it is annoying to give to them and it is annoying not to give to them.

And also sinners and bad consciences! Believe me, my friends: the bite of conscience teaches men to bite.

Worst of all, however, are petty thoughts. Verily, even evil deeds are better than petty thoughts.

To be sure, you say: "The pleasure in a lot of petty nastiness saves us from many a big evil deed." But here one should not wish to save.

An evil deed is like a boil: it itches and irritates and breaks open—it speaks honestly. "Behold, I am disease" —thus speaks the evil deed; that is its honesty.

But a petty thought is like a fungus: it creeps and stoops and does not want to be anywhere—until the whole body is rotten and withered with little fungi.

But to him who is possessed by the devil I whisper this word: "Better for you to rear up your devil! Even for you there is still a way to greatness!"

My brothers, one knows a little too much about everybody. And we can even see through some men and yet we can by no means *pass* through them.

It is difficult to live with people because it is so difficult to be silent. And not against him who is repugnant to us are we most unfair, but against him who is no concern of ours.

But if you have a suffering friend, be a resting place for his suffering, but a hard bed as it were, a field cot: thus will you profit him best.

And if a friend does you evil, then say: "I forgive you what you did to me; but that you have done it to *yourself*—how could I forgive that?" Thus speaks all great love: it overcomes even forgiveness and pity.

One ought to hold on to one's heart; for if one lets it go, one soon loses control of the head too. Alas, where in the world has there been more folly than among the pitying? And what in the world has caused more suffering than the folly of the pitying? Woe to all who love without having a height that is above their pity!

Thus spoke the devil to me once: "God too has his hell: that is his love of man." And most recently I heard him say this: "God is dead; God died of his pity for man."

Thus be warned of pity: from there a heavy cloud will yet come to man. Verily, I understand weather signs. But mark this too: all great love is even above all its pity; for it still wants to create the beloved.

"Myself I sacrifice to my love, *and my neighbor as myself*"—thus runs the speech of all creators. But all creators are hard.

Thus spoke Zarathustra.

ON PRIESTS

Once Zarathustra gave his disciples a sign and spoke these words to them:

"Here are priests; and though they are my enemies,

pass by them silently and with sleeping swords. Among them too there are heroes; many of them have suffered too much: therefore they want to make others suffer.

"They are evil enemies: nothing is more vengeful than their humility. And whoever attacks them, soils himself easily. Yet my blood is related to theirs, and I want to know that my blood is honored even in theirs."

And when they had passed, pain seized Zarathustra; and he had not wrestled long with his pain when he began to speak thus:

I am moved by compassion for these priests. I also find them repulsive; but that matters least of all to me since I have been among men. But I suffer and have suffered with them: prisoners they are to me, and marked men. He whom they call Redeemer has put them in fetters: in fetters of false values and delusive words. Would that someone would yet redeem them from their Redeemer!

Once when the sea cast them about, they thought they were landing on an island; but behold, it was a sleeping monster. False values and delusive words: these are the worst monsters for mortals; long does calamity sleep and wait in them. But eventually it comes and wakes and eats and devours what built huts upon it. Behold these huts which these priests built! Churches they call their sweet-smelling caves. Oh, that falsified light! That musty air! Here the soul is not allowed to soar to its height. For thus their faith commands: "Crawl up the stairs on your knees, ye sinners!"

Verily, rather would I see even the shameless than the contorted eyes of their shame and devotion! Who created for themselves such caves and stairways of repentance? Was it not such as wanted to hide themselves and were ashamed before the pure sky?

And only when the pure sky again looks through

broken ceilings and down upon grass and red poppies near broken walls, will I again turn my heart to the abodes of this god.

They have called "God" what was contrary to them and gave them pain; and verily, there was much of the heroic in their adoration. And they did not know how to love their god except by crucifying man.

As corpses they meant to live; in black they decked out their corpses; out of their speech, too, I still smell the bad odor of death chambers. And whoever lives near them lives near black ponds out of which an ominous frog sings its song with sweet melancholy. They would have to sing better songs for me to learn to have faith in their Redeemer: and his disciples would have to look more redeemed!

Naked would I see them: for only beauty should preach repentance. But who would be persuaded by this muffled melancholy? Verily, their redeemers themselves did not come out of freedom and the seventh heaven of freedom. Verily, they themselves have never walked on the carpets of knowledge. Of gaps was the spirit of these redeemers made up; but into every gap they put their delusion, their stopgap, which they called God.

Their spirit was drowned in their pity; and when they were swollen and overswollen with pity, it was always a great folly that swam on top. Eagerly and with much shouting they drove their herd over their path; as if there were but a single path to the future. Verily, these shepherds themselves belonged among the sheep. Small spirits and spacious souls these shepherds had; but my brothers, what small domains have even the most spacious souls proved to be so far!

They wrote signs of blood on the way they walked, and their folly taught that with blood one proved truth.

But blood is the worst witness of truth; blood poisons even the purest doctrine and turns it into delusion and hatred of the heart. And if a man goes through fire for his doctrine—what does that prove? Verily, it is more if your own doctrine comes out of your own fire.

A sultry heart and a cold head: where these two meet there arises the roaring wind, the "Redeemer." There have been greater ones, verily, and more highborn than those whom the people call redeemers, those roaring winds which carry away. And you, my brothers, must be redeemed from still greater ones than all the redeemers if you would find the way to freedom.

Never yet has there been an overman. Naked I saw both the greatest and the smallest man: they are still all-too-similar to each other. Verily, even the greatest I found all-too-human.

Thus spoke Zarathustra.

ON THE VIRTUOUS

Slack and sleeping senses must be addressed with thunder and heavenly fireworks. But the voice of beauty speaks gently: it creeps only into the most awakened souls. Gently trembled and laughed my shield today; that is the holy laughter and tremor of beauty. About you, the virtuous, my beauty laughed today. And thus its voice came to me: "They still want to be paid."

You who are virtuous still want to be paid! Do you want rewards for virtue, and heaven for earth, and the eternal for your today?

And now are you angry with me because I teach that there is no reward and paymaster? And verily, I do not even teach that virtue is its own reward.

Alas, that is my sorrow: they have lied reward and punishment into the foundation of things, and now also into the foundation of your souls, you who are virtuous. But like the boar's snout, my words shall tear open the foundation of your souls: a plowshare will I be to you. All the secrets of your foundation shall come to light; and when you lie uprooted and broken in the sun, then will your lies also be separated from your truths.

For this is your truth: you are too *pure* for the filth of the words: revenge, punishment, reward, retribution. You love your virtue as a mother her child; but when has a mother ever wished to be paid for her love? Your virtue is what is dearest to you. The thirst of the ring lives in you: every ring strives and turns to reach itself again. And like a dying star is every work of your virtue: its light is always still on its way and it wanders— and when will it no longer be on its way? Thus the light of your virtue is still on its way even when the work has been done. Though it be forgotten and dead, the ray of its light still lives and wanders. That your virtue is your self and not something foreign, a skin, a cloak, that is the truth from the foundation of your souls, you who are virtuous.

Yet there are those for whom virtue is the spasm under the scourge, and you have listened to their clamor too much.

And there are others who call it virtue when their vices grow lazy; and when their hatred and jealousy stretch their limbs for once, then their "justice" comes to life and rubs its sleepy eyes.

And there are others who are drawn downward: their devils draw them. But the more they sink, the more fervently glow their eyes and their lust for their god. Alas, their clamor too has reached your ears, you who are virtuous: "What I am not, that, that to me are God and virtue!"

And there are others who come along, heavy and

creaking like carts carrying stones downhill: they talk much of dignity and virtue—they call their brake virtue.

And there are others who are like cheap clocks that must be wound: they tick and they want the tick-tock to be called virtue. Verily, I have my pleasure in these: wherever I find such clocks, I shall wind and wound them with my mockery, and they shall whir for me.

And others are proud of their handful of justice and commit outrages against all things for its sake, till the world is drowned in their injustice. Oh, how ill the word virtue comes out of their mouths! And when they say, "I am just," it always sounds like "I am just—revenged." With their virtue they want to scratch out the eyes of their enemies, and they exalt themselves only to humble others.

And then again there are such as sit in their swamp and speak thus out of the reeds: "Virtue—that is sitting still in a swamp. We bite no one and avoid those who want to bite; and in all things we hold the opinion that is given to us."

And then again there are such as love gestures and think that virtue is some kind of gesture. Their knees always adore, and their hands are hymns to virtue, but their heart knows nothing about it.

And then again there are such as consider it virtue to say, "Virtue is necessary"; but at bottom they believe only that the police is necessary.

And some who cannot see what is high in man call it virtue that they see all-too-closely what is low in man: thus they call their evil eye virtue.

And some want to be edified and elevated, and they call that virtue, while others want to be bowled over, and they call that virtue too.

And thus almost all believe that they have a share in

virtue; and at the very least everyone wants to be an expert on good and evil.

Yet Zarathustra did not come to say to all these liars and fools: "What do *you* know of virtue? What *could* you know of virtue?"

Rather, that you, my friends, might grow weary of the old words you have learned from the fools and liars.

Weary of the words: reward, retribution, punishment, and revenge in justice.

Weary of saying: what makes an act good is that it is unselfish.

Oh, my friends, that your self be in your deed as the mother is in her child—let that be *your* word concerning virtue!

Verily, I may have taken a hundred words from you and the dearest toys of your virtue, and now you are angry with me, as children are angry. They played by the sea, and a wave came and carried off their toy to the depths: now they are crying. But the same wave shall bring them new toys and shower new colorful shells before them. Thus they will be comforted; and like them, you too, my friends, shall have your comfortings—and new colorful shells.

Thus spoke Zarathustra.

ON THE RABBLE

Life is a well of joy; but where the rabble drinks too, all wells are poisoned. I am fond of all that is clean, but I have no wish to see the grinning snouts and the thirst of the unclean. They cast their eye into the well: now their revolting smile shines up out of the well. They have poisoned the holy water with their lustfulness; and when they called their dirty dreams "pleasure," they poisoned the language too. The flame is vexed when their moist hearts come near the fire; the spirit itself seethes and smokes where the rabble steps near the fire. In their hands all fruit grows sweetish and overmellow; their glance makes the fruit tree a prey of the wind and withers its crown.

And some who turned away from life only turned away from the rabble: they did not want to share well and flame and fruit with the rabble.

And some who went into the wilderness and suffered thirst with the beasts of prey merely did not want to sit around the cistern with filthy camel drivers.

And some who came along like annihilators and like a hailstorm to all orchards merely wanted to put a foot into the gaping jaws of the rabble to plug up its throat.

The bite on which I gagged the most is not the knowledge that life itself requires hostility and death and torture-crosses—but once I asked, and I was almost choked by my question: What? does life require even the rabble? Are poisoned wells required, and stinking fires and soiled dreams and maggots in the bread of life?

Not my hatred but my nausea gnawed hungrily at my life. Alas, I often grew weary of the spirit when I found that even the rabble had *esprit*. And I turned my back on those who rule when I saw what they now call ruling: higgling and haggling for power—with the rabble. I have lived with closed ears among people with foreign tongues: would that the tongue of their higgling and their haggling for power might remain foreign to me. And, holding my nose, I walked disgruntled through all of yesterday and today: verily, all of yesterday and today smells foul of the writing rabble.

Like a cripple who has become deaf and blind and dumb: thus have I lived for many years lest I live with the power-, writing- and pleasure-rabble. Laboriously and cautiously my spirit climbed steps; alms of pleasure were its refreshment; and life crept along for the blind as on a cane.

What was it that happened to me? How did I redeem myself from nausea? Who rejuvenated my sight? How did I fly to the height where no more rabble sits by the well? Was it my nausea itself which created wings for me and water-divining powers? Verily, I had to fly to the highest spheres that I might find the fount of pleasure again.

Oh, I found it, my brothers! Here, in the highest spheres, the fount of pleasure wells up for me! And here is a life of which the rabble does not drink.

You flow for me almost too violently, fountain of pleasure. And often you empty the cup again by wanting to fill it. And I must still learn to approach you more modestly: all-too-violently my heart still flows toward you—my heart, upon which my summer burns, short, hot, melancholy, overblissful: how my summer-heart craves your coolness!

Gone is the hesitant gloom of my spring! Gone the malice of my snowflakes in June! Summer have I become entirely, and summer noon! A summer in the highest spheres with cold wells and blissful silence: oh, come, my friends, that the silence may become still more blissful!

For this is *our* height and our home: we live here too high and steep for all the unclean and their thirst. Cast your pure eyes into the well of my pleasure, friends! How should that make it muddy? It shall laugh back at you in its own purity.

On the tree, Future, we build our nest; and in our solitude eagles shall bring us nourishment in their beaks. Verily, no nourishment which the unclean might share: they would think they were devouring fire and they would burn their mouths. Verily, we keep no homes here for the unclean: our pleasure would be an ice cave to their bodies and their spirits.

And we want to live over them like strong winds, neighbors of the eagles, neighbors of the snow, neighbors of the sun: thus live strong winds. And like a wind I yet want to blow among them one day, and with my spirit take the breath of their spirit: thus my future wills it.

Verily, a strong wind is Zarathustra for all who are low; and this counsel he gives to all his enemies and all who spit and spew: "Beware of spitting *against* the wind!"

Thus spoke Zarathustra.

ON THE TARANTULAS

Behold, this is the hole of the tarantula. Do you want to see the tarantula itself? Here hangs its web; touch it, that it tremble!

There it comes willingly: welcome, tarantula! Your triangle and symbol sits black on your back; and I also know what sits in your soul. Revenge sits in your soul: wherever you bite, black scabs grow; your poison makes the soul whirl with revenge.

Thus I speak to you in a parable—you who make souls whirl, you preachers of *equality*. To me you are tarantulas, and secretly vengeful. But I shall bring your secrets to light; therefore I laugh in your faces with my laughter of the heights. Therefore I tear at your webs, that your rage may lure you out of your lie-holes and your revenge may leap out from behind your word justice. For *that man be delivered from revenge*, that is for me the bridge to the highest hope, and a rainbow after long storms.

The tarantulas, of course, would have it otherwise.

"What justice means to us is precisely that the world be filled with the storms of our revenge"—thus they speak to each other. "We shall wreak vengeance and abuse on all whose equals we are not"—thus do the tarantula-hearts vow. "And 'will to equality' shall henceforth be the name for virtue; and against all that has power we want to raise our clamor!"

You preachers of equality, the tyrannomania of impotence clamors thus out of you for equality: your most secret ambitions to be tyrants thus shroud themselves in words of virtue. Aggrieved conceit, repressed envy —perhaps the conceit and envy of your fathers—erupt from you as a flame and as the frenzy of revenge.

What was silent in the father speaks in the son; and often I found the son the unveiled secret of the father.

They are like enthusiasts, yet it is not the heart that fires them—but revenge. And when they become elegant and cold, it is not the spirit but envy that makes them elegant and cold. Their jealousy leads them even on the paths of thinkers; and this is the sign of their jealousy: they always go too far, till their weariness must in the end lie down to sleep in the snow. Out of every one of their complaints sounds revenge; in their praise there is always a sting, and to be a judge seems bliss to them.

But thus I counsel you, my friends: Mistrust all in whom the impulse to punish is powerful. They are people of a low sort and stock; the hangman and the bloodhound look out of their faces. Mistrust all who talk much of their justice! Verily, their souls lack more than honey. And when they call themselves the good and the just, do not forget that they would be pharisees, if only they had—power.

My friends, I do not want to be mixed up and confused with others. Some preach my doctrine of life and

are at the same time preachers of equality and tarantulas. Although they are sitting in their holes, these
poisonous spiders, with their backs turned on life, they
speak in favor of life, but only because they wish to
hurt. They wish to hurt those who now have power, for
among these the preaching of death is still most at
home. If it were otherwise, the tarantulas would teach
otherwise; they themselves were once the foremost slan-
derers of the world and burners of heretics.

I do not wish to be mixed up and confused with
these preachers of equality. For, to *me* justice speaks
thus: "Men are not equal." Nor shall they become
equal! What would my love of the overman be if I
spoke otherwise?

On a thousand bridges and paths they shall throng
to the future, and ever more war and inequality shall
divide them: thus does my great love make me speak.
In their hostilities they shall become inventors of images
and ghosts, and with their images and ghosts they shall
yet fight the highest fight against one another. Good
and evil, and rich and poor, and high and low, and all
the names of values—arms shall they be and clattering
signs that life must overcome itself again and again.

Life wants to build itself up into the heights with
pillars and steps; it wants to look into vast distances
and out toward stirring beauties: therefore it requires
height. And because it requires height, it requires steps
and contradiction among the steps and the climbers.
Life wants to climb and to overcome itself climbing.

And behold, my friends: here where the tarantula
has its hole, the ruins of an ancient temple rise; behold
it with enlightened eyes! Verily, the man who once
piled his thoughts to the sky in these stones—he, like
the wisest, knew the secret of all life. That struggle and
inequality are present even in beauty, and also war for

power and more power: that is what he teaches us here in the plainest parable. How divinely vault and arches break through each other in a wrestling match; how they strive against each other with light and shade, the godlike strivers—with such assurance and beauty let us be enemies too, my friends! Let us strive against one another like gods.

Alas, then the tarantula, my old enemy, bit me. With godlike assurance and beauty it bit my finger. "Punishment there must be and justice," it thinks; "and here he shall not sing songs in honor of enmity in vain."

Indeed, it has avenged itself. And alas, now it will make my soul, too, whirl with revenge. But to keep me from whirling, my friends, tie me tight to this column. Rather would I be a stylite even, than a whirl of revenge.

Verily, Zarathustra is no cyclone or whirlwind; and if he is a dancer, he will never dance the tarantella.

Thus spoke Zarathustra.

ON THE FAMOUS WISE MEN

You have served the people and the superstition of the people, all you famous wise men—and *not* truth. And that is precisely why you were accorded respect. And that is also why your lack of faith was tolerated: it was a joke and a circuitous route to the people. Thus the master lets his slaves have their way and is even amused by their pranks.

But the free spirit, the enemy of fetters, the non-adorer who dwells in the woods, is as hateful to the people as a wolf to dogs. To hound him out of his lair —that is what the people have ever called "a sense of decency"; and against him the people still set their fiercest dogs.

"Truth is there: after all, the people are there! Let those who seek beware!"—these words have echoed through the ages. You wanted to prove your people right in their reverence: that is what you called "will to truth," you famous wise men. And your hearts ever said to themselves: "From among the people I came, and from there too the voice of God came to me. As the people's advocates you have always been stiff-necked and clever like asses.

And many who were powerful and wanted to get along smoothly with the people harnessed in front of their horses a little ass, a famous wise man.

And now I should wish, you famous wise men, that you would at long last throw off the lion's skin completely. The skin of the beast of prey, mottled, and the mane of those who search, seek, and conquer.

Oh, to make me believe in your "truthfulness" you would first have to break your revering will.

Truthful I call him who goes into godless deserts, having broken his revering heart. In the yellow sands, burned by the sun, he squints thirstily at the islands abounding in wells, where living things rest under dark trees. Yet his thirst does not persuade him to become like these, dwelling in comfort; for where there are oases there are also idols.

Hungry, violent, lonely, godless: thus the lion-will wants itself. Free from the happiness of slaves, redeemed from gods and adorations, fearless and fearinspiring, great and lonely: such is the will of the truthful.

It was ever in the desert that the truthful have dwelt, the free spirits, as masters of the desert; but in the cities dwell the well-fed, famous wise men—the beasts of burden. For, as asses, they always pull the people's cart. Not that I am angry with them for that: but for me they remain such as serve and work in a harness, even when they shine in harnesses of gold. And often they have been good servants, worthy of praise. For thus speaks virtue: "If you must be a servant, seek him who profits most from your service. The spirit and virtue of your master shall grow by your being his servant: then you yourself will grow with his spirit and his virtue." And verily, you famous wise men, you servants of the people, you yourselves have grown with the spirit and virtue of the people—and the people through you. In your honor I say this. But even in your virtues you remain for me part of the people, the dumb-eyed people —the people, who do not know what spirit is.

Spirit is the life that itself cuts into life: with its own agony it increases its own knowledge. Did you know that?

And the happiness of the spirit is this: to be anointed and through tears to be consecrated as a sacrificial animal. Did you know that?

And the blindness of the blind and their seeking and groping shall yet bear witness to the power of the sun, into which they have looked. Did you know that?

And the lover of knowledge shall learn to *build* with mountains. It means little that the spirit moves mountains. Did you know that?

You know only the spark of the spirit, but you do not see the anvil it is, nor the cruelty of its hammer.

Verily, you do not know the pride of the spirit! But even less would you endure the modesty of the spirit, if ever it would speak.

And you have never yet been able to cast your spirit

into a pit of snow: you are not hot enough for that. Hence you also do not know the ecstasies of its coldness.

In all things, however, you act too familiarly with the spirit, and you have often made wisdom into a poorhouse and a hospital for bad poets.

You are no eagles: hence you have never experienced the happiness that is in the terror of the spirit. And he who is not a bird should not build his nest over abysses.

You are lukewarm to me, but all profound knowledge flows cold. Ice cold are the inmost wells of the spirit: refreshing for hot hands and men of action. You stand there honorable and stiff and with straight backs, you famous wise men: no strong wind and will drives you.

Have you never seen a sail go over the sea, rounded and taut and trembling with the violence of the wind? Like the sail, trembling with the violence of the spirit, my wisdom goes over the sea—my wild wisdom.

But you servants of the people, you famous wise men—how could you go with me?

Thus spoke Zarathustra.

THE NIGHT SONG

Night has come; now all fountains speak more loudly. And my soul too is a fountain.

Night has come; only now all the songs of lovers awaken. And my soul too is the song of a lover.

Something unstilled, unstillable is within me; it wants to be voiced. A craving for love is within me; it speaks the language of love.

Light am I; ah, that I were night! But this is my loneliness that I am girt with light. Ah, that I were dark and nocturnal! How I would suck at the breasts of light!

And even you would I bless, you little sparkling stars and glowworms up there, and be overjoyed with your gifts of light.

But I live in my own light; I drink back into myself the flames that break out of me. I do not know the happiness of those who receive; and I have often dreamed that even stealing must be more blessed than receiving. This is my poverty, that my hand never rests from giving; this is my envy, that I see waiting eyes and the lit-up nights of longing. Oh, wretchedness of all givers! Oh, darkening of my sun! Oh, craving to crave! Oh, ravenous hunger in satiation!

They receive from me, but do I touch their souls? There is a cleft between giving and receiving; and the narrowest cleft is the last to be bridged. A hunger grows out of my beauty: I should like to hurt those for whom I shine; I should like to rob those to whom I give; thus do I hunger for malice. To withdraw my hand when the other hand already reaches out to it; to linger like the waterfall, which lingers even while it plunges: thus do I hunger for malice. Such revenge my fullness plots: such spite wells up out of my loneliness. My happiness in giving died in giving; my virtue tired of itself in its overflow.

The danger of those who always give is that they lose their sense of shame; and the heart and hand of those who always mete out become callous from always meting out. My eye no longer wells over at the shame of those who beg; my hand has grown too hard for the trembling of filled hands. Where have the tears of my eyes gone and the down of my heart? Oh, the loneliness of all givers! Oh, the taciturnity of all who shine!

Many suns revolve in the void: to all that is dark they speak with their light—to me they are silent. Oh, this is the enmity of the light against what shines:

merciless it moves in its orbit. Unjust in its heart against all that shines, cold against suns—thus moves every sun.

The suns fly like a storm in their orbits: that is their motion. They follow their inexorable will: that is their coldness.

Oh, it is only you, you dark ones, you nocturnal ones, who create warmth out of that which shines. It is only you who drink milk and refreshment out of the udders of light.

Alas, ice is all around me, my hand is burned by the icy. Alas, thirst is within me that languishes after your thirst.

Night has come: alas, that I must be light! And thirst for the nocturnal! And loneliness!

Night has come: now my craving breaks out of me like a well; to speak I crave.

Night has come; now all fountains speak more loudly. And my soul too is a fountain.

Night has come; now all the songs of lovers awaken. And my soul too is the song of a lover.

Thus sang Zarathustra.

THE DANCING SONG

One evening Zarathustra walked through a forest with his disciples; and as he sought a well, behold, he came upon a green meadow, silently surrounded by trees and shrubs, and upon it girls were dancing with each other. As soon as the girls recognized Zarathustra they ceased dancing. But Zarathustra walked up to them with a friendly gesture and spoke these words:

"Do not cease dancing, you lovely girls! No killjoy has come to you with evil eyes, no enemy of girls. God's advocate am I before the devil: but the devil is the spirit of gravity. How could I, you lightfooted ones, be an enemy of godlike dances? Or of girls' feet with pretty ankles?

"Indeed, I am a forest and a night of dark trees: but he who is not afraid of my darkness will also find rose slopes under my cypresses. And he will also find the little god whom girls like best: beside the well he lies, still, with his eyes shut. Verily, in bright daylight he fell asleep, the sluggard! Did he chase after butterflies too much? Do not be angry with me, you beautiful dancers, if I chastise the little god a bit. He may cry and weep—but he is laughable even when he weeps. And with tears in his eyes he shall ask you for a dance, and I myself will sing a song for his dance: a dancing and mocking song on the spirit of gravity, my supreme and most powerful devil, of whom they say that he is 'the master of the world.' "

And this is the song that Zarathustra sang while Cupid and the girls danced together:

Into your eyes I looked recently, O life! And into the unfathomable I then seemed to be sinking. But you pulled me out with a golden fishing rod; and you laughed mockingly when I called you unfathomable.

"Thus runs the speech of all fish," you said; "what *they* do not fathom is unfathomable. But I am merely changeable and wild and a woman in every way, and not virtuous—even if you men call me profound, faithful, eternal, and mysterious. But you men always present us with your own virtues, O you virtuous men!"

Thus she laughed, the incredible one; but I never believe her and her laughter when she speaks ill of herself.

And when I talked in confidence with my wild wisdom she said to me in anger, "You will, you want, you love—that is the only reason why you *praise* life." Then

I almost answered wickedly and told the angry woman the truth; and there is no more wicked answer than telling one's wisdom the truth.

For thus matters stand among the three of us: Deeply I love only life—and verily, most of all when I hate life. But that I am well disposed toward wisdom, and often too well, that is because she reminds me so much of life. She has her eyes, her laugh, and even her little golden fishing rod: is it my fault that the two look so similar?

And when life once asked me, "Who is this wisdom?" I answered fervently, "Oh yes, wisdom! One thirsts after her and is never satisfied; one looks through veils, one grabs through nets. Is she beautiful? How should I know? But even the oldest carps are baited with her. She is changeable and stubborn; often I have seen her bite her lip and comb her hair against the grain. Perhaps she is evil and false and a female in every way; but just when she speaks ill of herself she is most seductive."

When I said this to life she laughed sarcastically and closed her eyes. "Of whom are you speaking?" she asked; "no doubt, of me. And even if you are right —should *that* be said to my face? But now speak of your wisdom too."

Ah, and then you opened your eyes again, O beloved life. And again I seemed to myself to be sinking into the unfathomable.

Thus sang Zarathustra. But when the dance was over and the girls had gone away, he grew sad.

"The sun has set long ago," he said at last; "the meadow is moist, a chill comes from the woods. Something unknown is around me and looks thoughtful. What? Are you still alive, Zarathustra?

"Why? What for? By what? Whither? Where? How? Is it not folly still to be alive?

"Alas, my friends, it is the evening that asks thus through me. Forgive me my sadness. Evening has come; forgive me that evening has come."

Thus spoke Zarathustra.

THE TOMB SONG

"There is the isle of tombs, the silent isle; there too are the tombs of my youth. There I wish to carry an evergreen wreath of life." Resolving this in my heart, I crossed the sea.

O you visions and apparitions of my youth! O all you glances of love, you divine moments! How quickly you died. Today I recall you like dead friends. From you, my dearest friends among the dead, a sweet scent comes to me, loosening heart and tears. Verily, it perturbs and loosens the heart of the lonely seafarer. I am still the richest and most enviable—I, the loneliest! For once I possessed you, and you still possess me: say, to whom fell, as to me, such rose apples from the bough? I am still the heir of your love and its soil, flowering in remembrance of you with motley wild virtues, O you most loved ones.

Alas, we were fashioned to remain close to each other, you fair and strange wonders; and you came to me and my craving, not like shy birds, but like trusting ones to him who trusts. Indeed, fashioned for loyalty, like myself, and for tender eternities—I must now call you after your disloyalty, you divine glances and moments: I have not yet learned any other name. Verily, you have died too soon for me, you fugitives. Yet you did not flee from me, nor did I flee from you: we are equally innocent in our disloyalty.

To kill *me*, they strangled you, songbirds of my hopes. Indeed, after you, my dearest friends, malice has ever shot its arrows—to hit *my* heart. And it hit! For you have always been closest to my heart, my possession and what possessed me: that is why you had to die young and all-too-early. The arrow was shot at my most vulnerable possession—at you, whose skin is like down and even more like a smile that dies of a glance.

But this word I want to speak to my enemies: What is all murder of human beings compared to that which you have done to me? What you have done to me is more evil than any murder of human beings; you have taken from me the irretrievable: thus I speak to you, my enemies. For you murdered the visions and dearest wonders of my youth. My playmates you took from me, the blessed spirits. In their memory I lay down this wreath and this curse. This curse against you, my enemies! For you have cut short my eternal bliss, as a tone that breaks off in a cold night. Scarcely as the gleam of divine eyes it came to me—passing swiftly as a glance.

Thus spoke my purity once in a fair hour: "All beings shall be divine to me." Then you assaulted me with filthy ghosts; alas, where has this fair hour fled now?

"All days shall be holy to me"—thus said the wisdom of my youth once; verily, it was the saying of a gay wisdom. But then you, my enemies, stole my nights from me and sold them into sleepless agony; alas, where has this gay wisdom fled now?

Once I craved happy omens from the birds; then you led a monster of an owl across my way, a revolting one. Alas, where did my tender desire flee then?

All nausea I once vowed to renounce: then you changed those near and nearest me into putrid boils. Alas, where did my noblest vow flee then?

I once walked as a blind man along blessed paths; then you threw filth in the path of the blind man, and now his old footpath nauseates him.

And when I did what was hardest for me and celebrated the triumph of my overcomings, then you made those who loved me scream that I was hurting them most.

Verily, this was always your practice: you galled my best honey and the industry of my best bees. To my charity you always dispatched the most impudent beggars; around my pity you always pushed the incurably shameless. Thus you wounded my virtue in its faith. And whenever I laid down for a sacrifice even what was holiest to me, your "piety" immediately placed its fatter gifts alongside, and in the fumes of your fat what was holiest to me suffocated.

And once I wanted to dance as I had never danced before: over all the heavens I wanted to dance. Then you persuaded my dearest singer. And he struck up a horrible dismal tune; alas, he tooted in my ears like a gloomy horn. Murderous singer, tool of malice, most innocent yourself! I stood ready for the best dance, when you murdered my ecstasy with your sounds. Only in the dance do I know how to tell the parable of the highest things: and now my highest parable remained unspoken in my limbs. My highest hope remained unspoken and unredeemed. And all the visions and consolations of my youth died! How did I endure it? How did I get over and overcome such wounds? How did my soul rise again out of such tombs?

Indeed, in me there is something invulnerable and unburiable, something that explodes rock: that is *my will*. Silent and unchanged it strides through the years. It would walk its way on my feet, my old will, and its mind is hard of heart and invulnerable.

Invulnerable am I only in the heel. You are still alive and your old self, most patient one. You have still broken out of every tomb. What in my youth was un-redeemed lives on in you; and as life and youth you sit there, full of hope, on yellow ruins of tombs.

Indeed, for me, you are still the shatterer of all tombs. Hail to thee, my will! And only where there are tombs are there resurrections.

Thus sang Zarathustra.

ON SELF-OVERCOMING

"Will to truth," you who are wisest call that which impels you and fills you with lust?

A will to the thinkability of all beings: this *I* call your will. You want to *make* all being thinkable, for you doubt with well-founded suspicion that it is already thinkable. But it shall yield and bend for you. Thus your will wants it. It shall become smooth and serve the spirit as its mirror and reflection. That is your whole will, you who are wisest: a will to power—when you speak of good and evil too, and of valuations. You still want to create the world before which you can kneel: that is your ultimate hope and intoxication.

The unwise, of course, the people—they are like a river on which a bark drifts; and in the bark sit the valuations, solemn and muffled up. Your will and your valuations you have placed on the river of becoming; and what the people believe to be good and evil, that betrays to me an ancient will to power.

It was you who are wisest who placed such guests in this bark and gave them pomp and proud names—you and your dominant will. Now the river carries your bark farther; it *has* to carry it. It avails nothing that the broken wave foams and angrily opposes the keel. Not the river is your danger and the end of your good and evil, you who are wisest, but that will itself, the will to power—the unexhausted procreative will of life.

But to make you understand my word concerning good and evil, I shall now say to you my word concerning life and the nature of all the living.

I pursued the living; I walked the widest and the narrowest paths that I might know its nature. With a hundredfold mirror I still caught its glance when its mouth was closed, so that its eyes might speak to me. And its eyes spoke to me.

But wherever I found the living, there I heard also the speech on obedience. Whatever lives, obeys.

And this is the second point: he who cannot obey himself is commanded. That is the nature of the living.

This, however, is the third point that I heard: that commanding is harder than obeying; and not only because he who commands must carry the burden of all who obey, and because this burden may easily crush him. An experiment and hazard appeared to me to be in all commanding; and whenever the living commands, it hazards itself. Indeed, even when it commands *itself*, it must still pay for its commanding. It must become the judge, the avenger, and the victim of its own law. How does this happen? I asked myself. What persuades the living to obey and command, and to practice obedience even when it commands?

Hear, then, my word, you who are wisest. Test in all seriousness whether I have crawled into the very heart of life and into the very roots of its heart.

Where I found the living, there I found will to power; and even in the will of those who serve I found the will to be master.

That the weaker should serve the stronger, to that it is persuaded by its own will, which would be master over what is weaker still: this is the one pleasure it does not want to renounce. And as the smaller yields to the greater that it may have pleasure and power over the smallest, thus even the greatest still yields, and for the sake of power risks life. That is the yielding of the greatest: it is hazard and danger and casting dice for death.

And where men make sacrifices and serve and cast amorous glances, there too is the will to be master. Along stealthy paths the weaker steals into the castle and into the very heart of the more powerful—and there steals power.

And life itself confided this secret to me: "Behold," it said, "I am *that which must always overcome itself*. Indeed, you call it a will to procreate or a drive to an end, to something higher, farther, more manifold: but all this is one, and one secret.

"Rather would I perish than forswear this; and verily, where there is perishing and a falling of leaves, behold, there life sacrifices itself—for power. That I must be struggle and a becoming and an end and an opposition to ends—alas, whoever guesses what is my will should also guess on what *crooked* paths it must proceed.

"Whatever I create and however much I love it— soon I must oppose it and my love; thus my will wills it. And you too, lover of knowledge, are only a path and footprint of my will; verily, my will to power walks also on the heels of your will to truth.

"Indeed, the truth was not hit by him who shot at it with the word of the 'will to existence': that will does not exist. For, what does not exist cannot will; but what is in existence, how could that still want existence? Only where there is life is there also will: not will to life but—thus I teach you—will to power.

"There is much that life esteems more highly than

life itself; but out of the esteeming itself speaks the will to power."

Thus life once taught me; and with this I shall yet solve the riddle of your heart, you who are wisest.

Verily, I say unto you: good and evil that are not transitory, do not exist. Driven on by themselves, they must overcome themselves again and again. With your values and words of good and evil you do violence when you value; and this is your hidden love and the splendor and trembling and overflowing of your soul. But a more violent force and a new overcoming grow out of your values and break egg and eggshell.

And whoever must be a creator in good and evil, verily, he must first be an annihilator and break values. Thus the highest evil belongs to the highest goodness: but this is creative.

Let us speak of this, you who are wisest, even if it be bad. Silence is worse; all truths that are kept silent become poisonous.

And may everything be broken that cannot brook our truths! There are yet many houses to be built!

Thus spoke Zarathustra.

ON THOSE WHO ARE SUBLIME

Still is the bottom of my sea: who would guess that it harbors sportive monsters? Imperturbable is my depth, but it sparkles with swimming riddles and laughters.

One who was sublime I saw today, one who was solemn, an ascetic of the spirit; oh, how my soul laughed at his ugliness! With a swelled chest and like one who holds in his breath, he stood there, the sublime one, silent, decked out with ugly truths, the spoil of his hunting, and rich in torn garments; many thorns too adorned him—yet I saw no rose.

As yet he has not learned laughter or beauty. Gloomy this hunter returned from the woods of knowledge. He came home from a fight with savage beasts; but out of his seriousness there also peers a savage beast—one not overcome. He still stands there like a tiger who wants to leap; but I do not like these tense souls, and my taste does not favor all these who withdraw.

And you tell me, friends, that there is no disputing of taste and tasting? But all of life is a dispute over taste and tasting. Taste—that is at the same time weight and scales and weigher; and woe unto all the living that would live without disputes over weight and scales and weighers!

If he grew tired of his sublimity, this sublime one, only then would his beauty commence; and only then will I taste him and find him tasteful. And only when he turns away from himself, will he jump over his shadow—and verily, into *his* sun. All-too-long has he been sitting in the shadow, and the cheeks of this ascetic of the spirit have grown pale; he almost starved to death on his expectations. Contempt is still in his eyes, and nausea hides around his mouth. Though he is resting now, his rest has not yet lain in the sun. He should act like a bull, and his happiness should smell of the earth, and not of contempt for the earth. I would like to see him as a white bull, walking before the plowshare, snorting and bellowing; and his bellowing should be in praise of everything earthly.

His face is still dark; the shadow of the hand plays upon him. His sense of sight is still in shadows. His deed itself still lies on him as a shadow: the hand still darkens the doer. As yet he has not overcome his deed.

Though I love the bull's neck on him, I also want to see the eyes of the angel. He must still discard his heroic will; he shall be elevated, not merely sublime: the ether itself should elevate him, the will-less one.

He subdued monsters, he solved riddles: but he must still redeem his own monsters and riddles, changing them into heavenly children. As yet his knowledge has not learned to smile and to be without jealousy; as yet his torrential passion has not become still in beauty.

Verily, it is not in satiety that his desire shall grow silent and be submerged, but in beauty. Gracefulness is part of the graciousness of the great-souled.

His arm placed over his head: thus should the hero rest; thus should he overcome even his rest. But just for the hero the *beautiful* is the most difficult thing. No violent will can attain the beautiful by exertion. A little more, a little less: precisely this counts for much here, this matters most here.

To stand with relaxed muscles and unharnessed will: that is most difficult for all of you who are sublime.

When power becomes gracious and descends into the visible—such descent I call beauty.

And there is nobody from whom I want beauty as much as from you who are powerful: let your kindness be your final self-conquest.

Of all evil I deem you capable: therefore I want the good from you.

Verily, I have often laughed at the weaklings who thought themselves good because they had no claws.

You shall strive after the virtue of the column: it grows more and more beautiful and gentle, but internally harder and more enduring, as it ascends.

Indeed, you that are sublime shall yet become beautiful one day and hold up a mirror to your own beauty.

Then your soul will shudder with godlike desires, and there will be adoration even in your vanity.

For this is the soul's secret: only when the hero has abandoned her, she is approached in a dream by the overhero.

Thus spoke Zarathustra.

ON THE LAND OF EDUCATION

I flew too far into the future: dread overcame me. and when I looked around, behold, time was my sole contemporary. Then I flew back toward home, faster and faster; and thus I came to you, O men of today, and into the land of education. For the first time I really had eyes for you, and a genuine desire; verily, it was with longing in my heart that I came.

But what happened to me? For all my anxiety I had to laugh. Never had my eyes beheld anything so dappled and motley. I laughed and laughed while my foot was still trembling, and my heart no less. "This is clearly the home of all paint pots," I said.

With fifty blotches painted on your faces and limbs you were sitting there, and I was amazed, you men of today. And with fifty mirrors around you to flatter and echo your color display! Verily, you could wear no better masks, you men of today, than your own faces! Who could possibly find you out?

With the characters of the past written all over you, and these characters in turn painted over with new characters: thus have you concealed yourselves perfectly from all interpreters of characters. And even if one could try the reins, who would be fool enough to believe that you have reins? You seem baked out of colors and pasted notes. Motley, all ages and peoples peek out of your veils; motley, all customs and faiths speak out of your gestures.

If one took the veils and wraps and colors and gestures away from you, just enough would be left to scare away the crows. Verily, I myself am the scared crow who once saw you naked and without color; and I flew away when the skeleton beckoned to me lovingly. Rather would I be a day laborer in Hades among the shades of the past! Even the underworldly are plumper and fuller than you.

This, indeed this, is bitterness for my bowels, that I can endure you neither naked nor clothed, you men of today. All that is uncanny in the future and all that has ever made fugitive birds shudder is surely more comfortable and cozy than your "reality." For thus you speak: "Real are we entirely, and without belief or superstition." Thus you stick out your chests—but alas, they are hollow! Indeed, how should you be *capable* of any belief, being so dappled and motley—you who are paintings of all that men have ever believed? You are walking refutations of all belief, and you break the limbs of all thought. Unbelievable: thus I call you, for all your pride in being real!

All ages prate against each other in your spirits; and the dreams and pratings of all ages were yet more real than your waking. You are sterile: that is why you lack faith. But whoever had to create also had his prophetic dreams and astral signs—and had faith in faith. You are half-open gates at which the gravediggers wait. And this is *your* reality: "Everything deserves to perish."

How you stand there, you who are sterile, how thin around the ribs! And some among you probably realized this and said, "Probably some god secretly took something from me while I slept. Verily, enough to make himself a little female! Strange is the poverty of my ribs." Thus have some men of today already spoken.

Indeed, you make me laugh, you men of today, and particularly when you are amazed at yourselves. And I should be in a sorry plight if I could not laugh at your amazement and had to drink down everything disgusting out of your bowls. But I shall take you more lightly, for I have a heavy burden; and what does it matter to me if bugs and winged worms still light on my bundle? Verily, that will not make it heavier. And not from you, you men of today, shall the great weariness come over me.

Alas, where shall I climb now with my longing? From all mountains I look out for fatherlands and motherlands. But home I found nowhere; a fugitive am I in all cities and a departure at all gates. Strange and a mockery to me are the men of today to whom my heart recently drew me; and I am driven out of fatherlands and motherlands. Thus I now love only my *children's land*, yet undiscovered, in the farthest sea: for this I bid my sails search and search.

In my children I want to make up for being the child of my fathers—and to all the future, for *this* today.

Thus spoke Zarathustra.

ON IMMACULATE PERCEPTION

When the moon rose yesterday I fancied that she wanted to give birth to a sun: so broad and pregnant she lay on the horizon. But she lied to me with her pregnancy; and I should sooner believe in the man in the moon than in the woman.

Indeed, he is not much of a man either, this shy nocturnal enthusiast. Verily, with a bad conscience he passes over the roofs. For he is lecherous and jealous, the monk in the moon, lecherous after the earth and all the joys of lovers.

No, I do not like him, this tomcat on the roofs! I loathe all that crawl about half-closed windows! Piously and silently he passes over carpets of stars; but I do not like softly treading men's feet, on which no spur jingles. The step of everything honest speaks; but the cat steals over the ground. Behold, like a cat the moon comes along, dishonestly.

This parable I offer you, sentimental hypocrites, you who are "pure perceivers." I call you—lechers.

You too love the earth and the earthly: I have seen through you; but there is shame in your love and bad conscience—you are like the moon. Your spirit has been persuaded to despise the earthly; but your entrails have not been persuaded, and they are what is strongest in you. And now your spirit is ashamed at having given in to your entrails, and, to hide from its shame, it sneaks on furtive and lying paths.

"This would be the highest to my mind"—thus says your lying spirit to itself—"to look at life without desire and not, like a dog, with my tongue hanging out. To be happy in looking, with a will that has died and without the grasping and greed of selfishness, the whole body cold and ashen, but with drunken moon eyes. This I should like best"—thus the seduced seduces himself—"to love the earth as the moon loves her, and to touch her beauty only with my eyes. And this is what the immaculate perception of all things shall mean to me: that I want nothing from them, except to be allowed to lie prostrate before them like a mirror with a hundred eyes."

O you sentimental hypocrites, you lechers! You lack innocence in your desire and therefore you slander all desire. Verily, it is not as creators, procreators, and those who have joy in becoming that you love the earth. Where is innocence? Where there is a will to procreate. And he who wants to create beyond himself has the purest will.

Where is beauty? Where I must will with all my will; where I want to love and perish that an image may not remain a mere image. Loving and perishing: that has rhymed for eternities. The will to love, that is to be willing also to die. Thus I speak to you cowards!

But now your emasculated leers wish to be called "contemplation." And that which permits itself to be touched by cowardly glances you would baptize "beautiful." How you soil noble names!

But this shall be your curse, you who are immaculate, you pure perceivers, that you shall never give birth, even if you lie broad and pregnant on the horizon. Verily, you fill your mouth with noble words; and are we to believe that your heart is overflowing, you liars? But *my* words are small, despised, crooked words: gladly I pick up what falls under the table at your meals. I can still use it to tell hypocrites the truth. Indeed, my fishbones, clamshells, and thorny leaves shall tickle the noses of hypocrites. Bad air always surrounds you and your meals: for your lecherous thoughts, your lies and secrets, are in the air. Would that you dared to believe yourselves—yourselves and your entrails. Whoever does not believe himself always lies.

Behind a god's mask you hide from yourselves, in your "purity"; your revolting worm has crawled into a god's mask. Verily, you deceive with your "contemplation." Zarathustra too was once fooled by your godlike skins and did not realize that they were stuffed with snakes' coils. I once fancied that I saw a god's soul at play in your play, you pure perceivers. No better art I once fancied than your arts. Snakes' filth and bad odors were concealed from me by the distance, and that the cunning of a lizard was crawling around lecherously.

But I came close to you, and the day dawned on me, and now it dawns on you too; the moon's love has come to an end. Look there! Caught and pale he stands there, confronted by the dawn. For already she approaches, glowing; her love for the earth approaches. All solar love is innocence and creative longing.

Look there: how she approaches impatiently over the sea. Do you not feel the thirst and the hot breath of her love? She would suck at the sea and drink its depth into her heights; and the sea's desire rises toward her with a thousand breasts. It wants to be kissed and sucked by the thirst of the sun; it wants to become air and height and a footpath of light, and itself light.

Verily, like the sun I love life and all deep seas. And this is what perceptive knowledge means to me: all that is deep shall rise up to my heights.

Thus spoke Zarathustra.

ON SCHOLARS

As I lay asleep, a sheep ate of the ivy wreath on my brow—ate and said, "Zarathustra is no longer a scholar." Said it and strutted away proudly. A child told it to me.

I like to lie here where the children play, beside the broken wall, among thistles and red poppies. I am still a scholar to the children, and also to the thistles and red poppies. They are innocent even in their malice. But to the sheep I am no longer a scholar; thus my lot decrees it—bless it!

For this is the truth: I have moved from the house of the scholars and I even banged the door behind me. My soul sat hungry at their table too long; I am not, like them, trained to pursue knowledge as if it were nut-cracking. I love freedom and the air over the fresh earth; rather would I sleep on ox hides than on their decorums and respectabilities.

I am too hot and burned by my own thoughts; often it nearly takes my breath away. Then I must go out into the open and away from all dusty rooms. But they sit cool in the cool shade: in everything they want to be mere spectators, and they beware of sitting where the sun burns on the steps. Like those who stand in the street and gape at the people who pass by, they too wait and gape at thoughts that others have thought.

If you seize them with your hands they raise a cloud of dust like flour bags, involuntarily; but who could guess that their dust comes from grain and from the yellow delight of summer fields? When they pose as wise, their little epigrams and truths chill me: their wisdom often has an odor as if it came from the swamps; and verily, I have also heard frogs croak out of it. They are skillful and have clever fingers: why would my simplicity want to be near their multiplicity? All threading and knotting and weaving their fingers under-stand: thus they knit the socks of the spirit.

They are good clockworks; but take care to wind them correctly! Then they indicate the hour without fail and make a modest noise. They work like mills and like stamps: throw down your seed-corn to them and they will know how to grind it small and reduce it to white dust.

They watch each other closely and mistrustfully. In-ventive in petty cleverness, they wait for those whose knowledge walks on lame feet: like spiders they wait. I have always seen them carefully preparing poison; and they always put on gloves of glass to do it. They also know how to play with loaded dice; and I have seen them play so eagerly that they sweated.

We are alien to each other, and their virtues are even more distasteful to me than their falseness and their loaded dice. And when I lived with them, I lived above them. That is why they developed a grudge against me. They did not want to hear how someone was living over their heads; and so they put wood and earth and filth between me and their heads. Thus they muffled the sound of my steps: and so far I have been heard least well by the most scholarly. Between themselves and me they laid all human faults and weaknesses: "false ceilings" they call them in their houses. And yet I live *over* their heads with my thoughts; and even if I wanted to walk upon my own mistakes, I would still be over their heads.

For men are *not* equal: thus speaks justice. And what I want, they would have no right to want!

Thus spoke Zarathustra.

ON POETS

"Since I have come to know the body better," Zarathustra said to one of his disciples, "the spirit is to me only quasi-spirit; and all that is 'permanent' is also a mere parable."

"I have heard you say that once before," the disciple replied; "and at that time you added, 'But the poets lie too much.' Why did you say that the poets lie too much?"

"Why?" said Zarathustra. "You ask, why? I am not one of those whom one may ask about their why. Is my experience but of yesterday? It was long ago that I experienced the reasons for my opinions. Would I not have to be a barrel of memory if I wanted to carry my reasons around with me? It is already too much for me to remember my own opinions; and many a bird flies away. And now and then I also find a stray in my dovecot that is strange to me and trembles when I place my hand on it. But what was it that Zarathustra once said to you? That the poets lie too much? But Zarathustra too is a poet. Do you now believe that he spoke the truth here? Why do you believe that?"

The disciple answered, "I believe in Zarathustra." But Zarathustra shook his head and smiled.

"Faith does not make me blessed," he said, "especially not faith in me. But suppose somebody said in all seriousness, the poets lie too much: he would be right; *we* do lie too much. We also know too little and we are bad learners; so we simply have to lie. And who among us poets has not adulterated his wine? Many a poisonous hodgepodge has been contrived in our cellars; much that is indescribable was accomplished there. And because we know so little, the poor in spirit please us heartily, particularly when they are young females. And we are covetous even of those things which the old females tell each other in the evening. That is what we ourselves call the Eternal-Feminine in us. And, as if there were a special secret access to knowledge, *buried* for those who learn something, we believe in the people and their 'wisdom.'

"This, however, all poets believe: that whoever pricks up his ears as he lies in the grass or on lonely slopes will find out something about those things that are between heaven and earth. And when they feel tender sentiments stirring, the poets always fancy that nature herself is in love with them; and that she is creeping to their ears to tell them secrets and amorous flatteries; and of this they brag and boast before all mortals.

"Alas, there are so many things between heaven and earth of which only the poets have dreamed.

"And especially *above* the heavens: for all gods are poets' parables, poets' prevarications. Verily, it always lifts us higher—specifically, to the realm of the clouds: upon these we place our motley bastards and call them gods and overmen. For they are just light enough for these chairs—all these gods and overmen. Ah, how weary I am of all the imperfection which must at all costs become event! Ah, how weary I am of poets!"

When Zarathustra spoke thus, his disciple was angry with him, but he remained silent. And Zarathustra too remained silent; and his eye had turned inward as if he were gazing into vast distances. At last he sighed and drew a deep breath.

"I am of today and before," he said then, "but there is something in me that is of tomorrow and the day after tomorrow and time to come. I have grown weary of the poets, the old and the new: superficial they all seem to me, and shallow seas. Their thoughts have not penetrated deeply enough; therefore their feelings did not touch bottom.

"Some lust and some boredom: that has so far been their best reflection. All their harp jingling is to me the breathing and flitting of ghosts; what have they ever known of the fervor of tones?

"Nor are they clean enough for me: they all muddy their waters to make them appear deep. And they like to pose as reconcilers: but mediators and mixers they remain for me, and half-and-half and unclean.

"Alas, I cast my net into their seas and wanted to catch good fish; but I always pulled up the head of some old god. Thus the sea gave him who was hungry a stone. And they themselves may well have come from the sea. Certainly, pearls are found in them: they are that much more similar to hard shellfish. And instead of a soul I often found salted slime in them.

"From the sea they learned even its vanity: is not the sea the peacock of peacocks? Even before the ugliest buffalo it still spreads out its tail, and never wearies of its lace fan of silver and silk. Sulky, the buffalo stares back, close to the sand in his soul, closer still to the thicket, closest of all to the swamp. What are beauty and sea and peacock's finery to him? This parable I offer the poets. Verily, their spirit itself is the peacock of peacocks and a sea of vanity! The spirit of the poet craves spectators—even if only buffaloes.

"But I have grown weary of this spirit; and I foresee that it will grow weary of itself. I have already seen the poets changed, with their glances turned back on themselves. I saw ascetics of the spirit approach; they grew out of the poets."

Thus spoke Zarathustra.

ON GREAT EVENTS

There is an island in the sea—not far from Zarathustra's blessed isles—on which a fire-spewing mountain smokes continually; and the people say of it, and especially the old women among the people say, that it has been placed like a huge rock before the gate to the underworld, and that the narrow path that leads to this gate to the underworld goes through the fire-spewing mountain.

Now it was during the time when Zarathustra was staying on the blessed isles that a ship anchored at the island with the smoking mountain and the crew went ashore to shoot rabbits. Around noon, however, when the captain and his men were together again, they suddenly saw a man approach through the air, and a voice said distinctly, "It is time! It is high time!" And when the shape had come closest to them—and it flew by swiftly as a shadow in the direction of the fire-spewing mountain—they realized with a great sense of shock that it was Zarathustra; for all of them had seen him before, except the captain, and they loved him as the people love—with a love that is mixed with an equal amount of awe. "Look there!" said the old helmsman. "There is Zarathustra descending to hell!"

At the time these seamen landed at the isle of fire there was a rumor abroad that Zarathustra had disappeared; and when his friends were asked, they said that he had embarked by night without saying where he intended to go. Thus uneasiness arose; and after three days the story of the seamen was added to this uneasiness; and now all the people said that the devil had taken Zarathustra. His disciples laughed at such talk to be sure, and one of them even said, "Sooner would I believe that Zarathustra has taken the devil." But deep in their souls they were all of them full of worry and longing; thus their joy was great when on the fifth day Zarathustra appeared among them.

And this is the story of Zarathustra's conversation with the fire hound:

"The earth," he said, "has a skin, and this skin has diseases. One of these diseases, for example, is called 'man.' And another one of these diseases is called 'fire hound': about *him* men have told each other, and believed, many lies. To get to the bottom of this mystery I went over the sea, and I have seen truth naked—verily, barefoot up to the throat. Now I am informed concerning the fire hound, and also concerning all scum-

and overthrow devils, of whom not only old women are afraid.

" 'Out with you, fire hound! Out from your depth!' I cried. 'And confess how deep this depth is! Whence comes what you are snorting up here? You drink copiously from the sea: your salty eloquence shows that. Indeed, for a hound of the depth you take your nourishment too much from the surface. At most, I take you for the earth's ventriloquist; and whenever I have heard overthrow- and scum-devils talking, I found them like you: salty, mendacious, and superficial. You know how to bellow and to darken with ashes. You are the best braggarts and great experts in the art of making mud seethe. Wherever you are, mud must always be nearby, and much that is spongy, cavernous, compressed—and wants freedom. Freedom is what all of you like best to bellow; but I have outgrown the belief in "great events" wherever there is much bellowing and smoke.

" 'Believe me, friend Hellishnoise: the greatest events —they are not our loudest but our stillest hours. Not around the inventors of new noise, but around the inventors of new values does the world revolve; it revolves *inaudibly*.

" 'Admit it! Whenever your noise and smoke were gone, very little had happened. What does it matter if a town became a mummy and a statue lies in the mud? And this word I shall add for those who overthrow statues: nothing is more foolish than casting salt into the sea and statues into the mud. The statue lay in the mud of your contempt; but precisely this is its law, that out of contempt life and living beauty come back to it. It rises again with more godlike features, seductive through suffering; and verily, it will yet thank you for having overthrown it, O you overthrowers. This counsel, however, I give to kings and churches and everything that is weak with age and weak in virtue: let yourselves be overthrown—so that you may return to life, and virtue return to you.'

"Thus I spoke before the fire hound; then he interrupted me crossly and asked, 'Church? What is that?'

" 'Church?' I answered. 'That is a kind of state—the most mendacious kind. But be still, you hypocritical hound! You know your own kind best! Like you, the state is a hypocritical hound; like you, it likes to talk with smoke and bellowing—to make himself believe, like you, that he is talking out of the belly of reality. For he wants to be by all means the most important beast on earth, the state; and they believe him too.'

"When I had said that, the fire hound carried on as if crazy with envy. 'What?' he cried, 'the most important beast on earth? And they believe him too?' And so much steam and so many revolting voices came out of his throat that I thought he would suffocate with anger and envy.

"At last, he grew calmer and his gasping eased; and as soon as he was calm I said, laughing, 'You are angry, fire hound; so I am right about you! And that I may continue to be right, let me tell you about another fire hound. He really speaks out of the heart of the earth. He exhales gold and golden rain; thus his heart wants it. What are ashes and smoke and hot slime to him? Laughter flutters out of him like colorful clouds; nor is he well disposed toward your gurgling and spewing and intestinal rumblings. This gold, however, and this laughter he takes from the heart of the earth; for— know this—*the heart of the earth is of gold.*'

"When the fire hound heard this he could no longer bear listening to me. Shamed, he drew in his tail, in a cowed manner said 'bow-wow,' and crawled down into his cave."

Thus related Zarathustra. But his disciples barely listened, so great was their desire to tell him of the seamen, the rabbits, and the flying man.

"What shall I think of that?" said Zarathustra; "am I a ghost then? But it must have been my shadow. I suppose you have heard of the wanderer and his shadow? This, however, is clear: I must watch it more closely—else it may yet spoil my reputation."

And once more Zarathustra shook his head and wondered. "What shall I think of that?" he said once more. "Why did the ghost cry, 'It is time! It is high time!' High time for *what*?"

Thus spoke Zarathustra.

THE SOOTHSAYER

"—And I saw a great sadness descend upon mankind. The best grew weary of their works. A doctrine appeared, accompanied by a faith: 'All is empty, all is the same, all has been!' And from all the hills it echoed: 'All is empty, all is the same, all has been!' Indeed we have harvested: but why did all our fruit turn rotten and brown? What fell down from the evil moon last night? In vain was all our work; our wine has turned to poison; an evil eye has seared our fields and hearts. We have all become dry; and if fire should descend on us, we should turn to ashes; indeed, we have wearied the fire itself. All our wells have dried up; even the sea has withdrawn. All the soil would crack, but the depth refuses to devour. 'Alas, where is there still a sea in which one might drown?' thus are we wailing across shallow swamps. Verily, we have become too weary even to die. We are still waking and living on—in tombs."

Thus Zarathustra heard a soothsayer speak, and the

prophecy touched his heart and changed him. He walked about sad and weary; and he became like those of whom the soothsayer had spoken.

"Verily," he said to his disciples, "little is lacking and this long twilight will come. Alas, how shall I save my light through it? It must not suffocate in this sadness. For it shall be a light for distant worlds and even more distant nights."

Thus grieved in his heart, Zarathustra walked about; and for three days he took neither food nor drink, had no rest, and lost his speech. At last he fell into a deep sleep. But his disciples sat around him in long night watches and waited with great concern for him to wake and speak again and recover from his melancholy.

And this is the speech of Zarathustra when he awoke; but his voice came to his disciples as if from a great distance:

"Listen to the dream which I dreamed, my friends, and help me guess its meaning. This dream is still a riddle to me; its meaning is concealed in it and imprisoned and does not yet soar above it with unfettered wings.

"I had turned my back on all life, thus I dreamed. I had become a night watchman and a guardian of tombs upon the lonely mountain castle of death. Up there I guarded his coffins: the musty vaults were full of such marks of triumph. Life that had been overcome, looked at me out of glass coffins. I breathed the odor of dusty eternities: sultry and dusty lay my soul. And who could have aired his soul there?

"The brightness of midnight was always about me; loneliness crouched next to it; and as a third, death-rattle silence, the worst of my friends. I had keys, the rustiest of all keys; and I knew how to use them to open the most creaking of all gates. Like a wickedly angry croaking, the sound ran through the long corridors when the gate's wings moved: fiendishly cried this bird, ferocious at being awakened. Yet still more terrible and heart-constricting was the moment when silence returned and it grew quiet about me, and I sat alone in this treacherous silence.

"Thus time passed and crawled, if time still existed—how should I know? But eventually that happened which awakened me. Thrice, strokes struck at the gate like thunder; the vaults echoed and howled thrice; then I went to the gate. 'Alpa,' I cried, 'who is carrying his ashes up the mountain? Alpa! Alpa! Who is carrying his ashes up the mountain?' And I pressed the key and tried to lift the gate and exerted myself; but still it did not give an inch. Then a roaring wind tore its wings apart; whistling, shrilling, and piercing, it cast up a black coffin before me.

"And amid the roaring and whistling and shrilling the coffin burst and spewed out a thousandfold laughter. And from a thousand grimaces of children, angels, owls, fools, and butterflies as big as children, it laughed and mocked and roared at me. Then I was terribly frightened; it threw me to the ground. And I cried in horror as I have never cried. And my own cry awakened me—and I came to my senses."

Thus Zarathustra told his dream and then became silent; for as yet he did not know the interpretation of his dream. But the disciple whom he loved most rose quickly, took Zarathustra's hand, and said:

"Your life itself interprets this dream for us, O Zarathustra. Are you not yourself the wind with the shrill whistling that tears open the gates of the castles of death? Are you not yourself the coffin full of colorful sarcasms and the angelic grimaces of life? Verily, like a thousandfold children's laughter Zarathustra enters all death chambers, laughing at all the night watchmen and guardians of tombs and at whoever else is rattling with gloomy keys. You will frighten and prostrate them with your laughter; and your power over them will make them faint and wake them. And even when the long twilight and the weariness of death come, you will not set in our sky, you advocate of life. New stars you have let us see, and new wonders of the night; verily, laughter itself you have spread over us like a colorful tent. Henceforth children's laughter will well forth from all coffins; henceforth a strong wind will come triumphantly to all weariness of death: of this you yourself are our surety and soothsayer. Verily, *this is what you dreamed of:* your enemies. That was your hardest dream. But as you woke from them and came to your senses, thus they shall awaken from themselves—and come to you."

Thus spoke the disciple; and all the others crowded around Zarathustra and took hold of his hands and wanted to persuade him to leave his bed and his sadness and to return to them. But Zarathustra sat erect on his resting place with a strange look in his eyes. Like one coming home from a long sojourn in strange lands, he looked at his disciples and examined their faces; and as yet he did not recognize them. But when they lifted him up and put him on his feet, behold, his eyes suddenly changed; he comprehended all that had happened, stroked his beard, and said in a strong voice:

"Now then, there is a time for this too. But see to it, my disciples, that we shall have a good meal, and soon. Thus I plan to atone for bad dreams. The soothsayer, however, shall eat and drink by my side; and verily, I shall show him a sea in which he can drown."

Thus spoke Zarathustra. But then he looked a long

time into the face of the disciple who had played the dream interpreter and he shook his head.

ON REDEMPTION

When Zarathustra crossed over the great bridge one day the cripples and beggars surrounded him, and a hunchback spoke to him thus: "Behold, Zarathustra. The people too learn from you and come to believe in your doctrine; but before they will believe you entirely one thing is still needed: you must first persuade us cripples. Now here you have a fine selection and, verily, an opportunity with more than one handle. You can heal the blind and make the lame walk; and from him who has too much behind him you could perhaps take away a little. That, I think, would be the right way to make the cripples believe in Zarathustra."

But Zarathustra replied thus to the man who had spoken: "When one takes away the hump from the hunchback one takes away his spirit—thus teach the people. And when one restores his eyes to the blind man he sees too many wicked things on earth, and he will curse whoever healed him. But whoever makes the lame walk does him the greatest harm: for when he can walk his vices run away with him—thus teach the people about cripples. And why should Zarathustra not learn from the people when the people learn from Zarathustra?

"But this is what matters least to me since I have been among men: to see that this one lacks an eye and that one an ear and a third a leg, while there are others who have lost their tongues or their noses or their heads. I see, and have seen, what is worse, and many things so vile that I do not want to speak of everything; and

concerning some things I do not even like to be silent:
for there are human beings who lack everything, except
one thing of which they have too much—human beings
who are nothing but a big eye or a big mouth or a big
belly or anything at all that is big. Inverse cripples I
call them.

"And when I came out of my solitude and crossed
over this bridge for the first time I did not trust my
eyes and looked and looked again, and said at last, 'An
ear! An ear as big as a man!' I looked still more closely
—and indeed, underneath the ear something was moving, something pitifully small and wretched and slender.
And, no doubt of it, the tremendous ear was attached
to a small, thin stalk—but this stalk was a human being!
If one used a magnifying glass one could even recognize
a tiny envious face; also, that a bloated little soul was
dangling from the stalk. The people, however, told me
that this great ear was not only a human being, but a
great one, a genius. But I never believed the people
when they spoke of great men; and I maintained my
belief that it was an inverse cripple who had too little
of everything and too much of one thing."

When Zarathustra had spoken thus to the hunchback
and to those whose mouthpiece and advocate the
hunchback was, he turned to his disciples in profound
dismay and said: "Verily, my friends, I walk among
men as among the fragments and limbs of men. This is
what is terrible for my eyes, that I find man in ruins and
scattered as over a battlefield or a butcher-field. And
when my eyes flee from the now to the past, they always find the same: fragments and limbs and dreadful
accidents—but no human beings.

"The now and the past on earth—alas, my friends,
that is what I find most unendurable; and I should not
know how to live if I were not also a seer of that which

must come. A seer, a willer, a creator, a future himself and a bridge to the future—and alas, also, as it were, a cripple at this bridge: all this is Zarathustra.

"And you too have often asked yourselves, 'Who is Zarathustra to us? What shall we call him?' And, like myself, you replied to yourselves with questions. Is he a promiser? or a fulfiller? A conqueror? or an inheritor? An autumn? or a plowshare? A physician? or one who has recovered? Is he a poet? or truthful? A liberator? or a tamer? good? or evil?

"I walk among men as among the fragments of the future—that future which I envisage. And this is all my creating and striving, that I create and carry together into One what is fragment and riddle and dreadful accident. And how could I bear to be a man if man were not also a creator and guesser of riddles and redeemer of accidents?

"To redeem those who lived in the past and to re-create all 'it was' into a 'thus I willed it'—that alone should I call redemption. Will—that is the name of the liberator and joy-bringer; thus I taught you, my friends. But now learn this too: the will itself is still a prisoner. Willing liberates; but what is it that puts even the liberator himself in fetters? 'It was'—that is the name of the will's gnashing of teeth and most secret melancholy. Powerless against what has been done, he is an angry spectator of all that is past. The will cannot will backwards; and that he cannot break time and time's covetousness, that is the will's loneliest melancholy.

"Willing liberates; what means does the will devise for himself to get rid of his melancholy and to mock his dungeon? Alas, every prisoner becomes a fool; and the imprisoned will redeems himself foolishly. That time does not run backwards, that is his wrath; 'that which was' is the name of the stone he cannot move. And so he moves stones out of wrath and displeasure, and he wreaks revenge on whatever does not feel wrath and displeasure as he does. Thus the will, the liberator, took to hurting; and on all who can suffer he wreaks revenge for his inability to go backwards. This, indeed this alone, is what *revenge* is: the will's ill will against time and its 'it was.'

"Verily, a great folly dwells in our will; and it has become a curse for everything human that this folly has acquired spirit.

"*The spirit of revenge,* my friends, has so far been the subject of man's best reflection; and where there was suffering, one always wanted punishment too.

"For 'punishment' is what revenge calls itself; with a hypocritical lie it creates a good conscience for itself.

"Because there is suffering in those who will, inasmuch as they cannot will backwards, willing itself and all life were supposed to be—a punishment. And now cloud upon cloud rolled over the spirit, until eventually madness preached, 'Everything passes away; therefore everything deserves to pass away. And this too is justice, this law of time that it must devour its children.' Thus preached madness.

" "Things are ordered morally according to justice and punishment. Alas, where is redemption from the flux of things and from the punishment called existence?' Thus preached madness.

" 'Can there be redemption if there is eternal justice? Alas, the stone *It was* cannot be moved: all punishments must be eternal too.' Thus preached madness.

" 'No deed can be annihilated: how could it be undone by punishment? This, this is what is eternal in the punishment called existence, that existence must eternally become deed and guilt again. Unless the will should at last redeem himself, and willing should become not willing.' But, my brothers, you know this fable of madness.

"I led you away from these fables when I taught you, 'The will is a creator.' All 'it was' is a fragment, a riddle, a dreadful accident—until the creative will says to it, 'But thus I willed it.' Until the creative will says to it, 'But thus I will it; thus shall I will it.'

"But has the will yet spoken thus? And when will that happen? Has the will been unharnessed yet from his own folly? Has the will yet become his own redeemer and joy-bringer? Has he unlearned the spirit of revenge and all gnashing of teeth? And who taught him reconciliation with time and something higher than any reconciliation? For that will which is the will to power must will something higher than any reconciliation; but how shall this be brought about? Who could teach him also to will backwards?"

At this point in his speech it happened that Zarathustra suddenly stopped and looked altogether like one who has received a severe shock. Appalled, he looked at his disciples; his eyes pierced their thoughts and the thoughts behind their thoughts as with arrows. But after a little while he laughed again and, pacified, he said: "It is difficult to live with people because silence is so difficult. Especially for one who is garrulous."

Thus spoke Zarathustra.

The hunchback, however, had listened to this discourse and covered his face the while; but when he heard Zarathustra laugh he looked up curiously and said slowly: "But why does Zarathustra speak otherwise to us than to his disciples?"

Zarathustra answered: "What is surprising in that? With hunchbacks one may well speak in a hunchbacked way."

"All right," said the hunchback; "and one may well tell pupils tales out of school. But why does Zarathustra speak otherwise to his pupils than to himself?"

ON HUMAN PRUDENCE

Not the height but the precipice is terrible. That precipice where the glance plunges *down* and the hand reaches *up*. There the heart becomes giddy confronted with its double will. Alas, friends, can you guess what is my heart's double will?

This, this is *my* precipice and my danger, that my glance plunges into the height and that my hand would grasp and hold on to the depth. My will clings to man; with fetters I bind myself to man because I am swept up toward the overman; for that way my other will wants to go. And therefore I live blind among men as if I did not know them, that my hand might not wholly lose its faith in what is firm.

I do not know you men: this darkness and consolation are often spread around me. I sit at the gateway, exposed to every rogue, and I ask: who wants to deceive me? That is the first instance of my human prudence, that I let myself be deceived in order not to be on guard against deceivers. Alas, if I were on guard against men, how could man then be an anchor for my ball? I should be swept up and away too easily. This providence lies over my destiny, that I must be without caution.

And whoever does not want to die of thirst among men must learn to drink out of all cups; and whoever would stay clean among men must know how to wash even with dirty water. And thus I often comforted myself, "Well then, old heart! One misfortune failed you; enjoy this as your good fortune."

This, however, is the second instance of my human prudence: I spare the *vain* more than the proud. Is not hurt vanity the mother of all tragedies? But where pride is hurt, there something better than pride is likely to grow.

That life may be good to look at, its play must be well acted; but for that good actors are needed. All the vain are good actors: they act and they want people to enjoy looking at them; all their spirit is behind this will. They enact themselves, they invent themselves; near them I love to look at life: that cures my melancholy. Therefore I spare the vain, for they are the physicians of my melancholy and keep me attached to life as to a play.

And then: who could fathom the full depth of the modesty of the vain man? I am well disposed to him and I pity his modesty. It is from you that he wants to acquire his faith in himself; he nourishes himself on your glances, he eats your praise out of your hands. He even believes your lies if you lie well about him; for, at bottom, his heart sighs: what am I? And if the true virtue is the one that is unaware of itself—well, the vain man is unaware of his modesty.

This, however, is the third instance of my human prudence: that I do not permit the sight of the *evil* to be spoiled for me by your timidity. I am delighted to see the wonders hatched by a hot sun: tigers and palms and rattlesnakes. Among men too a hot sun hatches a beautiful breed. And there are many wonderful things in those who are evil.

To be sure, even as your wisest men did not strike me as so very wise, I found men's evil too smaller than its reputation. And often I asked myself, shaking my head: why go on rattling, you rattlesnakes?

Verily, there is yet a future for evil too. And the hottest south has not yet been discovered for man. How many things are now called grossest wickedness and are yet only twelve shoes wide and three months long! One day, however, bigger dragons will come into this world. For in order that the overman should not lack his dragon, the overdragon that is worthy of him, much hot sunshine must yet glow upon damp jungles. Your wildcats must first turn into tigers, and your poisonous toads into crocodiles; for the good hunter shall have good hunting.

Verily, you who are good and just, there is much about you that is laughable, and especially your fear of that which has hitherto been called devil. What is great is so alien to your souls that the overman would be awesome to you in his kindness. And you who are wise and knowing, you would flee from the burning sun of that wisdom in which the overman joyously bathes his nakedness. You highest men whom my eyes have seen, this is my doubt concerning you and my secret laughter: I guess that you would call my over-man—devil.

Alas, I have wearied of these highest and best men: from their "height" I longed to get up, out, and away to the overman. A shudder came over me when I saw these best ones naked; then I grew wings to soar off into distant futures. Into more distant futures, into more southern souths than any artist ever dreamed of—where gods are ashamed of all clothes. But I want to see *you* disguised, my neighbors and fellow men, and well decked out, and vain, and dignified, as "the good and the just." And I myself want to sit among you dis-guised—*misjudging* you and myself: for that is the final instance of my human prudence.

Thus spoke Zarathustra.

THE STILLEST HOUR

What happened to me, my friends? You see me distracted, driven away, unwillingly obedient, prepared to go—alas, to go away from you. Indeed, Zarathustra must return once more to his solitude; but this time the bear goes back to his cave without joy. What happened to me? Who ordered this? Alas, my angry mistress wants it, she spoke to me; have I ever yet mentioned her name to you? Yesterday, toward evening, there spoke to me *my stillest hour:* that is the name of my awesome mistress. And thus it happened; for I must tell you everything lest your hearts harden against me for departing suddenly.

Do you know the fright of him who falls asleep? He is frightened down to his very toes because the ground gives under him and the dream begins. This I say to you as a parable. Yesterday, in the stillest hour, the ground gave under me, the dream began. The hand moved, the clock of my life drew a breath; never had I heard such stillness around me: my heart took fright.

Then it spoke to me without voice: "You know it, Zarathustra?" And I cried with fright at this whispering, and the blood left my face; but I remained silent.

Then it spoke to me again without voice: "You know it, Zarathustra, but you do not say it!" And at last I answered defiantly: "Yes, I know it, but I do not want to say it!"

Then it spoke to me again without voice: "You do not *want* to, Zarathustra? Is this really true? Do not hide in your defiance." And I cried and trembled like a child and spoke: "Alas, I would like to, but how can I? Let me off from this! It is beyond my strength!"

Then it spoke to me again without voice: "What do

you matter, Zarathustra? Speak your word and break!"

And I answered: "Alas, is it *my* word? Who am *I*? I await the worthier one; I am not worthy even of being broken by it."

Then it spoke to me again without voice: "What do you matter? You are not yet humble enough for me. Humility has the toughest hide." And I answered: "What has the hide of my humility not borne? I dwell at the foot of my height. How high are my peaks? No one has told me yet. But my valleys I know well."

Then it spoke to me again without voice: "O Zarathustra, he who has to move mountains also moves valleys and hollows." And I answered: "As yet my words have not moved mountains, and what I said did not reach men. Indeed, I have gone to men, but as yet I have not arrived."

Then it spoke to me again without voice: "What do you know of *that*? The dew falls on the grass when the night is most silent." And I answered: "They mocked me when I found and went my own way; and in truth my feet were trembling then. And thus they spoke to me: 'You have forgotten the way, now you have also forgotten how to walk.'"

Then it spoke to me again without voice: "What matters their mockery? You are one who has forgotten how to obey: now you shall command. Do you not know who is most needed by all? He that commands great things. To do great things is difficult; but to command great things is more difficult. This is what is most unforgivable in you: you have the power, and you do not want to rule." And I answered: "I lack the lion's voice for commanding."

Then it spoke to me again as a whisper: "It is the stillest words that bring on the storm. Thoughts that come on doves' feet guide the world. O Zarathustra, you shall go as a shadow of that which must come: thus you will command and, commanding, lead the way." And I answered: "I am ashamed."

Then it spoke to me again without voice: "You must yet become as a child and without shame. The pride of youth is still upon you; you have become young late; but whoever would become as a child must overcome his youth too." And I reflected for a long time and trembled. But at last I said what I had said at first: "I do not want to."

Then laughter surrounded me. Alas, how this laughter tore my entrails and slit open my heart! And it spoke to me for the last time: "O Zarathustra, your fruit is ripe, but you are not ripe for your fruit. Thus you must return to your solitude again; for you must yet become mellow." And again it laughed and fled; then it became still around me as with a double stillness. But I lay on the ground and sweat poured from my limbs.

Now you have heard all, and why I must return to my solitude. Nothing have I kept from you, my friends. But this too you have heard from me, who is still the most taciturn of all men—and wants to be. Alas, my friends, I still could tell you something, I still could give you something. Why do I not give it? Am I stingy?

But when Zarathustra had spoken these words he was overcome by the force of his pain and the nearness of his parting from his friends, and he wept loudly; and no one knew how to comfort him. At night, however, he went away alone and left his friends.

Thus Spoke Zarathustra: Third Part

You look up when you feel the need for elevation. And I look down because I am elevated. Who among you can laugh and be elevated at the same time? Whoever climbs the highest mountains laughs at all tragic plays and tragic seriousness. (Zarathustra, "On Reading and Writing," I, p. 40)

TRANSLATOR'S NOTES

1. *The Wanderer:* The contrast between Zarathustra's sentimentality and his praise of hardness remains characteristic of the rest of the book.

2. *On the Vision and the Riddle:* Zarathustra's first account of the eternal recurrence (see my *Nietzsche*, 11, II) is followed by a proto-surrealistic vision of a triumph over nausea.

3. *On Involuntary Bliss:* Zarathustra still cannot face the thought of the eternal recurrence.

4. *Before Sunrise:* An ode to the sky. Another quotation from Zweig's essay on Nietzsche seems pertinent: "His nerves immediately register every meter of height and every pressure of the weather as a pain in his organs, and they react rebelliously to every revolt in nature. Rain or gloomy skies lower his vitality ('overcast skies depress me deeply'), the weight of low clouds he feels down into his very intestines, rain 'lowers the potential,' humidity debilitates, dryness vivifies, sunshine is salvation, winter is a kind of paralysis and death. The quivering barometer needle of his April-like, changeable nerves never stands still—most nearly perhaps in cloudless landscapes, on the windless tablelands of the Engadine." In this chapter the phrase "beyond good and evil" is introduced; also one line, slightly varied, of the "Drunken Song" (see below). Another important

theme in Nietzsche's thought: the praise of chance and "a *little* reason" as opposed to any divine purpose.

5. *On Virtue That Makes Small:* "Do whatever you will, but . . .": What Nietzsche is concerned with is not casuistry but character, not a code of morals but a kind of man, not a syllabus of behavior but a state of being.

6. *Upon the Mount of Olives:* " 'The ice of knowledge will yet freeze him to *death!*' they moan." Compare Stefan George's poem on the occasion of Nietzsche's death (my *Nietzsche,* Prologue, II): "He came too late who said to thee imploring: There is no way left over icy cliffs."

7. *On Passing By:* Zarathustra's ape, or "grunting swine," unintentionally parodies Zarathustra's attitude and style. His denunciations are born of wounded vanity and vengefulness, while Zarathustra's contempt is begotten by love; and "where one can no longer love, there one should *pass by*."

8. *On Apostates:* Stylistically, Zarathustra is now often little better than his ape. But occasional epigrams show his old power: the third paragraph in section 2, for instance.

9. *The Return Home:* "Among men you will always seem wild and strange," his solitude says to Zarathustra. But "here all things come caressingly to your discourse and flatter you, for they want to ride on your back. On every parable you ride to every truth." The discipline of communication might have served the philosopher better than the indiscriminate flattery of his solitude. But in this respect too, it was not given to Nietzsche to live in blissful ignorance: compare, for example, "The Song of Melancholy" in Part Four.

10. *On the Three Evils:* The praise of so-called evil as an ingredient of greatness is central in Nietzsche's thought, from his early fragment, *Homer's Contest,* to his *Antichrist.* There are few problems the self-styled immoralist pursued so persistently. Whether he calls attention to the element of cruelty in the Greek *agon* or denounces Christianity for vilifying sex, whether he contrasts sublimation and extirpation or the egoism of the creative and the vengeful: all

these are variations of one theme. In German, the three evils in this chapter are *Wollust, Herrschsucht, Selbstsucht.* For the first there is no exact equivalent in English. In this chapter, "lust" might do in some sentences, "voluptuousness" in others, but each would be quite inaccurate half the time, and the context makes it imperative that the same word be used throughout. There is only one word in English that renders Nietzsche's meaning perfectly in every single sentence: sex. Its only disadvantage: it is, to put it mildly, a far less poetic word than *Wollust,* and hence modifies the tone though not Nietzsche's meaning. But if we reflect on the three things which, according to Nietzsche, had been maligned most, under the influence of Christianity, and which he sought to rehabilitate or revaluate—were they not selfishness, the will to power, and sex? Nietzsche's early impact was in some ways comparable to that of Freud or Havelock Ellis. But prudery was for him at most one of three great evils, one kind of hypocrisy, one aspect of man's betrayal of the earth and of himself.

11. *On the Spirit of Gravity:* It is not only the metaphor of the camel that points back to the first chapter of Part One: the dead weight of convention is a prime instance of what is meant by the spirit of gravity; and the bird that outsoars tradition is, like the child and the self-propelled wheel at the beginning of the book, a symbol of creativity. The creator, however, is neither an "evil beast" nor an "evil tamer of beasts"—neither a profligate nor an ascetic: he integrates what is in him, perfects and lavishes himself, and says, "This is *my* way; where is yours?" Michelangelo and Mozart do not offer us *"the* way" but a challenge and a promise of what is possible.

12. *On Old and New Tablets:* Attempt at a grand summary, full of allusions to, and quotations from, previous chapters Its unevenness is nowhere more striking than in section 12, with its puns on "crusades." Such sections as 5, 7, and 8, on the other hand, certainly deserve attention. The despot in section 11, who has all history rewritten, seems to point forward in time to Hitler, of whose racial legislation it

could indeed be said: "with the grandfather, however, time ends." Section 15 points back to Luther. Section 20 exposes in advance Stefan George's misconception when he ended his second poem on Nietzsche (my *Nietzsche*, p. 11): "The warner went—the wheel that downward rolls / To emptiness no arm now tackles in the spokes." The penultimate paragraph of this section is more "playful" in the original: *Ein Vorspiel bin ich besserer Spieler, oh meine Brüder! Ein Beispiel!* In section 25 the kéy word is *Versuch,* one of Nietzsche's favorite words, which means experiment, attempt, trial. Sometimes he associates it with *suchen,* searching. (In Chapter 2, "On the Vision and the Riddle," *Sucher, Versucher* has been rendered "searchers, researchers.") Section 29, finally, is used again, with minute changes, to conclude *Twilight of the Idols.*

13. *The Convalescent:* Zarathustra still cannot face the thought of the eternal recurrence but speaks about human speech and cruelty. In the end, his animals expound the eternal recurrence.

14. *On the Great Longing:* Hymn to his soul: Zarathustra and his soul wonder which of them should be grateful to the other.

15. *The Other Dancing Song:* Life and wisdom as women again; but in *this* dancing song, life is in complete control, and when Zarathustra's imagination runs away with him he gets his face slapped. What he whispers into the ear of life at the end of section 2 is, no doubt, that after his death he will yet recur eternally. The song at the end, punctuated by the twelve strokes of the bell, is interpreted in "The Drunken Song" in Part Four.

16. *The Seven Seals:* The eternal recurrence of the small man no longer nauseates Zarathustra. His affirmation now is boundless and without reservation: "For I love you, O eternity."

THE WANDERER

It was about midnight when Zarathustra started across the ridge of the island so that he might reach the other coast by early morning; for there he wanted to embark. There he would find a good roadstead where foreign ships too liked to anchor, and they often took along people who wanted to cross the sea from the blessed isles.

Now as Zarathustra was climbing the mountain he thought how often since his youth he had wandered alone and how many mountains and ridges and peaks he had already climbed.

I am a wanderer and a mountain climber, he said to his heart; I do not like the plains, and it seems I cannot sit still for long. And whatever may yet come to me as destiny and experience will include some wandering and mountain climbing: in the end, one experiences only oneself. The time is gone when mere accidents could still happen to me; and what could still come to me now that was not mine already? What returns, what finally comes home to me, is my own self and what of myself has long been in strange lands and scattered among all things and accidents. And one further thing I know: I stand before my final peak now and before that which has been saved up for me the longest. Alas, now I must face my hardest path! Alas, I have begun my loneliest walk! But whoever is of my kind cannot escape such an hour—the hour which says to him:

"Only now are you going your way to greatness! Peak and abyss—they are now joined together.

"You are going your way to greatness: now that which has hitherto been your ultimate danger has become your ultimate refuge.

"You are going your way to greatness: now this must give you the greatest courage that there is no longer any path behind you.

"You are going your way to greatness: here nobody shall sneak after you. Your own foot has effaced the path behind you, and over it there is written: impossibility.

"And if you now lack all ladders, then you must know how to climb on your own head: how else would you want to climb upward? On your own head and away over your own heart! Now what was gentlest in you must still become the hardest. He who has always spared himself much will in the end become sickly of so much consideration. Praised be what hardens! I do not praise the land where butter and honey flow.

"One must learn to *look away* from oneself in order to see *much*: this hardness is necessary to every climber of mountains.

"But the lover of knowledge who is obtrusive with his eyes—how could he see more of all things than their foregrounds? But you, O Zarathustra, wanted to see the ground and background of all things; hence you must climb over yourself—upward, up until even your stars are *under* you!"

Indeed, to look down upon myself and even upon my stars, that alone I should call my *peak*; that has remained for me as my *ultimate* peak.

Thus spoke Zarathustra to himself as he was climbing, comforting his heart with hard maxims; for his heart was sore as never before. And when he reached the height of the ridge, behold, the other sea lay spread out before him; and he stood still and remained silent a long time. But the night was cold at this height, and clear and starry bright.

I recognize my lot, he finally said sorrowfully. Well, I am ready. Now my ultimate loneliness has begun.

Alas, this black sorrowful sea below me! Alas, this pregnant nocturnal dismay! Alas, destiny and sea! To you I must now go *down!* Before my highest mountain I stand and before my longest wandering; to that end I must first go down deeper than ever I descended—deeper into pain than ever I descended, down into its blackest flood. Thus my destiny wants it. Well, I am ready.

Whence come the highest mountains? I once asked. Then I learned that they came out of the sea. The evidence is written in their rocks and in the walls of their peaks. It is out of the deepest depth that the highest must come to its height.

Thus spoke Zarathustra on the peak of the mountain, where it was cold; but when he came close to the sea and at last stood alone among the cliffs, he had become weary from walking and even more full of longing than before.

Everything is still asleep now, he said; even the sea is asleep. Drunk with sleep and strange it looks at me. But its breath is warm, that I feel. And I also feel that it is dreaming. In its dreams it tosses on hard pillows. Listen! Listen! How it groans with evil memories! Or evil forebodings? Alas, I am sad with you, you dark monster, and even annoyed with myself for your sake. Alas, that my hand does not have strength enough! Verily, I should like to deliver you from evil dreams.

And as Zarathustra was speaking thus he laughed at himself in melancholy and bitterness. What, Zarathustra, he said, would you sing comfort even to the sea? O you loving fool, Zarathustra, you are trust-overfull. But thus have you always been: you have always approached everything terrible trustfully. You have wanted to pet every monster. A whiff of warm breath, a little soft tuft on the paw—and at once you were ready to love and to lure it.

Love is the danger of the loneliest; love of everything if only it is alive. Laughable, verily, are my folly and my modesty in love.

Thus spoke Zarathustra and laughed for the second time. But then he recalled his friends whom he had left; and, as if he had wronged them with his thoughts, he was angry with himself for his thoughts. And soon it happened that he who had laughed wept: from wrath and longing Zarathustra wept bitterly.

ON THE VISION AND THE RIDDLE

1

When it got abroad among the sailors that Zarathustra was on board—for another man from the blessed isles had embarked with him—there was much curiosity and anticipation. But Zarathustra remained silent for two days and was cold and deaf from sadness and answered neither glances nor questions. But on the evening of the second day he opened his ears again, although he still remained silent, for there was much that was strange and dangerous to be heard on this ship, which came from far away and wanted to sail even farther. But Zarathustra was a friend of all who travel far and do not like to live without danger. And behold, eventually his own tongue was loosened as he listened, and the ice of his heart broke. Then he began to speak thus:

To you, the bold searchers, researchers, and whoever

embarks with cunning sails on terrible seas—to you, drunk with riddles, glad of the twilight, whose soul flutes lure astray to every whirlpool, because you do not want to grope along a thread with cowardly hand; and where you can *guess*, you hate to *deduce*—to you alone I tell the riddle that I *saw*, the vision of the loneliest.

Not long ago I walked gloomily through the deadly pallor of dusk—gloomy and hard, with lips pressed together. Not only one sun had set for me. A path that ascended defiantly through stones, malicious, lonely, not cheered by herb or shrub—a mountain path crunched under the defiance of my foot. Striding silently over the mocking clatter of pebbles, crushing the rock that made it slip, my foot forced its way upward. Upward— defying the spirit that drew it downward toward the abyss, the spirit of gravity, my devil and archenemy. Upward—although he sat on me, half dwarf, half mole, lame, making lame, dripping lead into my ear, leaden thoughts into my brain.

"O Zarathustra," he whispered mockingly, syllable by syllable; "you philosopher's stone! You threw yourself up high, but every stone that is thrown must fall. O Zarathustra, you philosopher's stone, you slingstone, you star-crusher! You threw yourself up so high; but every stone that is thrown must fall. Sentenced to yourself and to your own stoning—O Zarathustra, far indeed have you thrown the stone, but it will fall back on yourself."

Then the dwarf fell silent, and that lasted a long time. His silence, however, oppressed me; and such twosomeness is surely more lonesome than being alone. I climbed, I climbed, I dreamed, I thought; but everything oppressed me. I was like one sick whom his wicked torture makes weary, and who as he falls asleep is awakened by a still more wicked dream. But there is something in me that I call courage; that has so far slain my every discouragement. This courage finally bade me stand still and speak: "Dwarf! It is you or I!"

For courage is the best slayer, courage which *attacks;* for in every attack there is playing and brass.

Man, however, is the most courageous animal: hence he overcame every animal. With playing and brass he has so far overcome every pain; but human pain is the deepest pain.

Courage also slays dizziness at the edge of abysses: and where does man not stand at the edge of abysses? Is not seeing always—seeing abysses?

Courage is the best slayer: courage slays even pity. But pity is the deepest abyss: as deeply as man sees into life, he also sees into suffering.

Courage, however, is the best slayer—courage which attacks: which slays even death itself, for it says, "Was *that* life? Well then! Once more!"

In such words, however, there is much playing and brass. He that has ears to hear, let him hear!

2

"Stop, dwarf!" I said. "It is I or you! But I am the stronger of us two: you do not know my abysmal thought. *That* you could not bear!"

Then something happened that made me lighter, for the dwarf jumped from my shoulder, being curious; and he crouched on a stone before me. But there was a gateway just where we had stopped.

"Behold this gateway, dwarf!" I continued. "It has two faces. Two paths meet here; no one has yet followed either to its end. This long lane stretches back for an eternity. And the long lane out there, that is another eternity. They contradict each other, these paths; they offend each other face to face; and it is here at this gateway that they come together. The name of the gateway is inscribed above: 'Moment.' But whoever would follow one of them, on and on, farther and farther—do you believe, dwarf, that these paths contradict each other eternally?"

"All that is straight lies," the dwarf murmured contemptuously. "All truth is crooked; time itself is a circle."

"You spirit of gravity," I said angrily, "do not make things too easy for yourself! Or I shall let you crouch where you are crouching, lamefoot; and it was I that carried you to this *height*.

"Behold," I continued, "this moment! From this gateway, Moment, a long, eternal lane leads *backward*: behind us lies an eternity. Must not whatever *can* walk have walked on this lane before? Must not whatever *can* happen have happened, have been done, have passed by before? And if everything has been there before—what do you think, dwarf, of this moment? Must not this gateway too have been there before? And are not all things knotted together so firmly that this moment draws after it *all* that is to come? Therefore—itself too? For whatever *can* walk—in this long lane out *there* too, it *must* walk once more.

"And this slow spider, which crawls in the moonlight, and this moonlight itself, and I and you in the gateway, whispering together, whispering of eternal things—must not all of us have been there before? And return and walk in that other lane, out there, before us, in this long dreadful lane—must we not eternally return?"

Thus I spoke, more and more softly; for I was afraid of my own thoughts and the thoughts behind my thoughts. Then suddenly I heard a dog howl nearby. Had I ever heard a dog howl like this? My thoughts raced back. Yes, when I was a child, in the most distant childhood: then I heard a dog howl like this. And I saw him too, bristling, his head up, trembling, in the stillest midnight when even dogs believe in ghosts—and I took pity: for just then the full moon, silent as death, passed over the house; just then it stood still, a round glow—still on the flat roof, as if on another's property —that was why the dog was terrified, for dogs believe in thieves and ghosts. And when I heard such howling again I took pity again.

Where was the dwarf gone now? And the gateway? And the spider? And all the whispering? Was I dreaming, then? Was I waking up?

Among wild cliffs I stood suddenly alone, bleak, in the bleakest moonlight. *But there lay a man.* And there —the dog, jumping, bristling, whining—now he saw me coming; then he howled again, he *cried.* Had I ever heard a dog cry like this for help? And verily, what I saw—I had never seen the like. A young shepherd I saw, writhing, gagging, in spasms, his face distorted, and a heavy black snake hung out of his mouth. Had I ever seen so much nausea and pale dread on one face? He seemed to have been asleep when the snake crawled into his throat, and there bit itself fast. My hand tore at the snake and tore in vain; it did not tear the snake out of his throat. Then it cried out of me: "Bite! Bite its head off! Bite!" Thus it cried out of me— my dread, my hatred, my nausea, my pity, all that is good and wicked in me cried out of me with a single cry.

You bold ones who surround me! You searchers, researchers, and whoever among you has embarked with cunning sails on unexplored seas. You who are glad of riddles! Guess me this riddle that I saw then, interpret me the vision of the loneliest. For it was a vision and a foreseeing. *What* did I see then in a parable? And *who* is it who must yet come one day? *Who* is the shepherd into whose throat the snake crawled thus? *Who* is the man into whose throat all that is heaviest and blackest will crawl thus?

The shepherd, however, bit as my cry counseled him; he bit with a good bite. Far away he spewed the head of the snake—and he jumped up. No longer shepherd, no longer human—one changed, radiant, *laughing!* Never yet on earth has a human being laughed as he laughed! O my brothers, I heard a laughter that was no human laughter; and now a thirst gnaws at me, a longing that never grows still. My longing for this laughter gnaws at me; oh, how do I bear to go on living! And how could I bear to die now!

Thus spoke Zarathustra.

ON INVOLUNTARY BLISS

With such riddles and bitternesses in his heart Zarathustra crossed the sea. But when he was four days away from the blessed isles and from his friends, he had overcome all his pain; triumphant and with firm feet he stood on his destiny again. And then Zarathustra spoke thus to his jubilant conscience:

I am alone again and I want to be so; alone with the pure sky and open sea; again it is afternoon around me. It was in the afternoon that I once found my friends for the first time; it was afternoon the second time too, at the hour when all light grows quieter. For whatever of happiness is still on its way between heaven and earth now seeks a shelter in a bright soul; it is from happiness that all light has grown quieter.

O afternoon of my life! Once my happiness too descended to the valley to seek shelter; and found those open, hospitable souls. O afternoon of my life! What have I not given up to have one single thing: this living plantation of my thoughts and this morning light of my highest hope!

Companions the creator once sought, and children of his hope; and behold, it turned out that he could not find them, unless he first created them himself. Thus I am in the middle of my work, going to my children and returning from them: for his children's sake, Zarathustra must perfect himself. For from the depths one loves only one's child and work; and where there is great love of oneself it is the sign of pregnancy: thus I found it to be. My children are still verdant in their first spring, standing close together and shaken by the same winds—the trees of my garden and my best soil. And verily, where such trees stand together there are blessed isles. But one day I want to dig them up and place each by itself, so it may learn solitude and defiance and caution. Gnarled and bent and with supple hardness it shall then stand by the sea, a living lighthouse of invincible life.

Where the storms plunge down into the sea and the mountain stretches out its trunk for water, there every one shall once have his day and night watches for his testing and knowledge. He shall be known and tested, whether he is of my kind and kin, whether he is the master of a long will, taciturn even when he speaks, and yielding so that in giving he receives—so that he may one day become my companion and a fellow creator and fellow celebrant of Zarathustra—one who writes my will on my tablets to contribute to the greater perfection of all things. And for his sake and the sake of those like him I must perfect myself; therefore I now evade my happiness and offer myself to all unhappiness, for my final testing and knowledge.

And verily, it was time for me to leave; and the wanderer's shadow and the longest boredom and the stillest hour—they all urged me: "It is high time." The wind blew through my keyhole and said, "Come!" Cunningly, the door flew open and said to me, "Go!" But I lay there chained to the love for my children: desire set this snare for me—the desire for love that I might become my children's prey and lose myself to them. Desire—this means to me to have lost myself. *I have you, my children!* In this experience everything shall be security and nothing desire.

But, brooding, the sun of my love lay on me; Zarathustra was cooking in his own juice—then shadows and doubts flew over me. I yearned for frost and winter: "Oh, that frost and winter might make me crack and crunch again!" I sighed; then icy mists rose from me. My past burst its tombs; many a pain that had been buried alive awoke, having merely slept, hidden in burial shrouds.

Thus everything called out to me in signs: "It is time!" But I did not hear, until at last my abyss stirred and my thought bit me. Alas, abysmal thought that is *my* thought, when shall I find the strength to hear you burrowing, without trembling any more? My heart pounds to my very throat whenever I hear you burrowing. Even your silence wants to choke me, you who are so abysmally silent. As yet I have never dared to summon you; it was enough that I carried you with me. As yet I have not been strong enough for the final overbearing, prankish bearing of the lion. Your gravity was always terrible enough for me; but one day I shall yet find the strength and the lion's voice to summon you.

And once I have overcome myself that far, then I also want to overcome myself in what is still greater; and a victory shall seal my perfection.

Meanwhile I still drift on uncertain seas; smooth-tongued accident flatters me; forward and backward I look, and still see no end. As yet the hour of my final struggle has not come to me—or is it coming just now? Verily, with treacherous beauty sea and life look at me.

O afternoon of my life! O happiness before evening! O haven on the high seas! O peace in uncertainty! How I mistrust all of you! Verily, I am mistrustful of your treacherous beauty. I am like the lover who mistrusts the all-too-velvet smile. As he pushes his most beloved before him, tender even in his hardness, and jealous, thus I push this blessed hour before me.

Away with you, blessed hour: with you bliss came to me against my will. Willing to suffer my deepest pain, I stand here: you came at the wrong time.

Away with you, blessed hour: rather seek shelter there—with my children. Hurry and bless them before evening with *my* happiness.

There evening approaches even now: the sun sinks. Gone—my happiness!

Thus spoke Zarathustra. And he waited for his unhappiness the entire night, but he waited in vain. The night remained bright and still, and happiness itself came closer and closer to him. Toward morning, however, Zarathustra laughed in his heart and said mockingly, "Happiness runs after me. That is because I do not run after women. For happiness is a woman."

BEFORE SUNRISE

O heaven above me, pure and deep! You abyss of light! Seeing you, I tremble with godlike desires. To throw myself into your height, that is *my* depth. To hide in your purity, that is *my* innocence.

Gods are shrouded by their beauty; thus you conceal your stars. You do not speak; thus you proclaim your wisdom to me. Today you rose for me silently over the roaring sea; your love and your shyness are a revelation to my roaring soul. That you came to me, beautiful, shrouded in your beauty, that you speak to me silently, revealing your wisdom—oh, how should I not guess all that is shy in your soul! *Before* the sun you came to me, the loneliest of all.

We are friends from the beginning: we share grief and ground and gray dread; we even share the sun. We do not speak to each other, because we know too much; we are silent to each other, we smile our knowledge at each other. Are you not the light for my fire? Have you not the sister soul to my insight? Together we have learned everything; together we have learned to ascend over ourselves to ourselves and to smile cloudlessly—to smile down cloudlessly from bright eyes and from a vast distance when constraint and contrivance and guilt steam beneath us like rain.

And when I wandered alone, for *whom* did my soul hunger at night, on false paths? And when I climbed mountains, *whom* did I always seek on the mountains, if not you? And all my wandering and mountain climbing were sheer necessity and a help in my helplessness: what I want with all my will is to *fly*, to fly up into *you*.

And whom did I hate more than drifting clouds and

all that stains you? And I hated even my own hatred because it stained you. I loathe the drifting clouds, those stealthy great cats which prey on what you and I have in common—the uncanny, unbounded Yes and Amen. We loathe these mediators and mixers, the drifting clouds that are half-and-half and have learned neither to bless nor to curse from the heart.

Rather would I sit in a barrel under closed heavens, rather sit in the abyss without a heaven, than see you, bright heaven, stained by drifting clouds.

And often I had the desire to tie them fast with the jagged golden wires of the lightning, that, like thunder, I might beat the big drums on their kettle-belly— an angry kettle-drummer—because they rob me of your Yes and Amen, O heaven over me, pure and light! You abyss of light! Because they rob you of *my* Yes and Amen. For I prefer even noise and thunder and storm-curses to this deliberate, doubting cats' calm; and among men too I hate most of all the soft-treaders and those who are half-and-half and doubting, tottering drift clouds.

And "whoever cannot bless should *learn* to curse"— this bright doctrine fell to me from a bright heaven; this star stands in my heaven even in black nights.

But I am one who can bless and say Yes, if only you are about me, pure and light, you abyss of light; then I carry the blessings of my Yes into all abysses. I have become one who blesses and says Yes; and I fought long for that and was a fighter that I might one day get my hands free to bless. But this is my blessing: to stand over every single thing as its own heaven, as its round roof, its azure bell, and eternal security; and blessed is he who blesses thus.

For all things have been baptized in the well of

eternity and are beyond good and evil; and good and evil themselves are but intervening shadows and damp depressions and drifting clouds.

Verily, it is a blessing and not a blasphemy when I teach: "Over all things stand the heaven Accident, the heaven Innocence, the heaven Chance, the heaven Prankishness."

"By Chance"—that is the most ancient nobility of the world, and this I restored to all things: I delivered them from their bondage under Purpose. This freedom and heavenly cheer I have placed over all things like an azure bell when I taught that over them and through them no "eternal will" wills. This prankish folly I have put in the place of that will when I taught: "In everything one thing is impossible: rationality."

A *little* reason, to be sure, a seed of wisdom scattered from star to star—this leaven is mixed in with all things: for folly's sake, wisdom is mixed in with all things. A little wisdom is possible indeed; but this blessed certainty I found in all things: that they would rather *dance* on the feet of Chance.

O heaven over me, pure and high! That is what your purity is to me now, that there is no eternal spider or spider web of reason; that you are to me a dance floor for divine accidents, that you are to me a divine table for divine dice and dice players. But you blush? Did I speak the unspeakable? Did I blaspheme, wishing to bless you? Or is it the shame of twosomeness that makes you blush? Do you bid me go and be silent because the *day* is coming now?

The world is deep—and deeper than day had ever been aware. Not everything may be put into words in the presence of the day. But the day is coming, so let us part.

O heaven over me, bashful and glowing! O you, my happiness before sunrise! The day is coming, so let us part!

Thus spoke Zarathustra.

ON VIRTUE THAT MAKES SMALL

1

When Zarathustra was on land again he did not proceed straight to his mountain and his cave, but he undertook many ways and questions and found out this and that; so that he said of himself, joking: "Behold a river that flows, winding and twisting, back to its source!" For he wanted to determine what had happened to man meanwhile: whether he had become greater or smaller. And once he saw a row of new houses; then he was amazed and said:

"What do these houses mean? Verily, no great soul put them up as its likeness. Might an idiotic child have taken them out of his toy box? Would that another child might put them back into his box! And these rooms and chambers—can *men* go in and out of them? They look to me as if made for silken dolls, or for stealthy nibblers who probably also let themselves be nibbled stealthily."

And Zarathustra stood still and reflected. At last he said sadly: "Everything has become smaller! Everywhere I see lower gates: those who are of my kind probably still go through, but they must stoop. Oh, when shall I get back to my homeland, where I need no longer stoop—no longer stoop before *those who are small?*" And Zarathustra sighed and looked into the distance. On that same day, however, he made his speech on virtue that makes small.

2

I walk among this people and I keep my eyes open: they do not forgive me that I do not envy their virtues. They bite at me because I say to them: small people need small virtues—and because I find it hard to accept that small people are needed.

I am still like the rooster in a strange yard, where the hens also bite at him; but I am not angry with the hens on that account. I am polite to them as to all small annoyances; to be prickly to what is small strikes me as wisdom for hedgehogs.

They all speak of me when they sit around the fire in the evening; they speak of me, but no one thinks of me. This is the new stillness I have learned: their noise concerning me spreads a cloak over my thoughts.

They noise among themselves: "What would this gloomy cloud bring us? Let us see to it that it does not bring us a plague." And recently a woman tore back her child when it wanted to come to me. "Take the children away!" she cried; "such eyes scorch children's souls." They cough when I speak: they think that a cough is an argument against strong winds; they guess nothing of the roaring of my happiness. "We have no time yet for Zarathustra," they argue; but what matters a time that "has no time" for Zarathustra?

And when they praise me, how could I go to sleep on *their* praise? Their praise is a belt of thorns to me: it scratches me even as I shake it off. And this too I have learned among them: he who gives praise poses as if he were giving back; in truth, however, he wants more gifts.

Ask my foot whether it likes their way of lauding and luring! Verily, after such a beat and ticktock it has no wish either to dance or to stand still. They would laud and lure me into a small virtue; they would persuade my foot to the ticktock of a small happiness.

I walk among this people and I keep my eyes open: they have become smaller, and they are becoming smaller and smaller; *but this is due to their doctrine of happiness and virtue.* For they are modest in virtue, too—because they want contentment. But only a modest virtue gets along with contentment.

To be sure, even they learn in their way to stride and to stride forward: I call it their hobbling. Thus they become a stumbling block for everyone who is in a hurry. And many among them walk forward while looking backward with their necks stiff: I like running into them. Foot and eye should not lie nor give the lie to each other. But there is much lying among the small people. Some of them will, but most of them are only willed. Some of them are genuine, but most of them are bad actors. There are unconscious actors among them and involuntary actors; the genuine are always rare, especially genuine actors.

There is little of man here; therefore their women strive to be mannish. For only he who is man enough will release the woman in woman.

And this hypocrisy I found to be the worst among them, that even those who command, hypocritically feign the virtues of those who serve. "I serve, you serve, we serve"—thus prays even the hypocrisy of the rulers; and woe, if the first lord is *merely* the first servant!

Alas, into their hypocrisies too the curiosity of my eyes flew astray; and well I guessed their fly-happiness and their humming around sunny windowpanes. So much kindness, so much weakness do I see; so much justice and pity, so much weakness.

Round, righteous, and kind they are to each other,

round like grains of sand, righteous and kind with grains of sand. Modestly to embrace a small happiness—that they call "resignation"—and modestly they squint the while for another small happiness. At bottom, these simpletons want a single thing most of all: that nobody should hurt them. Thus they try to please and gratify everybody. This, however, is cowardice, even if it be called virtue.

And if they once speak roughly, these small people, *I* hear only their hoarseness, for every draft makes them hoarse. They are clever, their virtues have clever fingers. But they lack fists, their fingers do not know how to hide behind fists. Virtue to them is that which makes modest and tame: with that they have turned the wolf into a dog and man himself into man's best domestic animal.

"We have placed our chair in the middle," your smirking says to me; "and exactly as far from dying fighters as from amused sows." That, however, is mediocrity, though it be called moderation.

3

I walk among this people and I let many a word drop; but they know neither how to accept nor how to retain.

They are amazed that I did not come to revile venery and vice; and verily, I did not come to warn against pickpockets either.

They are amazed that I am not prepared to teach wit to their cleverness and to whet it—as if they did not have enough clever boys, whose voices screech like slate pencils!

And when I shout, "Curse all cowardly devils in you who like to whine and fold their hands and pray," they shout, "Zarathustra is godless." And their teachers of resignation shout it especially; but it is precisely into their ears that I like to shout, "Yes, I *am* Zarathustra the godless!" These teachers of resignation! Whatever is small and sick and scabby, they crawl to like lice; and only my nausea prevents me from squashing them.

Well then, this is my preaching for *their* ears: I am Zarathustra the godless, who speaks: "Who is more godless than I, that I may delight in his instruction?"

I am Zarathustra the godless: where shall I find my equal? And all those are my equals who give themselves their own will and reject all resignation.

I am Zarathustra the godless: I still cook every chance in my pot. And only when it has been cooked through there do I welcome it as my food. And verily, many a chance came to me domineeringly; but my will spoke to it still more domineeringly—and immediately it lay imploringly on its knees, imploring that it might find a hearth and heart in me, and urging with flattery, "Look, Zarathustra, how only a friend comes to his friend!"

But why do I speak where nobody has *my* ears? And so let me shout it into all the winds: You are becoming smaller and smaller, you small people! You are crumbling, you comfortable ones. You will yet perish of your many small virtues, of your many small abstentions, of your many small resignations. Too considerate, too yielding is your soil. But that a tree may become *great*, it must strike hard roots around hard rocks.

What you abstain from too weaves at the web of all human future; your nothing too is a spider web and a spider, which lives on the blood of the future. And when you receive it is like stealing, you small men of virtue; but even among rogues, *honor* says, "One should steal only where one cannot rob."

"It will give eventually"—that is another teaching of

resignation. But I tell you who are comfortable: *it will take* and will take more and more from you! Oh, that you would reject all *halfhearted* willing and would become resolute in sloth and deed!

Alas, that you would understand my word: "Do whatever you will, but first be such as are *able to will*.

"Do love your neighbor as yourself, but first be such as *love themselves*—loving with a great love, loving with a great contempt." Thus speaks Zarathustra the godless.

But why do I speak where nobody has *my* ears? It is still an hour too early for me here. I am my own precursor among this people, my own cock's crow through dark lanes. But *their* hour will come! And mine will come too! Hourly, they are becoming smaller, poorer, more sterile—poor herbs! poor soil! and *soon* they shall stand there like dry grass and prairie— and verily, weary of themselves and languishing even more than for water—for *fire*.

O blessed hour of lightning! O secret before noon! I yet hope to turn them into galloping fires and heralds with fiery tongues—they shall yet proclaim with fiery tongues: It is coming, it is near—*the great noon!*

Thus spoke Zarathustra.

UPON THE MOUNT OF OLIVES

Winter, a wicked guest, is sitting at home with me; my hands are blue from the handshake of his friendship. I honor this wicked guest, but I like to let him sit alone. I like to run away from him; and if one runs *well*, one escapes him. With warm feet and warm thoughts I run where the wind stands still, to the sunny nook of my mount of olives. There I laugh at my severe guest and am still well disposed toward him for catching the flies at home and for silencing much small noise. For he does not suffer it when a mosquito would sing, or even two; he even makes the lane lonely till the moonlight in it is afraid at night.

He is a hard guest, but I honor him, and I do not pray, like the pampered, to the potbellied fire idol. Even a little chattering of the teeth rather than adoring idols —thus my nature dictates. And I have a special grudge against all fire idols that are in heat, steaming and musty.

Whomever I love, I love better in winter than in summer; I mock my enemies better and more heartily since winter dwells in my home. Heartily, in truth, even when I crawl into bed; even then my hidden happiness still laughs and is full of pranks; even the dream that lies to me still laughs. I—a crawler? Never in my life have I crawled before the mighty; and if ever I lied, I lied out of love. Therefore I am glad in the wintry bed too. A simple bed warms me more than a rich one, for I am jealous of my poverty, and in winter it is most faithful to me.

I begin every day with a bit of malice: I mock the winter with a cold bath; that makes my severe house guest grumble. Besides, I like to tickle him with a little wax candle to make him let the sky come out of the ashen gray twilight at last. For I am especially malicious in the morning, in that early hour when the pail rattles at the well and the horses whinny warmly through gray lanes. Then I wait impatiently for the bright sky to rise before me at last, the snow-bearded winter sky, the old man with his white hair—the winter sky, so taciturn that it often tacitly hides even its sun.

Was it from him that I learned the long bright silence? Or did he learn it from me? Or did each of us invent it independently? The origin of all good things is thousandfold; all good prankish things leap into existence from sheer joy: how could one expect them to do that only once? Long silence too is a good prankish thing—and to look out of a bright round-eyed face, like the winter sky, and tacitly to hide one's sun and one's indomitable solar will: verily, this art and this winter prank I have learned well.

It is my favorite malice and art that my silence has learned not to betray itself through silence. Rattling with discourse and dice, I outwit those who wait solemnly: my will and purpose shall elude all these severe inspectors. That no one may discern my ground and ultimate will, for that I have invented my long bright silence. Many I found who were clever: they veiled their faces and muddied their waters that nobody might see through them, deep down. But precisely to them came the cleverer mistrusters and nutcrackers: precisely their most hidden fish were fished out. It is the bright, the bold, the transparent who are cleverest among those who are silent: their ground is down so deep that even the brightest water does not betray it.

You snow-bearded silent winter sky, you round-eyed white-head above me! O you heavenly parable of my soul and its pranks!

And *must* I not conceal myself like one who has swallowed gold, lest they slit open my soul? *Must* I not walk on stilts that they overlook my long legs—all these grudge-joys and drudge-boys who surround me? These smoky, room-temperature, used-up, wilted, fretful souls —how *could* their grudge endure my happiness? Hence I show them only the ice and the winter of my peaks— and not that my mountain still winds all the belts of the sun round itself. They hear only my winter winds whistling—and not that I also cross warm seas, like longing, heavy, hot south winds. They still have pity on my accidents; but *my* word says, "Let accidents come to me, they are innocent as little children."

How could they endure my happiness if I did not wrap my happiness in accidents and winter distress and polar-bear caps and covers of snowy heavens—if I myself did not have mercy on their *pity*, which is the pity of grudge-joys and drudge-boys, if I myself did not sigh before them and chatter with cold and patiently *suffer* them to wrap me in their pity. This is the wise frolicsomeness and friendliness of my soul, that it does not conceal its winter and its icy winds; nor does it conceal its chilblains.

Loneliness can be the escape of the sick; loneliness can also be escape *from* the sick.

Let them *hear* me chatter and sigh with the winter cold, all these poor jealous jokers around me! With such sighing and chattering I still escape their heated rooms.

Let them suffer and sigh over my chilblains. "The ice of knowledge will yet freeze him to death!" they moan.

Meanwhile I run crisscross on my mount of olives with warm feet; in the sunny nook of my mount of olives I sing and I mock all pity.

Thus sang Zarathustra.

ON PASSING BY

Thus, walking slowly among many peoples and through numerous towns, Zarathustra returned on roundabout paths to his mountains and his cave. And on the way he also came unexpectedly to the gate of the great city; but here a foaming fool jumped toward him with outspread hands and barred his way. This, however, was the same fool whom the people called "Zarathustra's ape": for he had gathered something of his phrasing and cadences and also liked to borrow from the treasures of his wisdom. But the fool spoke thus to Zarathustra:

"O Zarathustra, here is the great city; here you could find nothing and lose everything. Why do you want to wade through this mire? Have pity on your foot! Rather spit on the city gate and turn back. Here is hell for a hermit's thoughts: here great thoughts are boiled alive and cooked till they are small. Here all great feelings decay: only the smallest rattleboned feelings may rattle here. Don't you smell the slaughterhouses and ovens of the spirit even now? Does not this town steam with the fumes of slaughtered spirit?

"Don't you see the soul hanging like a limp, dirty rag? And they still make newspapers of these rags!

"Don't you hear how the spirit has here been reduced to plays on words? It vomits revolting verbal swill. And they still make newspapers of this swill!

"They hound each other and know not where. They overheat each other and know not why. They tinkle with their tin, they jingle with their gold. They are cold and seek warmth from brandy; they are heated and seek coolness from frozen spirits; they are all diseased and sick with public opinions.

"All lusts and vices are at home here; but there are also some here who are virtuous: there is much serviceable, serving virtue—much serviceable virtue with pen fingers and hard sitting- and waiting-flesh, blessed with little stars on the chest and with padded, rumpless daughters. There is also much piety, and there are many devout lickspittles, batteries of fakers and flattery-bakers before the God of Hosts. For it is 'from above' that the stars and the gracious spittle trickle; every starless chest longs above.

"The moon has her courtyard, and the courtyard has its mooncalves; to everything, however, that comes from the court, the beggarly mob and all serviceable beggar-virtue pray. 'I serve, you serve, we serve'—thus all serviceable virtue prays to the prince, that the deserved star may finally be pinned on the narrow chest.

"The moon, however, still revolves around all that is earthly: So too the prince still revolves around that which is earthliest—but that is the gold of the shop-keeper. The God of Hosts is no god of gold bars; the prince proposes, but the shopkeeper disposes.

"By everything in you that is bright and strong and good, O Zarathustra, spit on this city of shopkeepers and turn back! Here all blood flows putrid and luke-warm and spumy through all the veins; spit on the great city which is the great swill room where all the swill spumes together. Spit on the city of compressed souls and narrow chests, of popeyes and sticky fingers—on the city of the obtrusive, the impudent, the scribble- and scream-throats, the overheated ambitious-conceited —where everything infirm, infamous, lustful, dusky, overmusty, pussy, and plotting putrefies together: spit on the great city and turn back!"

Here, however, Zarathustra interrupted the foaming fool and put his hand over the fool's mouth. "Stop at last!" cried Zarathustra; "your speech and your manner have long nauseated me. Why did you live near the swamps so long, until you yourself have become a frog and a toad? Does not putrid, spumy swamp-blood flow through your own veins now that you have learned to croak and revile thus? Why have you not gone into the woods? Or to plow the soil? Does not the sea abound in green islands? I despise your despising; and if you warned me, why did you not warn yourself?

"Out of love alone shall my despising and my warn-ing bird fly up, not out of the swamp.

"They call you my ape, you foaming fool; but I call you my grunting swine: with your grunting you spoil for me my praise of folly. What was it that first made you grunt? That nobody flattered you sufficiently; you sat down to this filth so as to have reason to grunt much —to have reason for much *revenge*. For all your foaming is revenge, you vain fool; I guessed it well.

"But your fool's words injure me, even where you are right. And even if Zarathustra's words *were* a thousand times right, still *you* would always *do* wrong with my words."

Thus spoke Zarathustra; and he looked at the great city, sighed, and long remained silent. At last he spoke thus: "I am nauseated by this great city too, and not only by this fool. Here as there, there is nothing to better, nothing to worsen. Woe unto this great city! And I wish I already saw the pillar of fire in which it will be burned. For such pillars of fire must precede the great noon. But this has its own time and its own destiny.

"This doctrine, however, I give you, fool, as a parting present: where one can no longer love, there one should *pass by*."

Thus spoke Zarathustra, and he passed by the fool and the great city.

ON APOSTATES

1

Alas, all lies withered and gray that but recently stood green and colorful on this meadow. And how much honey of hope I carried from here to my beehives! These young hearts have all become old already—and not even old; only weary, ordinary, and comfortable. They put it, "We have become pious again."

Only recently I saw them run out in the morning on bold feet: but the feet of their thirst for knowledge have grown weary, and now they even slander the courage they had in the morning. Verily, many among them once lifted their legs like dancers, cheered by the laughter in my wisdom; then they thought better of it. Just now I saw one groveling—crawling back to the cross. Around light and freedom they once fluttered like mosquitoes and young poets. A little older, a little colder—and already they are musty mystifiers and hearth-squatters.

Did their hearts perhaps grow faint because solitude swallowed me like a whale? Did their ears perhaps listen longingly long, *in vain*, for me and my trumpet and herald's calls? Alas, there are always only a few whose hearts long retain their courageous bearing and overbearing prankishness, and whose spirits also remain patient. The rest, however, are cowards. The rest—those are always by far the most, the commonplace, the superfluous, the all-too-many: all these are cowards.

Whoever is of my kind will also encounter the experiences of my kind: so his first companions will have to be corpses and jesters. His second companions, however, will call themselves his *believers*: a living swarm, much love, much folly, much beardless veneration. To these believers, whoever is of my kind among men should not tie his heart; those who know the changeful, cowardly nature of mankind should not believe in these springtimes and colorful meadows.

Were their ability different, their will would be different too. Those who are half-and-half spoil all that is whole. That leaves wilt—what is there to wail about? Let them fly and fall, O Zarathustra, and do not wail! It is better to blow among them with rustling winds—

blow among these leaves, O Zarathustra, that everything wilted may run away from you even faster!

2

"We have become pious again"—so these apostates confess; and some among them are even too cowardly to confess it.

Those I look in the eye, and then I say it to their faces and to their blushing cheeks: you are such as pray again.

But it is a disgrace to pray! Not for everybody, but for you and me and whoever else has a conscience in his head too. For *you* it is a disgrace to pray!

You know it well: your cowardly devil within you, who would like to fold his hands and rest his hands in his lap and be more comfortable—this cowardly devil urges you, "There *is* a God." With this, however, you belong to the light-shunning kind who cannot rest where there is light; now you must daily bury your head deeper in night and haze.

And verily, you chose the hour well, for just now the nocturnal birds are flying again. The hour has come for all light-shunning folk, the hour of evening and rest, when they do not rest. I hear and smell it: their hour for chase and procession has come—not indeed for a wild chase, but for a tame, lame, snooping, pussyfooting, prayer-muttering chase—for a chase after soulful sneaks: all the heart's mousetraps have now been set again. And wherever I lift a curtain a little night moth rushes out. Did it perhaps squat there together with another little night moth? For everywhere I smell little hidden communities; and wherever there are closets, there are new canters praying inside and the fog of canters.

They sit together long evenings and say, "Let us become as little children again and say 'dear God!' "—their mouths and stomachs upset by pious confectioners.

Or they spend long evenings watching a cunning, ambushing, cross-marked spider, which preaches cleverness to the other spiders and teaches thus: "Under crosses one can spin well."

Or they spend the day sitting at swamps with fishing rods, thinking themselves profound; but whoever fishes where there are no fish, I would not even call superficial.

Or they learn to play the harp with pious pleasure—from a composer of songs who would like to harp himself right into the hearts of young females; for he has grown weary of old females and their praise.

Or they learn to shudder from a scholarly half-madman who waits in dark rooms for the spirits to come to him—so his spirit will flee completely.

Or they listen to an old traveling, caviling zany who has learned the sadness of tones from sad winds; now he whistles after the wind and preaches sadness in sad tones.

And some of them have even become night watchmen: now they know how to blow horns and to walk about at night and to awaken old things that had long gone to sleep. I heard five sayings about old things last night at the garden wall: they came from such old, saddened, dried-up night watchmen.

"For a father, he does not care enough about his children: human fathers do this better."

"He is too old. He does not care about his children at all any more"—thus the other night watchman replied.

"But does he *have* any children? Nobody can prove it, if he does not prove it himself. I have long wished he would for once prove it thoroughly."

"Prove? As if *he* had ever proved anything! Proof is difficult for him; he considers it terribly important that one should have *faith* in him."

"Sure! Sure! Faith makes him blessed, faith in him. That is the way of old people. We are no different ourselves."

Thus the two old night watchmen and scarelights spoke to each other and then tooted sadly on their horns: so it happened last night at the garden wall. In me, however, my heart twisted with laughter and wanted to break and did not know whither, and sank into my diaphragm. Verily, this will yet be my death, that I shall suffocate with laughter when I see asses drunk and hear night watchmen thus doubting God. Is not the time long past for all such doubts too? Who may still awaken such old sleeping, light-shunning things?

For the old gods, after all, things came to an end long ago; and verily, they had a good gay godlike end. They did not end in a "twilight," though this lie is told. Instead: one day they *laughed* themselves to death. That happened when the most godless word issued from one of the gods themselves—the word: "There is one god. Thou shalt have no other god before me!" An old grimbeard of a god, a jealous one, thus forgot himself. And then all the gods laughed and rocked on their chairs and cried, "Is not just this godlike that there are gods but no God?"

He that has ears to hear, let him hear!

Thus Zarathustra discoursed in the town which he loved and which is also called The Motley Cow. For from here he had only two more days to go to reach his cave and his animals again; but his soul jubilated continually because of the nearness of his return home.

THE RETURN HOME

O solitude! O my *home*, solitude! Too long have I lived wildly in wild strange places not to return home to you in tears. Now you may threaten me with your finger, as mothers threaten; now you may smile at me, as mothers smile; now you may say to me:

"And who was it that, like a storm, once stormed away from me? Who shouted in parting, 'Too long I have sat with solitude; I have forgotten how to be silent!' That, I suppose, you have learned again now? O Zarathustra, I know everything. Also that you were more forsaken among the many, being one, than ever with me. To be forsaken is one thing, to be lonely, another: that you have learned now. And that among men you will always seem wild and strange—wild and strange even when they love you; for above all things they want *consideration*.

"Here, however, you are in your own home and house; here you can talk freely about everything and pour out all the reasons; nothing here is ashamed of obscure, obdurate feelings. Here all things come caressingly to your discourse and flatter you, for they want to ride on your back. On every parable you ride to every truth. Here you may talk fairly and frankly to all things: and verily, it rings in their ears like praise when somebody talks straight to all things.

"To be forsaken, however, is another matter. For— do you still remember, Zarathustra? When your bird cried high above you, when you stood in the forest, undecided where to turn, ignorant, near a corpse—when you said, 'May my animals lead me! I found it more dangerous to be among men than among animals'—

then you were forsaken! And do you still remember, Zarathustra? When you sat on your island, a well of wine among empty pails, spending and expending, bestowing and flowing among the thirsty, until finally you sat thirsty among drunks and complained by night, 'Is it not more blessed to receive than to give, and to steal still more blessed than to receive?'—then you were forsaken! And do you still remember, Zarathustra? When your stillest hour came and drove you away from yourself, speaking in an evil whisper, 'Speak and break!'—when it made you repent all your waiting and silence and discouraged your humble courage—then you were forsaken."

O solitude! O my home, solitude! How happily and tenderly your voice speaks to me! We do not question each other, we do not complain to each other, we often walk together through open doors. For where you are, things are open and bright; and the hours too walk on lighter feet here. For in darkness, time weighs more heavily on us than in the light. Here the words and word-shrines of all being open up before me: here all being wishes to become word, all becoming wishes to learn from me how to speak.

Down there, however, all speech is in vain. There, forgetting and passing by are the best wisdom: *that* I have learned now. He who would grasp everything human would have to grapple with everything. But for that my hands are too clean. I do not even want to inhale their breath; alas, that I lived so long among their noises and vile breath!

O happy silence around me! O clean smells around me! Oh, how this silence draws deep breaths of clean air! Oh, how it listens, this happy silence!

But down there everyone talks and no one listens.

You could ring in your wisdom with bells: the shop-keepers in the market place would outjingle it with pennies.

Everyone among them talks; no one knows how to understand any more. Everything falls into the water, nothing falls into deep wells any longer.

Everyone among them talks; nothing turns out well any more and is finished. Everyone cackles; but who still wants to sit quietly in the nest and hatch eggs?

Everyone among them talks; everything is talked to pieces. And what even yesterday was still too hard for time itself and its tooth, today hangs, spoiled by scraping and gnawing, out of the mouths of the men of today.

Everyone among them talks; everything is betrayed. And what was once called the secret and the secrecy of deep souls today belongs to the street trumpeters and other butterflies.

Oh, everything human is strange, a noise on dark streets! But now it lies behind me again: my greatest danger lies behind me!

Consideration and pity have ever been my greatest dangers, and everything human wants consideration and pity. With concealed truths, with a fool's hands and a fond, foolish heart and a wealth of the little lies of pity: thus I always lived among men. Disguised I sat among them, ready to mistake *myself* that I might endure *them*, and willingly urging myself, "You fool, you do not know men."

One forgets about men when one lives among men; there is too much foreground in all men: what good are far-sighted, far-seeking eyes *there?* And whenever they mistook me, I, fool that I am, showed them more consideration than myself, being used to hardness against myself, and often I even took revenge on myself for being too considerate. Covered with the bites of poisonous flies and hollowed out like a stone by many drops of malice, thus I sat among them, and I still reminded myself, "Everything small is innocent of its smallness."

Especially those who call themselves "the good" I found to be the most poisonous flies: they bite in all innocence, they lie in all innocence; how could they possibly be just to me? Pity teaches all who live among the good to lie. Pity surrounds all free souls with musty air. For the stupidity of the good is unfathomable.

To conceal myself and my wealth, that I learned down there; for I have found everyone poor in spirit. The lie of my pity was this, that I knew I could see and smell in everyone what was spirit enough for him and what was too much spirit for him. Their stiff sages—I called them sagacious, not stiff; thus I learned to swallow words. Their gravediggers—I called them researchers and testers; thus I learned to change words. The gravediggers dig themselves sick; under old rubbish lie noxious odors. One should not stir up the morass. One should live on mountains.

With happy nostrils I again breathe mountain freedom. At last my nose is delivered from the smell of everything human. Tickled by the sharp air as by sparkling wines, my soul sneezes—sneezes and jubilates to itself: *Gesundheit!*

Thus spoke Zarathustra.

ON THE THREE EVILS

1

In a dream, in the last dream of the morning, I stood in the foothills today—beyond the world, held scales, and weighed the world. Alas, the jealous dawn came too early and glowed me awake! She is always jealous of my glowing morning dreams.

Measurable by him who has time, weighable by a good weigher, reachable by strong wings, guessable by divine nutcrackers: thus my dream found the world— my dream, a bold sailor, half ship, half hurricane, taciturn as butterflies, impatient as falcons: how did it have the patience or the time to weigh the world? Did my wisdom secretly urge it, my laughing, wide-awake day-wisdom which mocks all "infinite worlds"? For it speaks: "Wherever there is force, *number* will become mistress: she has more force."

How surely my dream looked upon this finite world, not inquisitively, not acquisitively, not afraid, not begging, as if a full apple offered itself to my hand, a ripe golden apple with cool, soft, velvet skin, thus the world offered itself to me; as if a tree waved to me, broad-branched, strong-willed, bent as a support, even as a footstool for one weary of his way, thus the world stood on my foothills; as if delicate hands carried a shrine toward me, a shrine open for the delight of bashful, adoring eyes, thus the world offered itself to me today; not riddle enough to frighten away human love, not solution enough to put to sleep human wisdom: a humanly good thing the world was to me today, though one speaks so much evil of it.

How shall I thank my morning dream that I thus weighed the world this morning? As a humanly good thing it came to me, this dream and heart-comforter. And to imitate it by day and to learn from it what was best in it, I shall now place the three most evil things on the scales and weigh them humanly well. He that taught to bless also taught to curse; what are the three best cursed things in the world? I shall put them on the scales.

Sex, the lust to rule, selfishness: these three have so far been best cursed and worst reputed and lied about; these three I will weigh humanly well.

Well then, here are my foothills and there the sea: *that* rolls toward me, shaggy, flattering, the faithful old hundred-headed canine monster that I love. Well then, here I will hold the scales over the rolling sea; and a witness I choose too, to look on—you, solitary tree, fragrant and broad-vaulted, that I love.

On what bridge does the present pass to the future? By what compulsion does the higher compel itself to the lower? And what bids even the highest grow still higher?

Now the scales are balanced and still: three weighty questions I threw on it; three weighty answers balance the other scale.

2

Sex: to all hair-shirted despisers of the body, their thorn and stake, and cursed as "world" among all the afterworldly because it mocks and fools all teachers of error and confusion.

Sex: for the rabble, the slow fire on which they are burned; for all worm-eaten wood and all stinking rags, the ever-ready rut and oven.

Sex: for free hearts, innocent and free, the garden happiness of the earth, the future's exuberant gratitude to the present.

Sex: only for the wilted, a sweet poison; for the lion-willed, however, the great invigoration of the heart and the reverently reserved wine of wines.

Sex: the happiness that is the great parable of a higher happiness and the highest hope. For to many is marriage promised, and more than marriage—to many who are stranger to each other than man and woman. And who can wholly comprehend *how* strange man and woman are to each other?

Sex—but I want to have fences around my thoughts and even around my words, lest swine and swooners break into my garden!

The lust to rule: the scalding scourge of the hardest among the hardhearted; the hideous torture that is saved up for the cruelest; the dark flame of living pyres.

The lust to rule: the malicious gadfly imposed on the vainest peoples; the mocker of all uncertain virtues; the rider on every horse and every pride.

The lust to rule: the earthquake that breaks and breaks open everything worm-eaten and hollow; the rumbling, grumbling punisher that breaks open whited sepulchers; the lightning-like question mark beside premature answers.

The lust to rule: before whose glances man crawls and ducks and slaves and becomes lower than snake and swine, until finally the great contempt cries out of him.

The lust to rule: the terrible teacher of the great contempt, who preaches "away with you" to the very faces of cities and empires, until it finally cries out of them themselves, "Away with *me!*"

The lust to rule: which, however, also ascends luringly to the pure and lonely and up to self-sufficient heights, glowing like a love that luringly paints crimson fulfillments on earthly skies.

The lust to rule—but who would call it *lust* when what is high longs downward for power? Verily, there is nothing diseased or lustful in such longing and condescending. That the lonely heights should not remain lonely and self-sufficient eternally; that the mountain should descend to the valley and the winds of the height to the low plains—oh, who were to find the right name for such longing? "Gift-giving virtue"—thus Zarathustra once named the unnamable.

And at that time it also happened—and verily, it happened for the first time—that his word pronounced *selfishness* blessed, the wholesome, healthy selfishness that wells from a powerful soul—from a powerful soul to which belongs the high body, beautiful, triumphant, refreshing, around which everything becomes a mirror —the supple, persuasive body, the dancer whose parable and epitome is the self-enjoying soul. The self-enjoyment of such bodies and souls calls itself "virtue."

With its words about good and bad, such self-enjoyment screens itself as with sacred groves; with the names of its happiness it banishes from its presence whatever is contemptible. From its presence it banishes whatever is cowardly; it says: bad—*that is* cowardly! Contemptible to its mind is anyone who always worries, sighs, is miserable, and also anyone who picks up even the smallest advantages. It also despises all wisdom that wallows in grief; for verily, there is also wisdom that blooms in the dark, a nightshade wisdom, which always sighs: all is vain.

Shy mistrust it holds in low esteem, also anyone who wants oaths instead of eyes and hands; also all wisdom that is all-too-mistrustful, for that is the manner of cowardly souls. In still lower esteem it holds the subservient, the doglike, who immediately lie on their backs, the humble; and there is wisdom too that is humble and doglike and pious and subservient. Altogether hateful and nauseating it finds those who never offer resistance, who swallow poisonous spittle and evil glances, the all-too-patient, all-suffering, always satisfied; for that is servile.

Whether one be servile before gods and gods' kicks or before men and stupid men's opinions—whatever is servile it spits on, this blessed selfishness. Bad: that is what it calls everything that is sorely stooped and sordidly servile, unfree blink-eyes, oppressed hearts, and that false yielding manner that kisses with wide cowardly lips.

And sham wisdom: that is what it calls the would-be wit of the servile and old and weary, and especially the whole wicked, nitwitted, witless foolishness of priests. The sham-wise, however—all the priests, the world-weary, and all those whose souls are womanish and servile—oh, what wicked tricks has their trickery always played on selfishness! And what was considered virtue and called virtue *was* playing wicked tricks on selfishness! And "selfless"—that is how all these world-weary cowards and cross-marked spiders wanted themselves, for good reasons.

But for all these the day is now at hand, the change, the sword of judgment, *the great noon:* much shall be revealed there.

And whoever proclaims the ego wholesome and holy, and selfishness blessed, verily, he will also tell what he knows, foretelling: "Verily, it is at hand, it is near, the great noon!"

Thus spoke Zarathustra.

ON THE SPIRIT OF GRAVITY

1

My tongue is of the people: I speak too crudely and heartily for Angora rabbits. And my speech sounds even stranger to all ink-fish and pen-hacks.

My hand is a fool's hand: beware, all tables and walls and whatever else still offer room for foolish frill or scribbling skill.

My foot is a cloven foot; with it I trample and trot over sticks and stones, crisscross, and I am happy as the devil while running so fast.

My stomach—is it an eagle's stomach? For it likes lamb best of all. Certainly it is the stomach of some bird. Nourished on innocent things and on little, ready and impatient to fly, to fly off—that happens to be my way: how could there not be something of the bird's way in that? And above all, I am an enemy of the spirit of gravity, that is the bird's way—and verily, a sworn enemy, archenemy, primordial enemy. Oh, where has not my enmity flown and misflown in the past?

Of that I could well sing a song—and *will* sing it, although I am alone in an empty house and must sing it to my own ears. There are other singers, of course, whose throats are made mellow, whose hands are made talkative, whose eyes are made expressive, whose hearts are awakened, only by a packed house. But I am not like those.

2

He who will one day teach men to fly will have moved all boundary stones; the boundary stones themselves will fly up into the air before him, and he will rebaptize the earth—"the light one."

The ostrich runs faster than the fastest horse, but even he buries his head gravely in the grave earth; even so, the man who has not yet learned to fly. Earth and life seem grave to him; and thus the spirit of gravity wants it. But whoever would become light and a bird must love himself: thus *I* teach.

Not, to be sure, with the love of the wilting and

wasting: for among those even self-love stinks. One must learn to love oneself—thus I teach—with a wholesome and healthy love, so that one can bear to be with oneself and need not roam. Such roaming baptizes itself "love of the neighbor": with this phrase the best lies and hypocrisies have been perpetrated so far, and especially by such as were a grave burden for all the world.

And verily, this is no command for today and tomorrow, to *learn* to love oneself. Rather, it is of all arts the subtlest, the most cunning, the ultimate, and the most patient. For whatever is his own is well concealed from the owner; and of all treasures, it is our own that we dig up last: thus the spirit of gravity orders it.

We are presented with grave words and values almost from the cradle: "good" and "evil" this gift is called. For its sake we are forgiven for living.

And therefore one suffers little children to come unto one—in order to forbid them betimes to love themselves: thus the spirit of gravity orders it.

And we—we carry faithfully what one gives us to bear, on hard shoulders and over rough mountains. And should we sweat, we are told: "Yes, life is a grave burden." But only man is a grave burden for himself! That is because he carries on his shoulders too much that is alien to him. Like a camel, he kneels down and lets himself be well loaded. Especially the strong, reverent spirit that would bear much: he loads too many *alien* grave words and values on himself, and then life seems a desert to him.

And verily, much that is our *own* is also a grave burden! And much that is inside man is like an oyster: nauseating and slippery and hard to grasp, so that a noble shell with a noble embellishment must plead for it. But this art too one must learn: to *have* a shell and shiny sheen and shrewd blindness. Moreover, one is deceived about many things in man because many a shell is shabby and sad and altogether too much shell. Much hidden graciousness and strength is never guessed; the most exquisite delicacies find no tasters. Women know this—the most exquisite do: a little fatter, a little slimmer—oh, how much destiny lies in so little!

Man is hard to discover—hardest of all for himself: often the spirit lies about the soul. Thus the spirit of gravity orders it. He, however, has discovered himself who says, "This is *my* good and evil"; with that he has reduced to silence the mole and dwarf who say, "Good for all, evil for all."

Verily, I also do not like those who consider everything good and this world the best. Such men I call the omni-satisfied. Omni-satisfaction, which knows how to taste everything, that is not the best taste. I honor the recalcitrant choosy tongues and stomachs, which have learned to say "I" and "yes" and "no." But to chew and digest everything—that is truly the swine's manner. Always to bray Yea-Yuh—that only the ass has learned, and whoever is of his spirit.

Deep yellow and hot red: thus *my* taste wants it; it mixes blood into all colors. But whoever whitewashes his house betrays a whitewashed soul to me. Some in love with mummies, the others with ghosts, and both alike enemies of all flesh and blood—oh, how both offend my taste. For I love blood.

And I do not want to reside and abide where everybody spits and spews: that happens to be *my* taste; rather I would live even among thieves and perjurers. Nobody has gold in his mouth. Still more revolting, however, I find all lickspittles; and the most revolting human animal that I found I baptized "parasite": it did not want to love and yet it wanted to live on love.

Cursed I call all who have only one choice: to become evil beasts or evil tamers of beasts; among such men I would not build my home.

Cursed I call those too who must always *wait;* they offend my taste: all the publicans and shopkeepers and kings and other land- and storekeepers. Verily, I too have learned to wait—thoroughly—but only to wait for *myself.* And above all I learned to stand and walk and run and jump and climb and dance. This, however, is my doctrine: he who would learn to fly one day must first learn to stand and walk and run and climb and dance: one cannot fly into flying. With rope ladders I have learned to climb to many a window; with swift legs I climbed high masts; and to sit on high masts of knowledge seemed to me no small happiness: to flicker like small flames on high masts—a small light only and yet a great comfort for shipwrecked sailors and castaways.

By many ways, in many ways, I reached my truth: it was not on one ladder that I climbed to the height where my eye roams over my distance. And it was only reluctantly that I ever inquired about the way: that always offended my taste. I preferred to question and try out the ways themselves.

A trying and questioning was my every move; and verily, one must also learn to answer such questioning. That, however, is my taste—not good, not bad, but *my* taste of which I am no longer ashamed and which I have no wish to hide.

"This is *my* way; where is yours?"—thus I answered those who asked me "the way." For *the* way—that does not exist.

Thus spoke Zarathustra.

ON OLD AND NEW TABLETS

1

Here I sit and wait, surrounded by broken old tablets and new tablets half covered with writing. When will my hour come? The hour of my going down and going under; for I want to go among men once more. For that I am waiting now, for first the signs must come to me that *my* hour has come: the laughing lion with the flock of doves. Meanwhile I talk to myself as one who has time. Nobody tells me anything new: so I tell myself—myself.

2

When I came to men I found them sitting on an old conceit: the conceit that they have long known what is good and evil for man. All talk of virtue seemed an old and weary matter to man; and whoever wanted to sleep well still talked of good and evil before going to sleep.

I disturbed this sleepiness when I taught: what is good and evil *no one knows yet,* unless it be he who creates. He, however, creates man's goal and gives the earth its meaning and its future. That anything at all is good and evil—that is his creation.

And I bade them overthrow their old academic chairs and wherever that old conceit had sat; I bade them laugh at their great masters of virtue and saints and poets and world-redeemers. I bade them laugh at their gloomy sages and at whoever had at any time sat on the tree of life like a black scarecrow. I sat down by their great tomb road among cadavers and vultures, and I laughed at all their past and its rotting, decaying glory.

Verily, like preachers of repentance and fools, I raised a hue and cry of wrath over what among them is great and small, and that their best is still so small. And that their greatest evil too is still so small—at that I laughed.

My wise longing cried and laughed thus out of me —born in the mountains, verily, a wild wisdom—my great broad-winged longing! And often it swept me away and up and far, in the middle of my laughter; and I flew, quivering, an arrow, through sun-drunken delight, away into distant futures which no dream had yet seen, into hotter souths than artists ever dreamed of, where gods in their dances are ashamed of all clothes— to speak in parables and to limp and stammer like poets; and verily, I am ashamed that I must still be a poet.

Where all becoming seemed to me the dance of gods and the prankishness of gods, and the world seemed free and frolicsome and as if fleeing back to itself—as an eternal fleeing and seeking each other again of many gods, as the happy controverting of each other, conversing again with each other, and converging again of many gods.

Where all time seemed to me a happy mockery of moments, where necessity was freedom itself playing happily with the sting of freedom.

Where I also found again my old devil and arch-enemy, the spirit of gravity, and all that he created: constraint, statute, necessity and consequence and purpose and will and good and evil.

For must there not be that *over* which one dances and dances away? For the sake of the light and the lightest, must there not be moles and grave dwarfs?

3

There it was too that I picked up the word "over-man" by the way, and that man is something that must be overcome—that man is a bridge and no end: proclaiming himself blessed in view of his noon and evening, as the way to new dawns—Zarathustra's word of the great noon, and whatever else I hung up over man like the last crimson light of evening.

Verily, I also let them see new stars along with new nights; and over clouds and day and night I still spread out laughter as a colorful tent.

I taught them all *my* creating and striving, to create and carry together into One what in man is fragment and riddle and dreadful accident; as creator, guesser of riddles, and redeemer of accidents, I taught them to work on the future and to redeem with their creation all that *has been*. To redeem what is past in man and to re-create all "it was" until the will says, "Thus I willed it! Thus I shall will it"—this I called redemption and this alone I taught them to call redemption.

Now I wait for my own redemption—that I may go to them for the last time. For I want to go to men once more; under their eyes I want to go under; dying, I want to give them my richest gift. From the sun I learned this: when he goes down, overrich; he pours gold into the sea out of inexhaustible riches, so that even the poorest fisherman still rows with golden oars. For this I once saw and I did not tire of my tears as I watched it.

Like the sun, Zarathustra too wants to go under; now he sits here and waits, surrounded by broken old tablets and new tablets half covered with writing.

4

Behold, here is a new tablet; but where are my brothers to carry it down with me to the valley and into hearts of flesh?

Thus my great love of the farthest demands it: *do not spare your neighbor!* Man is something that must be overcome.

There are many ways of overcoming: see to that *yourself!* But only a jester thinks: "Man can also be *skipped over.*"

Overcome yourself even in your neighbor: and a right that you can rob you should not accept as a gift.

What you do, nobody can do to you in turn. Behold, there is no retribution.

He who cannot command himself should obey. And many *can* command themselves, but much is still lacking before they also obey themselves.

5

This is the manner of noble souls: they do not want to have anything for nothing; least of all, life. Whoever is of the mob wants to live for nothing; we others, however, to whom life gave itself, we always think about what we might best give in return. And verily, that is a noble speech which says, "What life promises us, we ourselves want to keep to life."

One shall not wish to enjoy where one does not give joy. And one shall not *wish* to enjoy! For enjoyment and innocence are the most bashful things: both do not want to be sought. One shall *possess* them—but rather *seek* even guilt and suffering.

6

My brothers, the firstling is always sacrificed. We, however, are firstlings. All of us bleed at secret sacrificial altars; all of us burn and roast in honor of old idols. What is best in us is still young: that attracts old palates. Our flesh is tender, our hide is a mere lambskin: how could we fail to attract old idol-priests? *Even in ourselves* the old idol-priest still lives who roasts what is best in us for his feast. Alas, my brothers, how could firstlings fail to be sacrifices?

But thus our kind wants it; and I love those who do not want to preserve themselves. Those who are going under I love with my whole love: for they cross over.

7

To be true—only a few are *able!* And those who are still lack the will. But the good have this ability least of all. Oh, these good men! *Good men never speak the truth;* for the spirit, to be good in this way is a disease. They give in, these good men; they give themselves up; their heart repeats and their ground obeys: but whoever heeds commands does not heed *himself.*

Everything that the good call evil must come together so that one truth may be born. O my brothers, are you evil enough for this truth? The audacious daring, the long mistrust, the cruel No, the disgust, the cutting into the living—how rarely does all this come together. But from such seed is truth begotten.

Alongside the bad conscience, all science has grown so far. Break, break, you lovers of knowledge, the old tablets!

8

When the water is spanned by planks, when bridges and railings leap over the river, verily, those are not believed who say, "Everything is in flux." Even the blockheads contradict them. "How now?" say the blockheads. "Everything should be in flux? After all, planks and railings are *over* the river. Whatever is *over* the river is firm; all the values of things, the bridges, the concepts, all 'good' and 'evil'—all that is *firm*."

But when the hard winter comes, the river-animal tamer, then even the most quick-witted learn mistrust; and verily, not only the blockheads then say, "Does not everything *stand still?*"

"At bottom everything stands still"—that is truly a winter doctrine, a good thing for sterile times, a fine comfort for hibernators and hearth-squatters.

"At bottom everything stands still"—*against* this the thawing wind preaches. The thawing wind, a bull that is no plowing bull, a raging bull, a destroyer who breaks the ice with wrathful horns. Ice, however, *breaks bridges!*

O my brothers, is not everything in flux *now?* Have not all railings and bridges fallen into the water? Who could still cling to "good" and "evil"?

"Woe to us! Hail to us! The thawing wind blows!"— thus preach in every street, my brothers.

9

There is an old illusion, which is called good and evil. So far the wheel of this illusion has revolved around soothsayers and stargazers. Once man believed in soothsayers and stargazers, and therefore believed: "All is destiny: you ought to, for you must."

Then man again mistrusted all soothsayers and stargazers, and therefore believed: "All is freedom: you can, for you will."

O my brothers, so far there have been only illusions about stars and the future, not knowledge; and therefore there have been only illusions so far, not knowledge, about good and evil.

10

"Thou shalt not rob! Thou shalt not kill!" Such words were once called holy; one bent the knee and head and took off one's shoes before them. But I ask you: where have there ever been better robbers and killers in this world than such holy words?

Is there not in all life itself robbing and killing? And that such words were called holy—was not truth itself killed thereby? Or was it the preaching of death that was called holy, which contradicted and contravened all life? O my brothers, break, break the old tablets!

11

This is my pity for all that is past: I see how all of it is abandoned—abandoned to the pleasure, the spirit, the madness of every generation, which comes along and reinterprets all that has been as a bridge to itself.

A great despot might come along, a shrewd monster who, according to his pleasure and displeasure, might constrain and strain all that is past till it becomes a bridge to him, a harbinger and herald and cockcrow.

This, however, is the other danger and what prompts my further pity: whoever is of the rabble, thinks back as far as the grandfather; with the grandfather, however, time ends.

Thus all that is past is abandoned: for one day the rabble might become master and drown all time in shallow waters.

Therefore, my brothers, a *new nobility* is needed to be the adversary of all rabble and of all that is despotic and to write anew upon new tablets the word "noble."

For many who are noble are needed, and noble men of many kinds, that there may be a nobility. Or as I once said in a parable: "Precisely this is godlike that there are gods, but no God."

12

O my brothers, I dedicate and direct you to a new nobility: you shall become procreators and cultivators and sowers of the future—verily, not to a nobility that you might buy like shopkeepers and with shopkeepers' gold: for whatever has its price has little value.

Not whence you come shall henceforth constitute your honor, but whither you are going! Your will and your foot which has a will to go over and beyond yourselves—that shall constitute your new honor.

Verily, not that you have served a prince—what do princes matter now?—or that you became a bulwark for what stands that it might stand more firmly.

Not that your tribe has become courtly at court and that you have learned, like a flamingo, to stand for long hours in a colorful costume in shallow ponds—for the ability to stand is meritorious among courtiers; and all courtiers believe that blessedness after death must comprise permission to sit.

Nor that a spirit which they call holy led your ancestors into promised lands, which I do not praise—for where the worst of all trees grew, the cross, that land deserves no praise. And verily, wherever this "Holy Spirit" led his knights, on all such crusades goose aids goat in leading the way, and the contrary and crude sailed foremost.

O my brothers, your nobility should not look backward but ahead! Exiles shall you be from all father- and forefather-lands! Your *children's land* shall you love: this love shall be your new nobility—the undiscovered land in the most distant sea. For that I bid your sails search and search.

In your children you shall make up for being the children of your fathers: thus shall you redeem all that is past. This new tablet I place over you.

13

"Why live? All is vanity! Living—that is threshing straw; living—that is consuming oneself in flames without becoming warm." Such antiquarian babbling is still considered "wisdom"; it is honored all the more for being old and musty. Mustiness too ennobles.

Children might speak thus: they fear the fire because it burned them. There is much childishness in the old books of wisdom. And why should those who always "thresh *straw*" be allowed to blaspheme threshing? Such oxen should be muzzled after all.

Such men sit down to the table and bring nothing along, not even a good appetite; and then they blaspheme: "All is vanity." But eating and drinking well, O my brothers, is verily no vain art. Break, break the old tablets of the never gay!

14

"To the clean all is clean," the people say. But I say unto you, "To the mean all becomes mean."

Therefore the swooners and head-hangers, whose hearts also hang limply, preach, "The world itself is a filthy monster." For all these have an unclean spirit—but especially those who have neither rest nor repose except when they see the world from *abaft*, the afterworldly. To these I say to their faces, even though it may not sound nice: the world is like man in having a backside abaft; that much is true. There is much filth in the world; that much is true. But that does not make the world itself a filthy monster.

There is wisdom in this, that there is much in the world that smells foul: nausea itself creates wings and water-divining powers. Even in the best there is still something that nauseates; and even the best is something that must be overcome. O my brothers, there is much wisdom in this, that there is much filth in the world.

15

Such maxims I heard pious afterworldly people speak to their conscience—verily, without treachery or falseness, although there is nothing falser in the whole world, nothing more treacherous:

"Let the world go its way! Do not raise one finger against it!"

"Let him who wants to, strangle and stab and fleece and flay the people. Do not raise one finger against it! Thus will they learn to renounce the world."

"And your own reason—you yourself should stifle and strangle it; for it is a reason of this world; thus will you yourself learn to renounce the world."

Break, break, O my brothers, these old tablets of the pious. Break the maxims of those who slander the world.

16

"Whoever learns much will unlearn all violent desire" —that is whispered today in all the dark lanes.

"Wisdom makes weary; worth while is—nothing; thou shalt not desire!"—this new tablet I found hanging even in the open market places.

Break, O my brothers, break this *new* tablet too. The world-weary hung it up, and the preachers of death, and also the jailers; for behold, it is also an exhortation to bondage. Because they learned badly, and the best things not at all, and everything too early and everything too hastily; because they *ate* badly, therefore they got upset stomachs; for their spirit is an upset stomach which counsels death. For verily, my brothers, the spirit *is* a stomach. Life is a well of joy; but for those out of whom an upset stomach speaks, which is the father of melancholy, all wells are poisoned.

To gain knowledge is a *joy* for the lion-willed! But those who have become weary are themselves merely being "willed," and all the billows play with them. And this is always the manner of the weak: they get lost on the way. And in the end their weariness still asks, "Why did we ever pursue any way at all? It is all the same." *Their* ears appreciate the preaching, "Nothing is worth while! You shall not will!" Yet this is an exhortation to bondage.

O my brothers, like a fresh roaring wind Zarathustra comes to all who are weary of the way; many noses he will yet make sneeze. Through walls too, my free breath blows, and into prisons and imprisoned spirits. To will liberates, for to will is to create: thus I teach. And you shall learn solely in order to create.

And you shall first *learn* from me how to learn—how to learn well. He that has ears to hear, let him hear!

17

There stands the bark; over there perhaps the great nothing lies. But who would embark on this "perhaps"? No one of you wants to embark on the bark of death. Why then do you want to be world-weary? World-weary! And you are not even removed from the earth.

Lusting after the earth I have always found you, in love even with your own earth-weariness. Not for nothing is your lip hanging; a little earthly wish still sits on it. And in your eyes—does not a little cloud of unforgotten earthly joy float there?

There are many good inventions on earth, some useful, some pleasing: for their sake, the earth is to be loved. And there is such a variety of well-invented things that the earth is like the breasts of a woman: useful as well as pleasing.

But you who are world-weary, you who are earth-lazy, you should be lashed with switches: with lashes one should make your legs sprightly again. For when you are not invalids and decrepit wretches of whom the earth is weary, you are shrewd sloths or sweet-toothed, sneaky pleasure-cats. And if you do not want to *run* again with pleasure, then you should pass away. To the incurable, one should not try to be a physician—thus Zarathustra teaches—so you shall pass away!

But it takes more *courage* to make an end than to make a new verse: all physicians and poets know that.

18

O my brothers, there are tablets created by weariness and tablets created by rotten, rotting sloth; but though they speak alike, they must be understood differently.

Behold this man languishing here! He is but one span from his goal, but out of weariness he has defiantly lain down in the dust—this courageous man! Out of weariness he yawns at the way and the earth and the goal and himself: not one step farther will he go—this courageous man! Now the sun glows on him and the dogs lick his sweat; but he lies there in his defiance and would sooner die of thirst—die of thirst one span away from his goal! Verily, you will yet have to drag him by the hair into his heaven—this hero! Better yet, let him lie where he lay down, and let sleep, the comforter, come to him with cooling, rushing rain. Let him lie till he awakes by himself, till he renounces by himself all weariness and whatever weariness taught through him. Only, my brothers, drive the dogs away from him, the lazy creepers, and all the ravenous vermin—all the raving vermin of the "educated," who feast on every hero's sweat.

19

I draw circles around me and sacred boundaries; fewer and fewer men climb with me on ever higher mountains: I am building a mountain range out of ever more sacred mountains. But wherever you may climb with me, O my brothers, see to it that no *parasite* climbs with you. Parasites: creeping, cringing worms which would batten on your secret sores. And this is their art, that they find where climbing souls are weary; in your grief and discouragement, in your tender parts, they build their nauseating nests. Where the strong are weak and the noble all-too-soft—there they build their nauseating nests: the parasites live where the great have little secret sores.

What is the highest species of all being and what is the lowest? The parasite is the lowest species; but whoever is of the highest species will nourish the most parasites. For the soul that has the longest ladder and reaches down deepest—how should the most parasites not sit on that? The most comprehensive soul, which can run and stray and roam farthest within itself; the most necessary soul, which out of sheer joy plunges itself into chance; the soul which, having being, dives into becoming; the soul which *has*, but *wants* to want and will; the soul which flees itself and catches up with itself in the widest circle; the wisest soul, which folly exhorts most sweetly; the soul which loves itself most, in which all things have their sweep and countersweep and ebb and flood—oh, how should the highest soul not have the worst parasites?

20

O my brothers, am I cruel? But I say: what is falling, we should still push. Everything today falls and decays: who would check it? But I—I even want to push it.

Do you know the voluptuous delight which rolls stones into steep depths? These human beings of to-day—look at them, how they roll into my depth!

I am a prelude of better players, O my brothers! A precedent! Follow my precedent!

And he whom you cannot teach to fly, teach to fall faster!

21

I love the valiant; but it is not enough to wield a broadsword, one must also know against whom. And often there is more valor when one refrains and passes by, in order to save oneself for the worthier enemy.

You shall have only enemies who are to be hated, but not enemies to be despised: you must be proud of your enemy; thus I taught once before. For the worthier enemy, O my friends, you shall save yourselves; there-fore you must pass by much—especially much rabble who raise a din in your ears about the people and about peoples. Keep your eyes undefiled by their pro and con! There is much justice, much injustice; and whoever looks on becomes angry. Sighting and smiting here become one; therefore go away into the woods and lay your sword to sleep.

Go your *own* ways! And let the people and peoples

go theirs—dark ways, verily, on which not a single hope flashes any more. Let the shopkeeper rule where all that still glitters is—shopkeepers' gold. The time of kings is past: what calls itself a people today deserves no kings. Look how these peoples are now like shopkeepers: they pick up the smallest advantages from any rubbish. They lie around lurking and spy around smirking—and call that "being good neighbors." O blessed remote time when a people would say to itself, "I want to be *master* —over peoples." For, my brothers, the best should rule, the best also want to rule. And where the doctrine is different, there the best is *lacking*.

22

If *those* got free bread, alas! For what would they clamor? Their sustenance—that is what sustains their attention; and it should be hard for them. They are beasts of prey: in their "work" there is still an element of preying, in their "earning" still an element of over-reaching. Therefore it should be hard for them. Thus they should become better beasts of prey, subtler, more prudent, more *human*; for man is the best beast of prey. Man has already robbed all the beasts of their virtues, for of all beasts man has had the hardest time. Only the birds are still over and above him. And if man were to learn to fly—woe, to what heights would his rapacious-ness fly?

23

Thus I want man and woman: the one fit for war, the other fit to give birth, but both fit to dance with head and limbs. And we should consider every day lost on which we have not danced at least once. And we should call every truth false which was not accompanied by at least one laugh.

24

Your wedlock: see to it that it not be a bad lock. If you lock it too quickly, there follows wedlock-breaking: adultery And better even such wedlock-breaking than wedlock-picking, wedlock-tricking. Thus said a woman to me: "Indeed I committed adultery and broke my wedlock, but first my wedlock broke me!"

The worst among the vengeful I always found to be the ill-matched: they would make all the world pay for it that they no longer live singly.

Therefore I would have those who are honest say to each other, "We love each other; let us see to it that we remain in love. Or shall our promise be a mistake?"

"Give us a probation and a little marriage, so that we may see whether we are fit for a big marriage. It is a big thing always to be two."

Thus I counsel all who are honest; and what would my love for the overman and for all who shall yet come amount to if I counseled and spoke differently? Not merely to reproduce, but to produce something *higher* —toward that, my brothers, the garden of marriage should help you.

25

Whoever has gained wisdom concerning ancient origins will eventually look for wells of the future and for new origins. O my brothers, it will not be overlong before *new peoples* originate and new wells roar down into new depths. For earthquakes bury many wells and leave many languishing, but they also bring to light inner powers and secrets. Earthquakes reveal new wells. In earthquakes that strike ancient peoples, new wells break open.

And whoever shouts, "Behold, a well for many who

are thirsty, a heart for many who are longing, a will for many instruments"—around that man there will gather a *people;* that is: many triers.

Who can command, who must obey—*that is tried out there.* Alas, with what long trials and surmises and unpleasant surprises and learning and retrials!

Human society is a trial: thus I teach it—a long trial; and what it tries to find is the commander. A trial, O my brothers, and *not* a "contract." Break, break this word of the softhearted and half-and-half!

26

O my brothers, who represents the greatest danger for all of man's future? Is it not the good and the just? Inasmuch as they say and feel in their hearts, "We already know what is good and just, and we have it too; woe unto those who still seek here!" And whatever harm the evil may do, the harm done by the good is the most harmful harm. And whatever harm those do who slander the world, the harm done by the good is the most harmful harm.

O my brothers, one man once saw into the hearts of the good and the just and said, "They are the pharisees." But he was not understood. The good and the just themselves were not permitted to understand him: their spirit is imprisoned in their good conscience. The stupidity of the good is unfathomably shrewd. This, however, is the truth: the good *must* be pharisees— they have no choice. The good *must* crucify him who invents his own virtue. That is the truth!

The second one, however, who discovered their land —the land, heart, and soil of the good and the just— was he who asked, "Whom do they hate most?" The *creator* they hate most: he breaks tablets and old values. He is a breaker, they call him lawbreaker. For the good are *unable* to create; they are always the beginning of the end: they crucify him who writes new values on new tablets; they sacrifice the future to *themselves*— they crucify all man's future.

The good have always been the beginning of the end.

27

O my brothers, have you really understood this word? And what I once said concerning the "last man"? Who represents the greatest danger for all of man's future? Is it not the good and the just? *Break, break the good and the just!* O my brothers, have you really understood this word?

28

You flee from me? You are frightened? You tremble at this word?

O my brothers, when I bade you break the good and the tablets of the good, only then did I embark man on his high sea. And only now does there come to him the great fright, the great looking-around, the great sickness, the great nausea, the great seasickness.

False coasts and false assurances the good have taught you; in the lies of the good you were hatched and huddled. Everything has been made fraudulent and has been twisted through and through by the good.

But he who discovered the land "man," also discovered the land "man's future." Now you shall be seafarers, valiant and patient. Walk upright betimes, O my brothers; learn to walk upright. The sea is raging; many want to right themselves again with your help. The sea is raging; everything is in the sea. Well then, old sea dogs! What of fatherland? Our helm steers us toward our *children's land!* Out there, stormier than the sea, storms our great longing!

29

"Why so hard?" the kitchen coal once said to the diamond. "After all, are we not close kin?"

Why so soft? O my brothers, thus I ask you: are you not after all my brothers?

Why so soft, so pliant and yielding? Why is there so much denial, self-denial, in your hearts? So little destiny in your eyes?

And if you do not want to be destinies and inexorable ones, how can you triumph with me?

And if your hardness does not wish to flash and cut and cut through, how can you one day create with me?

For creators are hard. And it must seem blessedness to you to impress your hand on millennia as on wax,

Blessedness to write on the will of millennia as on bronze—harder than bronze, nobler than bronze. Only the noblest is altogether hard.

This new tablet, O my brothers, I place over you: *become hard!*

30

O thou my will! Thou cessation of all need, my *own* necessity! Keep me from all small victories! Thou destination of my soul, which I call destiny! Thou in-me! Over-me! Keep me and save me for a great destiny!

And thy last greatness, my will, save up for thy last feat that thou mayest be inexorable in thy victory. Alas, who was not vanquished in his victory? Alas, whose eye would not darken in this drunken twilight? Alas, whose foot would not reel in victory and forget how to stand?

That I may one day be ready and ripe in the great noon: as ready and ripe as glowing bronze, clouds pregnant with lightning, and swelling milk udders—

ready for myself and my most hidden will: a bow lusting for its arrow, an arrow lusting for its star—a star ready and ripe in its noon, glowing, pierced, enraptured by annihilating sun arrows—a sun itself and an inexorable solar will, ready to annihilate in victory!

O will, cessation of all need, my *own* necessity! Save me for a great victory!

Thus spoke Zarathustra.

THE CONVALESCENT

1

One morning, not long after his return to the cave, Zarathustra jumped up from his resting place like a madman, roared in a terrible voice, and acted as if somebody else were still lying on his resting place who refused to get up. And Zarathustra's voice resounded so that his animals approached in a fright, while out of all the caves and nooks that were near Zarathustra's cave all animals fled—flying, fluttering, crawling, jumping, according to the kind of feet or wings that were given to them. Zarathustra, however, spoke these words:

Up, abysmal thought, out of my depth! I am your cock and dawn, sleepy worm. Up! Up! My voice shall yet crow you awake! Unfasten the fetters of your ears: listen! For I want to hear you. Up! Up! Here is thunder enough to make even tombs learn to listen. And wipe sleep and all that is purblind and blind out of your eyes! Listen to me even with your eyes: my voice cures even those born blind. And once you are awake, you shall remain awake eternally. It is not my way to awaken great-grandmothers from their sleep to bid them sleep on!

You are stirring, stretching, wheezing? Up! Up! You shall not wheeze but speak to me. Zarathustra, the god-

less, summons you! I, Zarathustra, the advocate of life,
the advocate of suffering, the advocate of the circle; I
summon you, my most abysmal thought!

Hail to me! You are coming, I hear you. My abyss
speaks, I have turned my ultimate depth inside out into
the light. Hail to me! Come here! Give me your hand!
Huh! Let go! Huhhuh! Nausea, nausea, nausea—woe
unto me!

2

No sooner had Zarathustra spoken these words than
he fell down as one dead and long remained as one
dead. But when he regained his senses he was pale, and
he trembled and remained lying there, and for a long
time he wanted neither food nor drink. This behavior
lasted seven days; but his animals did not leave him by
day or night, except that the eagle flew off to get food.
And whatever prey he got together, he laid on Zarathustra's resting place; and eventually Zarathustra lay
among yellow and red berries, grapes, rose apples,
fragrant herbs, and pine cones. But at his feet two
lambs lay spread out, which the eagle had with difficulty robbed from their shepherds.

At last, after seven days, Zarathustra raised himself
on his resting place, took a rose apple into his hand,
smelled it, and found its fragrance lovely. Then his
animals thought that the time had come to speak to him.

"O Zarathustra," they said, "it is now seven days that
you have been lying like this with heavy eyes; won't
you at last get up on your feet again? Step out of your
cave: the world awaits you like a garden. The wind is
playing with heavy fragrances that want to get to you,
and all the brooks would run after you. All things have
been longing for you, while you have remained alone for

seven days. Step out of your cave! All things would be your physicians. Has perhaps some new knowledge come to you, bitter and hard? Like leavened dough you have been lying; your soul rose and swelled over all its rims."

"O my animals," replied Zarathustra, "chatter on like this and let me listen. It is so refreshing for me to hear you chattering: where there is chattering, there the world lies before me like a garden. How lovely it is that there are words and sounds! Are not words and sounds rainbows and illusive bridges between things which are eternally apart?

"To every soul there belongs another world; for every soul, every other soul is an afterworld. Precisely between what is most similar, illusion lies most beautifully; for the smallest cleft is the hardest to bridge.

"For me—how should there be any outside-myself? There is no outside. But all sounds make us forget this; how lovely it is that we forget. Have not names and sounds been given to things that man might find things refreshing? Speaking is a beautiful folly: with that man dances over all things. How lovely is all talking, and all the deception of sounds! With sounds our love dances on many-hued rainbows."

"O Zarathustra," the animals said, "to those who think as we do, all things themselves are dancing: they come and offer their hands and laugh and flee—and come back. Everything goes, everything comes back; eternally rolls the wheel of being. Everything dies, everything blossoms again; eternally runs the year of being. Everything breaks, everything is joined anew; eternally the same house of being is built. Everything parts, everything greets every other thing again; eternally the ring of being remains faithful to itself. In every Now, being begins; round every Here rolls the sphere There. The center is everywhere. Bent is the path of eternity."

"O you buffoons and barrel organs!" Zarathustra replied and smiled again. "How well you know what had to be fulfilled in seven days, and how that monster crawled down my throat and suffocated me. But I bit off its head and spewed it out. And you, have you already made a hurdy-gurdy song of this? But now I lie here, still weary of this biting and spewing, still sick from my own redemption. *And you watched all this?* O my animals, are even you cruel? Did you want to watch my great pain as men do? For man is the cruelest animal.

"At tragedies, bullfights, and crucifixions he has so far felt best on earth; and when he invented hell for himself, behold, that was his heaven on earth.

"When the great man screams, the small man comes running with his tongue hanging from lasciviousness. But he calls it his 'pity.'

"The small man, especially the poet—how eagerly he accuses life with words! Hear him, but do not fail to hear the delight that is in all accusation. Such accusers of life—life overcomes with a wink. 'Do you love me?' she says impudently. 'Wait a little while, just yet I have no time for you.'

"Man is the cruelest animal against himself; and whenever he calls himself 'sinner' and 'cross-bearer' and 'penitent,' do not fail to hear the voluptuous delight that is in all such lamentation and accusation.

"And I myself—do I thus want to be man's accuser? Alas, my animals, only this have I learned so far, that man needs what is most evil in him for what is best in him—that whatever is most evil is his best power and the hardest stone for the highest creator; and that man must become better and more evil.

"My torture was not the knowledge that man is evil —but I cried as no one has yet cried: 'Alas, that his greatest evil is so very small! Alas, that his best is so very small!'

"The great disgust with man—*this* choked me and had crawled into my throat; and what the soothsayer said: 'All is the same, nothing is worth while, knowledge chokes.' A long twilight limped before me, a sadness, weary to death, drunken with death, speaking with a yawning mouth. 'Eternally recurs the man of whom you are weary, the small man'—thus yawned my sadness and dragged its feet and could not go to sleep. Man's earth turned into a cave for me, its chest sunken; all that is living became human mold and bones and musty past to me. My sighing sat on all human tombs and could no longer get up; my sighing and questioning croaked and gagged and gnawed and wailed by day and night: 'Alas, man recurs eternally! The small man recurs eternally!'

"Naked I had once seen both, the greatest man and the smallest man: all-too-similar to each other, even the greatest all-too-human. All-too-small, the greatest!—that was my disgust with man. And the eternal recurrence even of the smallest—that was my disgust with all existence. Alas! Nausea! Nausea! Nausea!"

Thus spoke Zarathustra and sighed and shuddered, for he remembered his sickness. But then his animals would not let him go on.

"Do not speak on, O convalescent!" thus his animals answered him; "but go out where the world awaits you like a garden. Go out to the roses and bees and dovecots. But especially to the songbirds, that you may learn from them how to sing! For singing is for the convalescent; the healthy can speak. And when the healthy man also wants songs, he wants different songs from the convalescent."

"O you buffoons and barrel organs, be silent!" Zarathustra replied and smiled at his animals. "How well you know what comfort I invented for myself in seven days! That I must sing again, this comfort and convalescence I invented for myself. Must you immediately turn this too into a hurdy-gurdy song?"

"Do not speak on!" his animals answered him again; "rather even, O convalescent, fashion yourself a lyre first, a new lyre! For behold, Zarathustra, new lyres are needed for your new songs. Sing and overflow, O Zarathustra; cure your soul with new songs that you may bear your great destiny, which has never yet been any man's destiny. For your animals know well, O Zarathustra, who you are and must become: behold, *you are the teacher of the eternal recurrence*—that is your destiny! That you as the first must teach this doctrine— how could this great destiny not be your greatest danger and sickness too?

"Behold, we know what you teach: that all things recur eternally, and we ourselves too; and that we have already existed an eternal number of times, and all things with us. You teach that there is a great year of becoming, a monster of a great year, which must, like an hourglass, turn over again and again so that it may run down and run out again; and all these years are alike in what is greatest as in what is smallest; and we ourselves are alike in every great year, in what is greatest as in what is smallest.

"And if you wanted to die now, O Zarathustra, behold, we also know how you would then speak to yourself. But your animals beg you not to die yet. You would speak, without trembling but breathing deeply with happiness, for a great weight and sultriness would be taken from you who are most patient.

" 'Now I die and vanish,' you would say, 'and all at once I am nothing. The soul is as mortal as the body. But the knot of causes in which I am entangled recurs and will create me again. I myself belong to the causes of the eternal recurrence. I come again, with this sun, with this earth, with this eagle, with this serpent—*not* to a new life or a better life or a similar life: I come back eternally to this same, selfsame life, in what is greatest as in what is smallest, to teach again the eternal recurrence of all things, to speak again the word of the great noon of earth and man, to proclaim the overman again to men. I spoke my word, I break of my word: thus my eternal lot wants it; as a proclaimer I perish. The hour has now come when he who goes under should bless himself. Thus *ends* Zarathustra's going under.' "

When the animals had spoken these words they were silent and waited for Zarathustra to say something to them; but Zarathustra did not hear that they were silent. Rather he lay still with his eyes closed, like one sleeping, although he was not asleep; for he was conversing with his soul. The serpent, however, and the eagle, when they found him thus silent, honored the great stillness around him and cautiously stole away.

ON THE GREAT LONGING

O my soul, I taught you to say "today" and "one day" and "formerly" and to dance away over all Here and There and Yonder.

O my soul, I delivered you from all nooks; I brushed dust, spiders, and twilight off you.

O my soul, I washed the little bashfulness and the

nook-virtue off you and persuaded you to stand naked before the eyes of the sun. With the storm that is called "spirit" I blew over your wavy sea; I blew all clouds away; I even strangled the strangler that is called "sin."

O my soul, I gave you the right to say No like the storm, and to say Yes as the clear sky says Yes: now you are still as light whether you stand or walk through storms of negation.

O my soul, I gave you back the freedom over the created and uncreated; and who knows, as you know, the voluptuous delight of what is yet to come?

O my soul, I taught you the contempt that does not come like the worm's gnawing, the great, the loving contempt that loves most where it despises most.

O my soul, I taught you to persuade so well that you persuade the very ground—like the sun who persuades even the sea to his own height.

O my soul, I took from you all obeying, knee-bending, and "Lord"-saying; I myself gave you the name "cessation of need" and "destiny."

O my soul, I gave you new names and colorful toys; I called you "destiny" and "circumference of circumferences" and "umbilical cord of time" and "azure bell."

O my soul, I gave your soil all wisdom to drink, all the new wines and also all the immemorially old strong wines of wisdom.

O my soul, I poured every sun out on you, and every night and every silence and every longing: then you grew up like a vine.

O my soul, overrich and heavy you now stand there, like a vine with swelling udders and crowded brown gold-grapes—crowded and pressed by your happiness, waiting in your superabundance and still bashful about waiting.

O my soul, now there is not a soul anywhere that

would be more loving and comprehending and comprehensive. Where would future and past dwell closer together than in you?

O my soul, I gave you all, and I have emptied all my hands to you; and now—now you say to me, smiling and full of melancholy, "Which of us has to be thankful? Should not the giver be thankful that the receiver received? Is not giving a need? Is not receiving mercy?"

O my soul, I understand the smile of your melancholy: now your own overrichness stretches out longing hands. Your fullness gazes over roaring seas and seeks and waits; the longing of overfullness gazes out of the smiling skies of your eyes. And verily, O my soul, who could see your smile and not be melted by tears? The angels themselves are melted by tears because of the overgraciousness of your smile. Your graciousness and overgraciousness do not want to lament and weep; and yet, O my soul, your smile longs for tears and your trembling mouth for sobs. "Is not all weeping a lamentation? And all lamentation an accusation?" Thus you speak to yourself, and therefore, my soul, you would sooner smile than pour out your suffering—pour out into plunging tears all your suffering over your fullness and over the vine's urge for the vintager and his knife.

But if you will not weep, not weep out your crimson melancholy, then you will have to *sing*, O my soul. Behold, I myself smile as I say this before you: sing with a roaring song till all seas are silenced, that they may listen to your longing—till over silent, longing seas the bark floats, the golden wonder around whose gold all good, bad, wondrous things leap—also many great and small animals and whatever has light, wondrous feet for running on paths blue as violets—toward the golden wonder, the voluntary bark and its master; but that is the vintager who is waiting with his diamond knife—

your great deliverer, O my soul, the nameless one for whom only future songs will find names. And verily, even now your breath is fragrant with future songs; even now you are glowing and dreaming and drinking thirstily from all deep and resounding wells of comfort; even now your melancholy is resting in the happiness of future songs.

O my soul, now I have given you all, and even the last I had, and I have emptied all my hands to you: *that I bade you sing*, behold, that was the last I had. That I bade you sing—speak now, speak: which of us has to be thankful now? Better yet, however: sing to me, sing, O my soul! And let me be thankful.

Thus spoke Zarathustra.

THE OTHER DANCING SONG

1

Into your eyes I looked recently, O life: I saw gold blinking in your night-eye; my heart stopped in delight: a golden boat I saw blinking on nocturnal waters, a golden rocking-boat, sinking, drinking, and winking again. At my foot, frantic to dance, you cast a glance, a laughing, questioning, melting rocking-glance: twice only you stirred your rattle with your small hands, and my foot was already rocking with dancing frenzy.

My heels twitched, then my toes hearkened to understand you, and rose: for the dancer has his ear in his toes.

I leaped toward you, but you fled back from my leap, and the tongue of your fleeing, flying hair licked me in its sweep.

Away from you I leaped, and from your serpents' ire; and already you stood there, half turned, your eyes full of desire.

With crooked glances you teach me—crooked ways; on crooked ways my foot learns treachery.

I fear you near, I love you far; your flight lures me, your seeking cures me: I suffer, but what would I not gladly suffer for you?

You, whose coldness fires, whose hatred seduces, whose flight binds, whose scorn inspires:

Who would not hate you, you great binder, entwiner, temptress, seeker, and finder? Who would not love you, you innocent, impatient, wind-swift, child-eyed sinner?

Whereto are you luring me now, you never-tame extreme? And now you are fleeing from me again, you sweet wildcat and ingrate!

I dance after you, I follow wherever your traces linger. Where are you? Give me your hand! Or only one finger!

Here are caves and thickets; we shall get lost. Stop! Stand still! Don't you see owls and bats whirring past?

You owl! You bat! Intent to confound! Where are we? Such howling and yelping you have learned from a hound.

Your lovely little white teeth are gnashing at me; out of a curly little mane your evil eyes are flashing at me.

That is a dance up high and down low: I am the hunter; would you be my dog or my doe?

Alongside me now! And swift, you malicious leaping belle! Now up and over there! Alas, as I leaped I fell.

Oh, see me lying there, you prankster, suing for grace. I should like to walk with you in a lovelier place.

Love's paths through silent bushes, past many-hued plants. Or there along that lake: there goldfish swim and dance.

You are weary now? Over there are sunsets and sheep: when shepherds play on their flutes—is it not lovely to sleep?

You are so terribly weary? I'll carry you there; just let your arms sink. And if you are thirsty—I have got something, but your mouth does not want it to drink.

Oh, this damned nimble, supple snake and slippery witch! Where are you? In my face two red blotches from your hand itch.

I am verily weary of always being your sheepish shepherd. You witch, if *I* have so far sung to you, now you shall cry.

Keeping time with my whip, you shall dance and cry! Or have I forgotten the whip? Not I!

2

Then life answered me thus, covering up her delicate ears: "O Zarathustra, don't crack your whip so frightfully! After all, you know that noise murders thought—and just now such tender thoughts are coming to me. We are both two real good-for-nothings and evil-for-nothings. Beyond good and evil we found our island and our green meadow—we two alone. Therefore we had better like each other. And even if we do not love each other from the heart—need we bear each other a grudge if we do not love each other from the heart? And that I like you, often too well, that you know; and the reason is that I am jealous of your wisdom. Oh, this mad old fool of a wisdom! If your wisdom ever ran away from you, then my love would quickly run away from you too."

Then life looked back and around thoughtfully and said softly: "O Zarathustra, you are not faithful enough to me. You do not love me nearly as much as you say; I know you are thinking of leaving me soon. There is an old heavy, heavy growl-bell that growls at night all the way up to your cave; when you hear this bell strike the hour at midnight, then you think between one and twelve—you think, O Zarathustra, I know it, of how you want to leave me soon."

"Yes," I answered hesitantly, "but you also know—" and I whispered something into her ear, right through her tangled yellow foolish tresses.

"You *know* that, O Zarathustra? Nobody knows that."

And we looked at each other and gazed on the green meadow over which the cool evening was running just then, and we wept together. But then life was dearer to me than all my wisdom ever was.

Thus spoke Zarathustra.

3

One!

O man, take care!

Two!

What does the deep midnight declare?

Three!

"I was asleep—

Four!

"From a deep dream I woke and swear:

Five!

"The world is deep,

Six!

"Deeper than day had been aware.

Seven!

"Deep is its woe;

Eight!

"Joy—deeper yet than agony:

Nine!

"Woe implores: Go!

Ten!

"But all joy wants eternity—

Eleven!
"Wants deep, wants deep eternity."
Twelve!

THE SEVEN SEALS
(OR: THE YES AND AMEN SONG)

1

If I am a soothsayer and full of that soothsaying spirit which wanders on a high ridge between two seas, wandering like a heavy cloud between past and future, an enemy of all sultry plains and all that is weary and can neither die nor live—in its dark bosom prepared for lightning and the redemptive flash, pregnant with lightning bolts that say Yes and laugh Yes, soothsaying lightning bolts—blessed is he who is thus pregnant! And verily, long must he hang on the mountains like a dark cloud who shall one day kindle the light of the future: Oh, how should I not lust after eternity and after the nuptial ring of rings, the ring of recurrence?

Never yet have I found the woman from whom I wanted children, unless it be this woman whom I love: for I love you, O eternity.

For I love you, O eternity!

2

If ever my wrath burst tombs, moved boundary stones, and rolled old tablets, broken, into steep depths; if ever my mockery blew moldy words into the wind, and I came as a broom to the cross-marked spiders and as a sweeping gust to old musty tomb chambers; if ever I sat jubilating where old gods lie buried, world-blessing, world-loving, beside the monuments of old world-slanders—for I love even churches and tombs of gods, once the sky gazes through their broken roofs with its

pure eyes, and like grass and red poppies, I love to sit
on broken churches: Oh, how should I not lust after
eternity and after the nuptial ring of rings, the ring of
recurrence?

Never yet have I found the woman from whom I
wanted children, unless it be this woman whom I love:
for I love you, O eternity.

For I love you, O eternity!

3

If ever one breath came to me of the creative breath
and of that heavenly need that constrains even accidents
to dance star-dances; if I ever laughed the laughter of
creative lightning which is followed obediently but
grumblingly by the long thunder of the deed; if I ever
played dice with gods at the gods' table, the earth, till
the earth quaked and burst and snorted up floods of
fire—for the earth is a table for gods and trembles with
creative new words and gods' throws: Oh, how should
I not lust after eternity and after the nuptial ring of
rings, the ring of recurrence?

Never yet have I found the woman from whom I
wanted children, unless it be this woman whom I love:
for I love you, O eternity.

For I love you, O eternity!

4

If ever I drank full drafts from that foaming spice-
and blend-mug in which all things are well blended; if
my hand ever poured the farthest to the nearest, and
fire to spirit, and joy to pain, and the most wicked to
the most gracious; if I myself am a grain of that re-
deeming salt which makes all things blend well in the
blend-mug—for there is a salt that unites good with
evil; and even the greatest evil is worthy of being used

as spice for the last foaming over: Oh, how should I not lust after eternity and after the nuptial ring of rings, the ring or recurrence?

Never yet have I found the woman from whom I wanted children, unless it be this woman whom I love: for I love you, O eternity.

For I love you, O eternity!

5

If I am fond of the sea and of all that is of the sea's kind, and fondest when it angrily contradicts me; if that delight in searching which drives the sails toward the undiscovered is in me, if a seafarer's delight is in my delight; if ever my jubilation cried, "The coast has vanished, now the last chain has fallen from me; the boundless roars around me, far out glisten space and time; be of good cheer, old heart!" Oh, how should I not lust after eternity and after the nuptial ring of rings, the ring of recurrence?

Never yet have I found the woman from whom I wanted children, unless it be this woman whom I love: for I love you, O eternity.

For I love you, O eternity!

6

If my virtue is a dancer's virtue and I have often jumped with both feet into golden-emerald delight; if my sarcasm is a laughing sarcasm, at home under rose slopes and hedges of lilies—for in laughter all that is evil comes together, but is pronounced holy and absolved by its own bliss; and if this is my alpha and omega, that all that is heavy and grave should become light; all that is body, dancer; all that is spirit, bird—and verily, that is my alpha and omega: Oh, how should

I not lust after eternity and after the nuptial ring of rings, the ring of recurrence?

Never yet have I found the woman from whom I wanted children, unless it be this woman whom I love: for I love you, O eternity.

For I love you, O eternity!

7

If ever I spread tranquil skies over myself and soared on my own wings into my own skies; if I swam playfully in the deep light-distances, and the bird-wisdom of my freedom came—but bird-wisdom speaks thus: "Behold, there is no above, no below! Throw yourself around, out, back, you who are light! Sing! Speak no more! Are not all words made for the grave and heavy? Are not all words lies to those who are light? Sing! Speak no more!" Oh, how should I not lust after eternity and after the nuptial ring of rings, the ring of recurrence?

Never yet have I found the woman from whom I wanted children, unless it be this woman whom I love: for I love you, O eternity.

For I love you, O eternity!

Thus Spoke Zarathustra:
Fourth and Last Part

Alas, where in the world has there been more folly than among the pitying? And what in the world has caused more suffering than the folly of the pitying? Woe to all who love without having a height that is above their pity!

Thus spoke the devil to me once: "God too has his hell: that is his love of man." And most recently I heard him say this: "God is dead; God died of his pity for man." (Zarathustra, II, p. 90)

TRANSLATOR'S NOTES

Part Four was originally intended as an intermezzo, not as the end of the book. The very appearance of a collection of sayings is abandoned: Part Four forms a whole, and as such represents a new stylistic experiment—as well as a number of widely different stylistic experiments, held together by a unity of plot and a pervasive sense of humor.

1. *The Honey Sacrifice:* Prologue. The "queer fish" are not long in coming: the first of them appears in the next chapter.

2. *The Cry of Distress:* Beginning of the story that continues to the end of the book. The soothsayer of Part Two reappears, and Zarathustra leaves in search of the higher man. Now that he has overcome his nausea, his final trial is: pity.

3. *Conversation with the Kings:* The first of seven encounters in each of which Zarathustra meets men who have accepted some part of his teaching without, however, embodying the type he envisages. Their revolting and tiresome flatteries might be charged to their general inadequacy. But Zarathustra's own personality, as it emerges in chapter after chapter, poses a more serious problem. At least in part, this is clearly due to the author's deliberate malice: he does not want to be a "new idol": "I do not want to be a saint, rather even a buffoon. Perhaps I am a buffoon. And nevertheless, or rather *not* nevertheless—for there has never been anybody more mendacious than saints—truth speaks out of me" (*Ecce Homo*). Earlier in the same work he says of Shakespeare: "What must a man have suffered to have found it that necessary to be a buffoon!" In these pages Nietzsche would resemble the

dramatist rather than the hagiographer, and a Shakespear-
ean fool rather than the founder of a new cult.

4. *The Leech:* Encounter with "the conscientious in spirit."

5. *The Magician:* In the magician some of Nietzsche's
own features blend with some of Wagner's as conceived
by Nietzsche. The poem appears again in a manuscript of
1888, which bears the title "Dionysus Dithyrambs" and
the motto: "These are the songs of Zarathustra which he
sang to himself to endure his ultimate loneliness." In this
later context, the poem is entitled "Ariadne's Lament,"
and a new conclusion has been added by Nietzsche:

(*Lightning. Dionysus becomes visible in emerald
beauty.*)

> DIONYSUS: Be clever, Ariadne!
> You have small ears, you have my ears:
> Put a clever word into them!
> Must one not first hate each other
> if one is to love each other?
> I am your labyrinth.

The song is not reducible to a single level of meaning. The
outcry is (1) Nietzsche's own; and the unnamable, terrible
thought near the beginning is surely that of the eternal
recurrence; it is (2) projected onto Wagner, who is here
imagined as feeling desperately forsaken after Nietzsche
left him (note especially the penultimate stanza); it is
(3) wishfully projected onto Cosima Wagner—Nietzsche's
Ariadne (see my *Nietzsche*, 1, II)—who is here imagined as desiring and possessed by Nietzsche-Dionysus.
Part Four is all but made up of similar projections. *All* the
characters are caricatures of Nietzsche. And like the magician, he too would lie if he said: " 'I did all this *only* as a
game.' There was *seriousness* in it too."

6. *Retired:* Encounter with the last pope. Reflections on
the death and inadequacies of God.

7. *The Ugliest Man:* The murderer of God. The sentence
beginning "Has not all success . . ." reads in German:

War nicht aller Erfolg bisher bei den Gut-Verfolgten? Und wer gut verfolgt, lernt leicht folgen:—ist er doch einmal— hinterher!

8. *The Voluntary Beggar:* A sermon on a mount—about cows.

9. *The Shadow:* An allusion to Nietzsche's earlier work, *The Wanderer and His Shadow* (1880).

10. *At Noon:* A charming intermezzo.

11. *The Welcome:* Zarathustra rejects his guests, though together they form a kind of higher man compared to their contemporaries. He repudiates these men of great longing and nausea as well as all those who enjoy his diatribes and denunciations and desire recognition and consideration for being out of tune with their time. What Nietzsche envisages is the creator for whom all negation is merely incidental to his great affirmation: joyous spirits, "laughing lions."

12. *The Last Supper:* One of the persistent themes of Part Four reaches its culmination in this chapter: Nietzsche not only satirizes the Gospels, and all hagiography generally, but he also makes fun of and laughs at himself.

13. *On the Higher Man:* A summary comparable to "On Old and New Tablets" in Part Three. Section 5 epitomizes Nietzsche's praise of "evil"—too briefly to be clear apart from the rest of his work—and the conclusion should be noted. The opening paragraph of section 7 takes up the same theme: Nietzsche opposes sublimation to both license and what he elsewhere calls "castratism." A fine epigram is mounted in the center of section 9. The mellow moderation of the last lines of section 15 is not usually associated with Nietzsche. And the chapter ends with a praise of laughter.

14. *The Song of Melancholy:* In the 1888 manuscript of the "Dionysus Dithyrambs" this is the first poem and it bears the title "Only Fool! Only Poet!" The two introductory sections of this chapter help to dissociate Nietzsche from the poem, while the subsquent references to this song show that he considered it far more depressing than it

appears in its context. Though his solitude sometimes flattered him, "On every parable you ride to every truth" ("The Return Home"), he also knew moments when he said to himself, "I am ashamed that I must still be a poet" ("On Old and New Tablets"). Although Zarathustra's buffooneries are certainly intended as such by the author, the thought that he might be *only* a fool, *only* a poet "climbing around on mendacious word bridges," made Nietzsche feel more than despondent. Soon it led him to abandon further attempts to ride on parables in favor of some of the most supple prose in German literature.

15. *On Science:* Only the origin of science is considered. The attempt to account for it in terms of fear goes back to the period of *The Dawn* (1881), in which Nietzsche tried to see how far he could reduce different phenomena to fear and power. Zarathustra suggests that courage is crucial —that is, the will to power over fear.

16. *Among Daughters of the Wilderness:* Zarathustra, about to slip out of his cave for the second time because he cannot stand the bad smell of the "higher men," is called back by his shadow, who has nowhere among men smelled better air—except once. In the following song Nietzsche's buffoonery reaches its climax. But though it can and should be read as thoroughly delightful nonsense, it is not entirely void of personal significance. *Wüste* means "desert" or "wilderness," and *wüst* can also mean wild and dissolute; and the "flimsy little fan-, flutter-, and tinsel-skirts" seem to have been suggested by the brothel to which a porter in Cologne once took the young Nietzsche, who had asked to be shown to a hotel. (He ran away, shocked; cf. my *Nietzsche*, 1, I.) Certainly the poem is full of sexual fantasies. But the double meaning of "date" is not present in the original.

17. *The Awakening:* The titles of this and the following chapter might well be reversed; for it is this chapter that culminates in the ass festival, Nietzsche's version of the Black Mass. But "the awakening" here does not refer to the moment when an angry Moses holds his people accountable

for their worship of the golden calf, but to the moment when "they have learned to laugh at themselves." In this art, incidentally, none of the great philosophers excelled the author of Part Four of *Zarathustra*.

18. *The Ass Festival*: Five of the participants try to justify themselves. The pope satirizes Catholicism (Luther was last made fun of at the end of the song in Chapter 16), while the conscientious in spirit develops a new theology —and suggests that Zarathustra himself is pretty close to being an ass.

19. *The Drunken Song*: Nietzsche's great hymn to joy invites comparison with Schiller's—minus Beethoven's music. That they use different German words is the smallest difference. Schiller writes:

> Suffer bravely, myriads!
> Suffer for the better world!
> Up above the firmament
> A great God will give rewards.

Nietzsche wants the eternity of *this* life with all its agonies —and seeing that it flees, its eternal recurrence. As it is expressed in sections 9, 10, and 11, the conception of the eternal recurrence is certainly meaningful; but its formulation as a doctrine depended on Nietzsche's mistaken belief that science compels us to accept the hypothesis of the eternal recurrence of the same events at gigantic intervals. (See "On the Vision and the Riddle" and "The Convalescent," both in Part Three, and, for a detailed discussion, my *Nietzsche*, 11, II.)

20. *The Sign*: In "The Welcome," Zarathustra repudiated the "higher men" in favor of "laughing lions." Now a lion turns up and laughs, literally. And in place of the single dove in the New Testament, traditionally understood as a symbol of the Holy Ghost, we are presented with a whole flock. Both the lion and the doves were mentioned before ("On Old and New Tablets," section 1) as the signs for which Zarathustra must wait, and now afford Nietzsche an

opportunity to preserve his curious blend of myth, irony, and hymn to the very end.

THE HONEY SACRIFICE

And again months and years passed over Zarathustra's soul, and he did not heed them; but his hair turned white. One day when he sat on a stone before his cave and looked out—and one looks on the sea from there, across winding abysses—his animals walked about him thoughtfully and at last stood still before him.

"O Zarathustra," they said, "are you perhaps looking out for your happiness?"

"What matters happiness?" he replied; "I have long ceased to be concerned with happiness; I am concerned with my work."

"O Zarathustra," the animals spoke again, "you say that as one having overmuch of the good. Do you not lie in a sky-blue lake of happiness?"

"You buffoons," Zarathustra replied and smiled; "how well you chose your metaphor. But you also know that my happiness is heavy and not like a flowing wave of water: it presses me and will not leave me and acts like melted tar."

Again the animals walked about him thoughtfully and then stood still before him. "O Zarathustra," they said, "is *that* why you yourself are becoming ever yellower and darker, although your hair wants to look white and flaxen? You are in a dreadful mess!"

"What are you saying there, my animals?" Zarathustra said and laughed; "verily, I was abusive when I spoke of tar. What is happening to me, happens to every fruit when it grows ripe. It is the *honey* in my veins that makes my blood thicker and my soul calmer."

"That is what it will be, Zarathustra," the animals answered and nestled against him; "but do you not want to climb a high mountain today? The air is clear and one sees more of the world today than ever before."

"Yes, my animals," he replied, "your advice is excellent and quite after my own heart: I want to climb a high mountain today. But see to it that honey will be at hand there: yellow, white, good, ice-fresh, golden comb honey. For you should know that up there I want to offer the honey sacrifice."

But when Zarathustra had reached the height he sent back the animals who had accompanied him, and he found himself alone. Then he laughed heartily, looked around, and spoke thus:

That I spoke of sacrifices and honey sacrifices was mere cunning and, verily, a useful folly. Up here I may speak more freely than before hermits' caves and hermits' domestic animals.

Why sacrifice? I squander what is given to me, I— a squanderer with a thousand hands; how could I call that sacrificing? And when I desired honey, I merely desired bait and sweet mucus and mucilage, which make even growling bears and queer, sullen, evil birds put out their tongues—the best bait, needed by hunters and fishermen. For if the world is like a dark jungle and a garden of delight for all wild hunters, it strikes me even more, and so I prefer to think of it, as an abysmal, rich sea—a sea full of colorful fish and crabs, which even gods might covet, that for their sakes they would wish to become fishermen and net-throwers: so rich is the world in queer things, great and small. Especially the human world, the human sea: *that* is where I now cast my golden fishing rod and say: Open up, you human abyss!

Open up and cast up to me your fish and glittering crabs! With my best bait I shall today bait the queerest human fish. My happiness itself I cast out far and wide, between sunrise, noon, and sunset, to see if many human fish might not learn to wriggle and wiggle from my happiness until, biting at my sharp hidden hooks, they must come up to *my* height—the most colorful abysmal groundlings, to the most sarcastic of all who fish for men. For *that* is what I am through and through: reeling, reeling in, raising up, raising, a raiser, cultivator, and disciplinarian, who once counseled himself, not for nothing: Become who you are!

Thus men may now come *up* to me; for I am still waiting for the sign that the time has come for my descent; I still do not myself go under, as I must do, under the eyes of men. That is why I wait here, cunning and mocking on high mountains, neither impatient nor patient, rather as one who has forgotten patience too, because his "passion" is over. For my destiny leaves me time; perhaps it has forgotten me. Or does it sit in the shade behind a big stone, catching flies? And verily, I like it for this, my eternal destiny: it does not hurry and press me, and it leaves me time for jests and sarcasm, so that I could climb this high mountain today to catch fish.

Has a man ever caught fish on high mountains? And even though what I want and do up here be folly, it is still better than if I became solemn down there from waiting, and green and yellow—a swaggering wrath-snorter from waiting, a holy, howling storm out of the mountains, an impatient one who shouts down into the valleys, "Listen or I shall whip you with the scourge of God!"

Not that I bear such angry men a grudge! They are good enough for my laughter. They must surely be impatient—these big noisy drums, which find their chance to speak today or never. I, however, and my destiny— we do not speak to the Today, nor do we speak to the Never; we have patience and time and overmuch time in which to speak. For one day it must yet come and may not pass. What must come one day and may not pass? Our great *Hazar:* that is, our great distant human kingdom, the Zarathustra kingdom of a thousand years. How distant may this "distant" be? What is that to me? But for all that, this is no less certain: with both feet I stand firmly on this ground, on eternal ground, on hard primeval rock, on this highest, hardest, primeval mountain range to which all winds come as to the "weather- shed" and ask: where? and whence? and whither?

Laugh, laugh, my bright, wholesome sarcasm! From high mountains cast down your glittering mocking laughter! With your glitter bait me the most beautiful human fish! And whatever in all the seas belongs to *me,* my in-and-for-me in all things—*that* fish out for me, *that* bring up to me: for that I, the most sarcastic of all fishermen, am waiting.

Out, out, my fishing rod! Down, down, bait of my happiness! Drip your sweetest dew, honey of my heart! Bite, my fishing rod, into the belly of all black melan- choly!

Out there, out there, my eye! Oh, how many seas sur- round me, what dawning human futures! And over me —what rose-red stillness! What unclouded silence!

THE CRY OF DISTRESS

The next day Zarathustra again sat on his stone be- fore his cave, while the animals were roaming through the outside world to find new nourishment—also new honey, for Zarathustra had spent and squandered the old honey down to the last drop. But as he was sitting there, a stick in his hand, tracing his shadow on the ground, thinking—and verily, not about himself and his shadow—he was suddenly frightened, and he started: for beside his own shadow he saw another shadow. And as he looked around quickly and got up, behold, the soothsayer stood beside him—the same he had once feted at his table, the proclaimer of the great weariness who taught, "All is the same, nothing is worth while, the world is without meaning, knowledge strangles." But his face had changed meanwhile; and when Zarathustra looked into his eyes, his heart was frightened again: so many ill tidings and ashen lightning bolts ran over this face.

The soothsayer, who had noticed what went on in Zarathustra's soul, wiped his hand over his face as if he wanted to wipe it away; and Zarathustra did likewise. And when both had thus silently composed and strengthened themselves, they shook hands as a sign that they wanted to recognize each other.

"Welcome," said Zarathustra, "you soothsayer of the great weariness; not for nothing were you once my guest. Eat and drink with me again today, and forgive a cheerful old man for sitting at the table with you."

"A cheerful old man?" the soothsayer replied, shaking his head; "but whatever you may be or want to be, Zarathustra, you shall not be up here much longer: soon your bark shall not be stranded any more."

"But am I stranded?" Zarathustra asked, laughing.

"The waves around your mountain," replied the soothsayer, "are climbing and climbing, the waves of great distress and melancholy; soon they will lift up your bark too, and carry you off."

Zarathustra fell silent at that and was surprised.

"Do you not hear anything yet?" continued the sooth-sayer. "Does it not rush and roar up from the depth?"

Zarathustra remained silent and listened, and he heard a long, long cry, which the abysses threw to each other and handed on, for none wanted to keep it: so evil did it sound.

"You proclaimer of ill tidings," Zarathustra said finally, "this is a cry of distress and the cry of a man; it might well come out of a black sea. But what is human distress to me? My final sin, which has been saved up for me—do you know what it is?"

"*Pity!*" answered the soothsayer from an overflowing heart, and he raised both hands. "O Zarathustra, I have come to seduce you to your final sin."

And no sooner had these words been spoken than the cry resounded again, and longer and more anxious than before; also much closer now.

"Do you hear? Do you hear, O Zarathustra?" the soothsayer shouted. "The cry is for you. It calls you: Come, come, come! It is time! It is high time!"

Then Zarathustra remained silent, confused and shaken. At last he asked, as one hesitant in his own mind, "And who is it that calls me?"

"But you know that," replied the soothsayer violently; "why do you conceal yourself? It is *the higher man* that cries for you!"

"The higher man?" cried Zarathustra, seized with horror. "What does he want? What does he want? The higher man! What does he want here?" And his skin was covered with perspiration.

The soothsayer, however, made no reply to Zara-thustra's dread, but listened and listened toward the depth. But when there was silence for a long time, he turned his glance back and saw Zarathustra standing there trembling. "O Zarathustra," he began in a sad tone of voice, "you are not standing there as one made giddy by his happiness: you had better dance lest you fall. But even if you would dance before me, leaping all your side-leaps, no one could say to me, 'Behold, here dances the last gay man!' Anybody coming to this height, looking for *that* man, would come in vain: caves he would find, and caves behind caves, hiding-places for those addicted to hiding, but no mines of happiness or treasure rooms or new gold veins of happiness. Happiness—how should one find happiness among hermits and those buried like this? Must I still seek the last happiness on blessed isles and far away between forgotten seas? But all is the same, nothing is worth while, no seeking avails, nor are there any blessed isles any more."

Thus sighed the soothsayer. At his last sigh, however, Zarathustra grew bright and sure again, like one emerging into the light out of a deep gorge. "No! No! Three times no!" he shouted with a strong voice and stroked his beard. "*That* I know better: there still are blessed isles. Be quiet about *that*, you sighing bag of sadness! Stop splashing about *that*, you raincloud in the morning! Do I not stand here even now, wet from your melancholy and drenched like a dog? Now I shake myself and run away from you to dry again; you must not be surprised at that. Do I strike you as discourteous? But this is *my* court. As for your higher man—well then, I shall look for him at once in those woods: *thence* came his cry. Perhaps an evil beast troubles him there. He is in *my* realm: there he shall not come to grief. And verily, there are many evil beasts around me."

With these words Zarathustra turned to leave. Then the soothsayer said, "O Zarathustra, you are a rogue! I know it: you want to get rid of me. You would sooner run into the woods and look for evil beasts. But what will it avail you? In the evening you will have me back anyway; in your own cave I shall be sitting, patient and heavy as a block—waiting for you."

"So be it!" Zarathustra shouted back as he was walking away. "And whatever is mine in my cave belongs to you too, my guest. And if you should find honey in there—well, then, lick it up, you growling bear, and sweeten your soul. For in the evening we should both be cheerful—cheerful and gay that this day has come to an end. And you yourself shall dance to my songs as my dancing bear. You do not believe it? You shake your head? Well then, old bear! But I too am a soothsayer."

Thus spoke Zarathustra.

CONVERSATION WITH THE KINGS

1

Zarathustra had not yet walked an hour in his mountains and woods when he suddenly saw a strange procession. On the very path he wanted to follow down, two kings were approaching, adorned with crowns and crimson belts and colorful as flamingos; and they were driving a laden ass before them. "What do these kings want in my realm?" Zarathustra said in his heart, surprised, and quickly he hid behind a bush. But when the kings came close he said half aloud, as if talking to himself, "Strange! Strange! How does this fit together? Two kings I see—and only one ass!"

The two kings stopped, smiled, looked in the direction from which the voice had come, and then looked at each other. "Something of the sort may have occurred to one of us too," said the king at the right; "but one does not say it." The king at the left, however, shrugged his shoulders and replied, "It may well be a goatherd.

Or a hermit who has lived too long among rocks and trees. For no society at all also spoils good manners."

"Good manners?" the other king retorted angrily and bitterly; "then what is it that we are trying to get away from? Is it not 'good manners'? Our 'good society'? It is indeed better to live among hermits and goatherds than among our gilded, false, painted mob—even if they call themselves 'good society,' even if they call themselves 'nobility.' They are false and foul through and through, beginning with the blood, thanks to bad old diseases and worse quacks. Best and dearest to me today is a healthy peasant, coarse, cunning, stubborn, enduring: that is the noblest species today. The peasant is the best type today, and the peasant type should be master. But it is the realm of the mob; I shall not be deceived any more. Mob, however, means hodgepodge. Mob-hodgepodge: there everything is mixed up in every way, saint and scamp and Junker and Jew and every kind of beast out of Noah's ark. Good manners! Everything among us is false and foul. Nobody knows how to revere any longer: we are trying to get away from precisely that. They are saccharine, obtrusive curs; they gild palm leaves.

"This nausea suffocates me: we kings ourselves have become false, overhung and disguised with ancient yellowed grandfathers' pomp, showpieces for the most stupid and clever and anyone who haggles for power today. We are not the first and yet must represent them: it is this deception that has come to disgust and nauseate us. We have tried to get away from the rabble, all these scream-throats and scribbling bluebottles, the shopkeepers' stench, the ambitious wriggling, the foul breath—phew for living among the rabble! Phew for representing the first among the rabble! Nausea! Nausea! Nausea! What do we kings matter now?"

"Your old illness is upon you," the king at the left said at this point; "nausea is seizing you, my poor brother. But you know that somebody is listening to us."

Immediately Zarathustra, who had opened his ears and eyes wide at this talk, rose from his hiding-place, walked toward the kings, and began, "He who is listening to you, he who likes to listen to you, O kings, is called Zarathustra. I am Zarathustra, who once said, 'What do kings matter now?' Forgive me, I was delighted when you said to each other, 'What do we kings matter now?' Here, however, is *my* realm and my dominion: what might you be seeking in my realm? But perhaps you found on your way what I am looking for: the higher man."

When the kings heard this, they beat their breasts and said as with one voice, "We have been found out. With the sword of this word you cut through our hearts' thickest darkness. You have discovered our distress, for behold, we are on our way to find the higher man—the man who is higher than we, though we are kings. To him we are leading this ass. For the highest man shall also be the highest lord on earth. Man's fate knows no harsher misfortune than when those who have power on earth are not also the first men. That makes everything false and crooked and monstrous. And when they are even the last, and more beast than man, then the price of the mob rises and rises, and eventually the virtue of the mob even says, 'Behold, I alone am virtue!' "

"What did I just hear?" replied Zarathustra. "What wisdom in kings! I am delighted and, verily, even feel the desire to make a rhyme on this—even if it should be a rhyme which is not fit for everybody's ears. I have long become unaccustomed to any consideration for long ears. Well then!" (But at this point it happened that the ass too got in a word; but he said clearly and with evil intent, Yea-Yuh.)

"Once—in the year of grace number one, I think—
The Sibyl said, drunken without any drink,
'Now everything goes wrong! Oh, woe!
Decay! The world has never sunk so low!
Rome sank to whoredom and became a stew,
The Caesars became beasts, and God—a Jew!' "

2

These rhymes of Zarathustra delighted the kings; but the king at the right said, "O Zarathustra, how well we did to go forth to see you! For your enemies showed us your image in their mirror: there you had the mocking grimace of a devil, so that we were afraid of you. But what could we do? Again and again you pierced our ears and hearts with your maxims. So we said at last: what difference does it make how he looks? We must *hear* him who teaches: 'You shall love peace as a means to new wars, and the short peace more than the long!' Nobody ever spoke such warlike words: 'What is good? To be brave is good. It is the good war that hallows any cause.' Zarathustra, the blood of our fathers stirred in our bodies at such words: it was like the speech of spring to old wine barrels. When the swords ran wild like snakes with red spots, our fathers grew fond of life; the sun of all peace struck them as languid and lukewarm, and any long peace caused shame. How our fathers sighed when they saw flashing dried-up swords on the wall! Like them, they thirsted for war. For a sword wants to drink blood and glistens with desire."

When the kings talked thus and chatted eagerly of the happiness of their fathers, Zarathustra was overcome with no small temptation to mock their eagerness: for obviously they were very peaceful kings with old and fine faces. But he restrained himself. "Well!" he said, "that is where the path leads; there lies Zarathustra's cave; and this day shall yet have a long evening. Now, however, a cry of distress calls me away from you urgently. My cave is honored if kings want to sit in it and wait: only, you will have to wait long. But what does it matter? Where does one now learn better how to wait than at court? And all the virtue left to kings today—is it not called: being able to wait?"

Thus spoke Zarathustra.

THE LEECH

And thoughtfully Zarathustra went farther and deeper, through woods and past swampy valleys; but as happens to everybody who reflects on grave matters, he stepped on a man unwittingly. And behold, all at once a cry of pain and two curses and twenty bad insults splashed into his face and startled him so that he raised his stick and beat the man on whom he had stepped. A moment later, however, he recovered his senses, and his heart laughed at the folly he had just committed.

"Forgive me," he said to the man he had stepped on, who had angrily risen and sat down; "forgive me and, above all, listen to a parable first. As a wanderer who dreams of distant matters will unwittingly stumble over a sleeping dog on a lonely road—a dog lying in the sun—and both start and let fly at each other like mortal enemies, because both are mortally frightened: thus it happened to us. And yet—and yet, how little was lacking, and they might have caressed each other, this dog and this lonely man. For after all they were both lonely."

"Whoever you may be," said the man he had stepped on, still angry, "your parable too offends me, and not only your foot. After all, am I a dog?" And at that the seated man got up and pulled his bare arm out of the swamp. For at first he had been lying stretched out on the ground, concealed and unrecognizable, as one lying in wait for some swamp animal.

"But what are you doing?" cried Zarathustra, startled, for he saw that much blood was flowing down the bare arm. "What has happened to you? Did a bad animal bite you, you poor wretch?"

The bleeding man laughed, still angry. "What is that to you?" he said and wanted to go on. "Here I am at home and in my realm. Let whoever wants to, ask me; but I certainly won't answer a bumpkin."

"You are wrong," said Zarathustra, full of pity, and he held him back. "You are wrong. This is not your realm but mine, and here nobody shall come to grief. Call me whatever you like; I am who I must be. I call myself Zarathustra. Well! Up there runs the path to Zarathustra's cave, which is not far. Do you not want to look after your wounds in my place? Things have gone badly for you in this life, you poor wretch; first the beast bit you and then man stepped on you."

When the man who had been stepped on heard Zarathustra's name he changed completely. "What is happening to me?" he cried out. "*Who* else matters to me any more in this life but this one man, Zarathustra, and that one beast which lives on blood, the leech? For the leech's sake I lay here beside this swamp like a fisherman, and my arm, which I had cast, had already been bitten ten times when a still more beautiful leech bit, seeking my blood, Zarathustra himself. O happiness! O miracle! Praised be this day that lured me into this swamp! Praised be the best, the most alive cupper living today, praised be the great leech of the conscience, Zarathustra!"

Thus spoke the man who had been stepped on; and Zarathustra enjoyed his words and their fine, respectful manner. "Who are you?" he asked and offered him his hand. "There is much between us that remains to be cleared up and cheered up; but even now, it seems to me, the day dawns pure and bright."

"I am *the conscientious in spirit*," replied the man; "and in matters of the spirit there may well be none stricter, narrower, and harder than I, except he from whom I have learned it, Zarathustra himself.

"Rather know nothing than half-know much! Rather be a fool on one's own than a sage according to the opinion of others! I go to the ground—what does it matter whether it be great or small? whether it be called swamp or sky? A hand's breadth of ground suffices me, provided it is really ground and foundation. A hand's breadth of ground—on that one can stand. In the conscience of science there is nothing great and nothing small."

"Then perhaps you are the man who knows the leech?" Zarathustra asked. "And do you pursue the leech to its ultimate grounds, my conscientious friend?"

"O Zarathustra," replied the man who had been stepped on, "that would be an immensity; how could I presume so much! That of which I am the master and expert is the *brain* of the leech: that is *my* world. And it really is a world too. Forgive me that here my pride speaks up, for I have no equal here. That is why I said, 'Here is my home.' How long have I been pursuing this one thing, the brain of the leech, lest the slippery truth slip away from me here again! Here is *my* realm. For its sake I have thrown away everything else; for its sake everything else has become indifferent to me; and close to my knowledge lies my black ignorance.

"The conscience of my spirit demands of me that I know one thing and nothing else: I loathe all the half in spirit, all the vaporous that hover and rave.

"Where my honesty ceases, I am blind and I also want to be blind. But where I want to know, I also want to be honest—that is, hard, strict, narrow, cruel, and inexorable.

"That *you*, O Zarathustra, once said, 'Spirit is the life that itself cuts into life,' that introduced and seduced me to your doctrine. And verily, with my own blood I increased my own knowledge."

"As is quite apparent," Zarathustra interrupted, for the blood still flowed down the bare arm of the conscientious man, ten leeches having bitten deep into it. "O you strange fellow, how much I learn from what is apparent here, namely from you. And perhaps I had better not pour all of it into your strict ears. Well! Here we part. But I should like to find you again. Up there goes the path to my cave: tonight you shall be my dear guest there. To your body too, I should like to make up for Zarathustra's having stepped on you with his feet: I shall reflect on that. Now, however, a cry of distress urgently calls me away from you."

Thus spoke Zarathustra.

THE MAGICIAN

1

But when Zarathustra came around a rock he beheld, not far below on the same path, a man who threw his limbs around like a maniac and finally flopped down on his belly. "Wait!" Zarathustra said to his heart; "that must indeed be the higher man; from him came that terrible cry of distress; let me see if he can still be helped." But when he ran to the spot where the man lay on the ground he found a trembling old man with vacant eyes; and however Zarathustra exerted himself to help the man to get up on his feet again, it was all in vain. Nor did the unfortunate man seem to notice that anybody was with him; rather he kept looking around with piteous gestures, like one abandoned and forsaken by all the world. At last, however, after many shudders, convulsions, and contortions, he began to moan thus:

"Who warms me, who loves me still?
Give hot hands!
Give a heart as glowing coals!
Stretched out, shuddering,
Like something half dead whose feet one warms—
Shaken, alas, by unknown fevers,
Shivering with piercing icy frost-arrows,
Hunted by thee, O thought!
Unnamable, shrouded, terrible one!
Thou hunter behind clouds!
Struck down by thy lightning bolt,
Thou mocking eye that stares at me from the dark:
Thus I lie
Writhing, twisting, tormented
With all eternal tortures,
Hit
By thee, cruelest hunter,
Thou unknown *god!*

Hit deeper!
Hit once more yet!
Drive a stake through and break this heart!

Why this torture
With blunt-toothed arrows?
Why dost thou stare again,
Not yet weary of human agony,
With gods' lightning eyes that delight in suffering?
Thou wouldst not kill,
Only torture, torture?
Why torture *me*,
Delighted by suffering, thou unknown god?

Hah! hah! Thou art crawling close?
In such midnight—
What dost thou want? Speak!
Thou art crowding, pressing me—
Hah! Far too close!
Away! Away!
Thou art listening to me breathe,
Thou art listening to my heart,
Thou jealous one—
Jealous of what?
Away! Away! Why the ladder?
Wouldst thou *enter*
The heart,
Climb in, deep into my
Most secret thoughts?
Shameless one! Unknown thief!
What wouldst thou steal?
What wouldst thou gain by listening?
What wouldst thou gain by torture,
Thou torturer!
Thou hangman-god!
Or should I, doglike,
Roll before thee?
Devotedly, frantic, beside myself,
Wag love to thee?

In vain! Pierce on,
Cruelest thorn! No,
No dog—only thy game am I,
Cruelest hunter!
Thy proudest prisoner,
Thou robber behind clouds!
Speak at last!
What wouldst thou, waylayer, from *me*?
Thou lightning-shrouded one! Unknown one! Speak,
What wilt thou, unknown—god?

What? Ransom?
Why wilt thou ransom?
Demand much! Thus my pride advises.
And make thy speech short! That my other pride
    advises.

Hah, hah!
Me thou wilt have? Me?
Me—entirely?

Hah, hah!
And art torturing me, fool that thou art,
Torturing my pride?
Give love to me—who warms me still?
Who loves me still?—Give hot hands,
Give a heart as glowing coals,
Give me, the loneliest
Whom ice, alas, sevenfold ice
Teaches to languish for enemies,
Even for enemies,
Give, yes, give wholly,
Cruelest enemy,
Give me—*thyself!*

Away!
He himself fled,
My last, only companion,
My great enemy,
My unknown,
My hangman-god.

No! Do come back
With all thy tortures!
To the last of all that are lonely,
Oh, come back!
All my tear-streams run
Their course to thee;
And my heart's final flame—
Flares up for *thee!*
Oh, come back,
My unknown god! My *pain!* My last—happiness!"

2

At this point, however, Zarathustra could not restrain himself any longer, raised his stick, and started to beat the moaning man with all his might. "Stop it!" he shouted at him furiously. "Stop it, you actor! You counterfeiter! You liar from the bottom! I recognize you well! I'll warm your legs for you, you wicked magician. I know well how to make things hot for such as you."

"Leave off!" the old man said and leaped up from the ground. "Don't strike any more, Zarathustra! I did all this only as a game. Such things belong to my art; it was you that I wanted to try when I treated you to this tryout. And verily, you have seen through me very well. But you too have given me no small sample of yourself to try out: you are hard, wise Zarathustra. Hard do you hit with your 'truths'; your stick forces this truth out of me."

"Don't flatter!" replied Zarathustra, still excited and angry, "you actor from the bottom! You are false; why do you talk of truth? You peacock of peacocks, you sea of vanity, *what* were you playing before me, you wicked magician? In *whom* was I to believe when you were moaning in this way?"

"*The ascetic of the spirit*," said the old man, "I played *him*—you yourself once coined this word—the poet and magician who at last turns his spirit against himself, the changed man who freezes to death from his evil science and conscience. And you may as well confess it: it took a long time, O Zarathustra, before you saw through my art and lie. You *believed* in my distress when you held my head with both your hands; I heard you moan, 'He has been loved too little, loved too little.' That I deceived you to that extent made my malice jubilate inside me."

"You may have deceived people subtler than I," Zarathustra said harshly. "I do not guard against deceivers; I have to be without caution; thus my lot wants it. You, however, have to deceive: that far I know you. You always have to be equivocal—tri-, quadri-, quinquevocal. And what you have now confessed, that too was not nearly true enough or false enough to suit me. You wicked counterfeiter, how could you do otherwise? You would rouge even your disease when you show yourself naked to your doctor. In the same way you have just now rouged your lie when you said to me, 'I did all this *only* as a game.' There was *seriousness* in it too: you *are* something of an ascetic of the spirit. I solve your riddle: your magic has enchanted everybody, but no lie or cunning is left to you to use against yourself: you are disenchanted for yourself. You have harvested nausea as your one truth. Not a word of yours is genuine any more, except your mouth—namely, the nausea that sticks to your mouth."

"Who are you?" cried the old magician at this point, his voice defiant. "Who may speak thus to *me*, the greatest man alive today?" And a green lightning bolt flashed from his eye toward Zarathustra. But immediately afterward he changed and said sadly, "O Zarathustra, I am weary of it; my art nauseates me; I am not *great*—why do I dissemble? But you know it too: I sought greatness. I wanted to represent a great human being and I persuaded many; but this lie went beyond my strength. It is breaking me. O Zarathustra, everything about me is a lie; but that I am breaking—this, my breaking, is genuine."

"It does you credit," said Zarathustra gloomily, looking aside to the ground, "it does you credit that you sought greatness, but it also betrays you. You are not great. You wicked old magician, this is what is best and most honest about you, and this I honor: that you wearied of yourself and said it outright: 'I am not great.' In this I honor you as an ascetic of the spirit; and even if it was only a wink and a twinkling, in this one moment you were genuine.

"But speak, what are you seeking here in *my* woods and rocks? And lying down on *my* path, how did you want to try me? In what way were you seeking to test *me?*" Thus spoke Zarathustra, and his eyes flashed.

The old magician remained silent for a while, then said, "Did I seek to test you? I—merely seek. O Zarathustra, I seek one who is genuine, right, simple, unequivocal, a man of all honesty, a vessel of wisdom, a saint of knowledge, a great human being. Do you not know it, Zarathustra? *I seek Zarathustra.*"

And at this point there began a long silence between the two. But Zarathustra became deeply absorbed and

closed his eyes. Then, however, returning to his partner
in the conversation, he seized the hand of the magician
and said, full of kindness and cunning, "Well! Up there
goes the path; there lies Zarathustra's cave. There you
may seek him whom you would find. And ask my
animals for advice, my eagle and my serpent: they shall
help you seek. But my cave is large. I myself, to be
sure—I have not yet seen a great human being. For
what is great, even the eyes of the subtlest today are
too coarse. It is the realm of the mob. Many have I seen,
swollen and straining, and the people cried, 'Behold a
great man!' But what good are all bellows? In the end,
the wind comes out. In the end, a frog which has
puffed itself up too long will burst: the wind comes out.
To stab a swollen man in the belly, I call that a fine
pastime. Hear it well, little boys!

"Today belongs to the mob: who could still know
what is great and what small? Who could still success-
fully seek greatness? Only a fool: fools succeed. You
seek great human beings, you queer fool? Who *taught*
you that? Is today the time for that? O you wicked
seeker, why did you seek to test me?"

Thus spoke Zarathustra, his heart comforted, and he
continued on his way, laughing.

RETIRED

Not long, however, after Zarathustra had got away
from the magician, he again saw somebody sitting by
the side of his path: a tall man in black, with a gaunt
pale face; and *this* man displeased him exceedingly.
"Alas!" he said to his heart, "there sits muffled-up
melancholy, looking like the tribe of priests: what do
they want in my realm? How now? I have scarcely
escaped that magician; must another black artist cross

my way so soon—some wizard with laying-on of hands, some dark miracle worker by the grace of God, some anointed world-slanderer whom the devil should fetch? But the devil is never where he should be: he always comes too late, this damned dwarf and clubfoot!"

Thus cursed Zarathustra, impatient in his heart, and he wondered how he might sneak past the black man, looking the other way. But behold, it happened otherwise. For at the same moment the seated man had already spotted him; and not unlike one on whom unexpected good fortune has been thrust, he jumped up and walked toward Zarathustra.

"Whoever you may be, you wanderer," he said, "help one who has lost his way, a seeker, an old man who might easily come to grief here. This region is remote and strange to me, and I have heard wild animals howling; and he who might have offered me protection no longer exists himself. I sought the last pious man, a saint and hermit who, alone in his forest, had not yet heard what all the world knows today."

"What does all the world know today?" asked Zarathustra. "Perhaps this, that the old god in whom all the world once believed no longer lives?"

"As you say," replied the old man sadly. "And I served that old god until his last hour. But now I am retired, without a master, and yet not free, nor ever cheerful except in my memories. That is why I climbed these mountains, that I might again have a festival at last, as is fitting for an old pope and church father—for behold, I am the last pope—a festival of pious memories and divine services. But now he himself is dead, the most pious man, that saint in the forest who constantly praised his god with singing and humming. I did not find him when I found his cave; but there were two wolves inside, howling over his death, for all animals

loved him. So I ran away. Had I then come to these
woods and mountains in vain? Then my heart decided
that I should seek another man, the most pious of all
those who do not believe in God—that I should seek
Zarathustra!"

Thus spoke the old man, and he looked with sharp
eyes at the man standing before him; but Zarathustra
seized the hand of the old pope and long contemplated
it with admiration. "Behold, venerable one!" he said
then; "what a beautiful long hand! That is the hand of
one who has always dispensed blessings. But now it
holds him whom you seek, me, Zarathustra. It is I, the
godless Zarathustra, who speaks: who is more godless
than I, that I may enjoy his instruction?"

Thus spoke Zarathustra, and with his glances he
pierced the thoughts and the thoughts behind the
thoughts of the old pope. At last the pope began, "He
who loved and possessed him most has also lost him
most now; behold, now I myself am probably the more
godless of the two of us. But who could rejoice in that?"

"You served him to the last?" Zarathustra asked
thoughtfully after a long silence. "You know *how* he
died? Is it true what they say, that pity strangled him,
that he saw how *man* hung on the cross and that he
could not bear it, that love of man became his hell, and
in the end his death?"

The old pope, however, did not answer but looked
aside, shy, with a pained and gloomy expression. "Let
him go!" Zarathustra said after prolonged reflection,
still looking the old man straight in the eye. "Let him
go! He is gone. And although it does you credit that
you say only good things about him who is now dead,
you know as well as I *who* he was, and that his ways
were queer."

"Speaking in the confidence of three eyes," the old

pope said cheerfully (for he was blind in one eye), "in what pertains to God, I am—and have the right to be —more enlightened than Zarathustra himself. My love served him many years, my will followed his will in everything. A good servant, however, knows everything, including even things that his master conceals from himself. He was a concealed god, addicted to secrecy. Verily, even a son he got himself in a sneaky way. At the door of his faith stands adultery.

"Whoever praises him as a god of love does not have a high enough opinion of love itself. Did this god not want to be a judge too? But the lover loves beyond reward and retribution.

"When he was young, this god out of the Orient, he was harsh and vengeful and he built himself a hell to amuse his favorites. Eventually, however, he became old and soft and mellow and pitying, more like a grandfather than a father, but most like a shaky old grandmother. Then he sat in his nook by the hearth, wilted, grieving over his weak legs, weary of the world, weary of willing, and one day he choked on his all-too-great pity."

"You old pope," Zarathustra interrupted at this point, "did you see that with your own eyes? Surely it might have happened that way—that way, and also in some other way. When gods die, they always die several kinds of death. But—well then! This way or that, this way and that—he is gone! He offended the taste of my ears and eyes; I do not want to say anything worse about him now that he is dead.

"I love all that looks bright and speaks honestly. But he—you know it, you old priest, there was something of your manner about him, of the priest's manner: he was equivocal. He was also indistinct. How angry he got with us, this wrath-snorter, because we understood him badly! But why did he not speak more cleanly? And if it was the fault of our ears, why did he give us ears that heard him badly? If there was mud in our ears—well, who put it there? He bungled too much, this potter who had never finished his apprenticeship. But that he wreaked revenge on his pots and creations for having bungled them himself, that was a sin against *good taste*. There is good taste in piety too; and it was this that said in the end, 'Away with *such* a god! Rather no god, rather make destiny on one's own, rather be a fool, rather be a god oneself!' "

"What is this I hear?" said the old pope at this point, pricking up his ears. "O Zarathustra, with such disbelief you are more pious than you believe. Some god in you must have converted you to your godlessness. Is it not your piety itself that no longer lets you believe in a god? And your overgreat honesty will yet lead you beyond good and evil too. Behold, what remains to you? You have eyes and hands and mouth, predestined for blessing from all eternity. One does not bless with the hand alone. Near you, although you want to be the most godless, I scent a secret, sacred, pleasant scent of long blessings: it gives me gladness and grief. Let me be your guest, O Zarathustra, for one single night! Nowhere on earth shall I now feel better than with you."

"Amen! So be it!" said Zarathustra in great astonishment. "Up there goes the way, there lies Zarathustra's cave. I should indeed like to accompany you there myself, you venerable one, for I love all who are pious. But now a cry of distress urgently calls me away from you. In my realm no one shall come to grief; my cave is a good haven. And I wish that I could put everyone who is sad back on firm land and firm legs.

"But who could take *your* melancholy off your shoulders? For that I am too weak. Verily, we might wait long before someone awakens your god again. For this old god lives no more: he is thoroughly dead."

Thus spoke Zarathustra.

THE UGLIEST MAN

And again Zarathustra's feet ran over mountains and through woods, and his eyes kept seeking, but he whom they wanted to see was nowhere to be seen: the great distressed one who had cried out. All along the way, however, Zarathustra jubilated in his heart and was grateful. "What good things," he said, "has this day given me to make up for its bad beginning! What strange people have I found to talk with! Now I shall long chew their words like good grains; my teeth shall grind them and crush them small till they flow like milk into my soul."

But when the path turned around a rock again the scenery changed all at once, and Zarathustra entered a realm of death. Black and red cliffs rose rigidly: no grass, no tree, no bird's voice. For it was a valley that all animals avoided, even the beasts of prey; only a species of ugly fat green snakes came here to die when they grew old. Therefore the shepherds called this valley Snakes' Death.

Zarathustra, however, sank into a black reminiscence, for he felt as if he had stood in this valley once before. And much that was grave weighed on his mind; he walked slowly, and still more slowly, and finally stood still. But when he opened his eyes he saw something sitting by the way, shaped like a human being, yet scarcely like a human being—something inexpressible. And all at once a profound sense of shame overcame Zarathustra for having laid eyes on such a thing: blushing right up to his white hair, he averted his eyes and raised his feet to leave this dreadful place. But at that moment the dead waste land was filled with a noise, for something welled up from the ground, gurgling and rattling, as water gurgles and rattles by night in clogged waterpipes; and at last it became a human voice and human speech—thus:

"Zarathustra! Zarathustra! Guess my riddle! Speak, speak! What is *the revenge against the witness?* I lure you back, here is slippery ice. Take care, take care that your pride does not break its legs here! You think yourself wise, proud Zarathustra. Then guess the riddle, you cracker of hard nuts—the riddle that I am. Speak then: who am I?"

But when Zarathustra had heard these words—what do you suppose happened to his soul? *Pity seized him;* and he sank down all at once, like an oak tree that has long resisted many woodcutters—heavily, suddenly, terrifying even those who had wanted to fell it. But immediately he rose from the ground again, and his face became hard.

"I recognize you well," he said in a voice of bronze; *"you are the murderer of God!* Let me go. You could not *bear* him who saw *you*—who always saw you through and through, you ugliest man! You took revenge on this witness!"

Thus spoke Zarathustra, and he wanted to leave; but the inexpressible one seized a corner of his garment and began again to gurgle and seek for words. "Stay!" he said finally. "Stay! Do not pass by! I have guessed what ax struck you to the ground: hail to you, O Zarathustra, that you stand again! You have guessed, I know it well, how he who killed him feels—the murderer of God. Stay! Sit down here with me! It is not for nothing. Whom did I want to reach, if not you? Stay! Sit down! But do not look at me! In that way honor my ugliness!

They persecute me; now *you* are my last refuge. *Not* with their hatred, *not* with their catchpoles: I would mock such persecution and be proud and glad of it!

"Has not all success hitherto been with the well-persecuted? And whoever persecutes well, learns readily how to *follow;* for he is used to going after somebody else. But it is their *pity*—it is their pity that I flee, fleeing to you. O Zarathustra, protect me, you my last refuge, the only one who has solved my riddle: you guessed how he who killed him feels. Stay! And if you would go, you impatient one, do not go the way I came. *That* way is bad. Are you angry with me that I have even now stammered too long—and even advise you? But know, it is I, the ugliest man, who also has the largest and heaviest feet. Where *I* have gone, the way is bad. I tread all ways till they are dead and ruined.

"But that you passed me by, silent; that you blushed, I saw it well; that is how I recognized you as Zarathustra. Everyone else would have thrown his alms to me, his pity, with his eyes and words. But for that I am not beggar enough, as you guessed; for that I am too rich, rich in what is great, in what is terrible, in what is ugliest, in what is most inexpressible. Your shame, Zarathustra, honored me! With difficulty I escaped the throng of the pitying, to find the only one today who teaches, 'Pity is obtrusive'—you, O Zarathustra. Whether it be a god's pity or man's—pity offends the sense of shame. And to be unwilling to help can be nobler than that virtue which jumps to help.

"But today that is called virtue itself among all the little people—pity. They have no respect for great misfortune, for great ugliness, for great failure. Over this multitude I look away as a dog looks away over the backs of teeming flocks of sheep. They are little gray people, full of good wool and good will. As a heron looks away contemptuously over shallow ponds, its head leaning back, thus I look away over the teeming mass of gray little waves and wills and souls. Too long have we conceded to them that they are right, these little people; so that in the end we have also conceded them might. Now they teach: 'Good is only what little people call good.'

"And today 'truth' is what the preacher said, who himself came from among them, that queer saint and advocate of the little people who bore witness about himself: 'I am the truth.' This immodest fellow has long given the little people swelled heads—he who taught no small error when he taught, 'I am the truth.' Has an immodest fellow ever been answered more politely? You, however, O Zarathustra, passed him by and said, 'No! No! Three times no!' You warned against his error, you, as the first, warned against pity—not all, not none, but you and your kind.

"You are ashamed of the shame of the great sufferer; and verily, when you say, 'From pity, a great cloud approaches; beware, O men!'; when you teach, 'All creators are hard, all great love is over and above its pity'—O Zarathustra, how well you seem to me to understand storm signs. But you—warn yourself also against *your* pity. For many are on their way to you, many who are suffering, doubting, despairing, drowning, freezing. And I also warn you against myself. You guessed my best, my worst riddle: myself and what I did. I know the ax that fells you.

"But he *had to* die: he saw with eyes that saw everything; he saw man's depths and ultimate grounds, all his concealed disgrace and ugliness. His pity knew no shame: he crawled into my dirtiest nooks. This most curious, overobtrusive, overpitying one had to die. He always saw me: on such a witness I wanted to have revenge or not live myself. The god who saw everything, *even man*—this god had to die! Man cannot bear it that such a witness should live."

Thus spoke the ugliest man. But Zarathustra rose and was about to leave, for he felt frozen down to his very entrails. "You inexpressible one," he said, "you have warned me against *your* way. In thanks I shall praise mine to you. Behold, up there lies Zarathustra's cave. My cave is large and deep and has many nooks; even the most hidden can find a hiding-place there. And close by there are a hundred dens and lodges for crawling, fluttering, and jumping beasts. You self-exiled exile, would you not live among men and men's pity? Well then! Do as I do. Thus you also learn from me; only the doer learns. And speak first of all to my animals. The proudest animal and the wisest animal—they should be the right counselors for the two of us."

Thus spoke Zarathustra, and he went his way, still more reflectively and slowly than before; for he asked himself much, and he did not know how to answer himself readily. "How poor man is after all," he thought in his heart; "how ugly, how wheezing, how full of hidden shame! I have been told that man loves himself: ah, how great must this self-love be! How much contempt stands against it! This fellow too loved himself, even as he despised himself: a great lover he seems to me, and a great despiser. None have I found yet who despised himself more deeply: that too is a kind of height. Alas, was *he* perhaps the higher man whose cry I heard? I love the great despisers. Man, however, is something that must be overcome."

THE VOLUNTARY BEGGAR

When Zarathustra had left the ugliest man, he felt frozen and lonely: for much that was cold and lonely passed through his mind and made his limbs too feel colder. But as he climbed on and on, up and down, now past green pastures, then again over wild stony places where an impatient brook might once have made its bed, all at once he felt warmer and more cheerful again.

"What happened to me?" he asked himself. "Something warm and alive refreshes me, something that must be near me. Even now I am less alone; unknown companions and brothers roam about me; their warm breath touches my soul."

But when he looked around to find those who had comforted his loneliness, behold, they were cows, standing together on a knoll; their proximity and smell had warmed his heart. These cows, however, seemed to be listening eagerly to a speaker and did not heed him that was approaching. But when Zarathustra had come quite close to them, he heard distinctly that a human voice was speaking in the middle of the herd; and they had evidently all turned their heads toward the speaker.

Thereupon Zarathustra jumped up eagerly and pushed the animals apart, for he was afraid that somebody had suffered some harm here, which the pity of cows could scarcely cure. But he was wrong, for behold, there sat a man on the ground, and he seemed to be urging the animals to have no fear of him, a peaceful man and sermonizer on the mount out of whose eyes goodness itself was preaching. "What do you seek here?" shouted Zarathustra, amazed.

"What do I seek here?" he replied. "The same thing

you are seeking, you disturber of the peace: happiness on earth. But I want to learn that from these cows. For, you know, I have already been urging them half the morning, and just now they wanted to tell me. Why do you disturb them?

"Except we turn back and become as cows, we shall not enter the kingdom of heaven. For we ought to learn one thing from them: chewing the cud. And verily, what would it profit a man if he gained the whole world and did not learn this one thing: chewing the cud! He would not get rid of his melancholy—his great melancholy; but today that is called *nausea*. Who today does not have his heart, mouth, and eyes full of nausea? You too! You too! But behold these cows!"

Thus spoke the sermonizer on the mount, and then he turned his own eyes toward Zarathustra, for until then they had dwelt lovingly on the cows. But then his eyes changed. "Who is this to whom I am talking?" he cried, startled, and jumped up from the ground. "This is the man without nausea, this is Zarathustra himself, the man who overcame the great nausea; this is the eye, this is the mouth, this is the heart of Zarathustra himself." And as he spoke thus, he kissed the hands of the man to whom he was talking, and his eyes welled over, and he behaved exactly as one to whom a precious gift and treasure falls unexpectedly from the sky. But the cows watched all this with amazement.

"Do not speak of me, you who are so strange, so lovely!" Zarathustra said and restrained his tender affection. "First speak to me of yourself. Are you not the voluntary beggar who once threw away great riches? Who was ashamed of his riches and of the rich, and fled to the poorest to give them his fullness and his heart? But they did not accept him."

"But they did not accept me," said the voluntary beggar; "you know it. So I finally went to the animals and to these cows."

"There you have learned," Zarathustra interrupted the speaker, "how right giving is harder than right receiving, and that to give presents well is an *art* and the ultimate and most cunning master-art of graciousness."

"Especially today," answered the voluntary beggar; "today, I mean, when everything base has become rebellious and shy and, in its own way, arrogant—I mean, in the way of the mob. For the hour has come, you know it, for the great, bad, long, slow revolt of the mob and slaves: it grows and grows. Now the base are outraged by any charity and any little giving away; and the overrich should beware. Whoever drips today, like bulging bottles out of all-too-narrow necks—such bottles they like to seize today to break their necks. Lascivious greed, galled envy, aggrieved vengefulness, mob pride: all that leaped into my face. It is no longer true that the poor are blessed. But the kingdom of heaven is among the cows."

"And why is it not among the rich?" asked Zarathustra temptingly as he warded off the cows, which were breathing trustingly on the peaceful man.

"Why do you tempt me?" he replied. "You yourself know it even better than I. What was it after all that drove me to the poorest, O Zarathustra? Was it not that I was nauseated by our richest men? By the convicts of riches, who pick up their advantage out of any rubbish, with cold eyes, lewd thoughts; by this rabble that stinks to high heaven; by this gilded, false mob whose fathers have been pickpockets or carrion birds or ragpickers—with women, obliging, lascivious, and forgetful: for none of them is too far from the whores—mob above and mob below! What do 'poor' and 'rich' matter today? This difference I have forgotten. I fled, farther, ever farther, till I came to these cows."

Thus spoke the peaceful man, and he himself breathed hard and sweated as he spoke, so that the cows were amazed again. But Zarathustra kept looking into his face, smiling as he spoke so harshly, and silently he shook his head. "You do yourself violence, you sermonizer on the mount, when you use such harsh words. Your mouth was not formed for such harshness, nor your eyes. Nor, it seems to me, your stomach either: it is offended by all such wrath and hatred and frothing. Your stomach wants gentler things: you are no butcher. You seem much more like a plant-and-root man to me. Perhaps you gnash grain. Certainly, however, you are averse to the joys of the flesh and you love honey."

"You have unriddled me well," answered the voluntary beggar, his heart relieved. "I love honey; I also gnash grain, for I sought what tastes lovely and gives a pure breath; also what takes a long time, a day's and a mouth's work for gentle idlers and loafers. Nobody, to be sure, has achieved more than these cows: they invented for themselves chewing the cud and lying in the sun. And they abstain from all grave thoughts, which bloat the heart."

"Well then!" said Zarathustra. "You should also see *my* animals, my eagle and my serpent: their like is not to be found on earth today. Behold, there goes the way to my cave: be its guest tonight. And talk with my animals of the happiness of animals—till I myself return home. For now a cry of distress urgently calls me away from you. You will also find new honey in my cave, ice-fresh golden comb honey: eat that! But now quickly take leave from your cows, you who are so strange, so lovely!—though it may be hard for you. For they are your warmest friends and teachers."

"Excepting one whom I love still more," answered the voluntary beggar. "You yourself are good, and even better than a cow, O Zarathustra."

"Away, away with you, you wicked flatterer!" Zarathustra cried with malice. "Why do you corrupt me with such praise and honeyed flattery? Away, away from me!" he cried once more and brandished his stick at the affectionate beggar, who ran away quickly.

THE SHADOW

But as soon as the voluntary beggar had run away and Zarathustra was alone again, he heard a new voice behind him, shouting, "Stop, Zarathustra! Wait! It is I, O Zarathustra, I, your shadow!" But Zarathustra did not wait, for a sudden annoyance came over him at the many intruders and obtruders in his mountains. "Where has my solitude gone?" he said. "Verily, it is becoming too much for me; this mountain range is teeming, my kingdom is no longer of *this* world, I need new mountains. My shadow calls me? What does my shadow matter? Let him run after me! I shall run away from him."

Thus spoke Zarathustra to his heart, and he ran away. But he who was behind him followed him, so that soon there were three runners, one behind the other, first the voluntary beggar, then Zarathustra, and third and last his shadow. It was not long that they ran this way before Zarathustra realized his folly and with a single shrug shook off all discontent and disgust. "Well!" he said; "have not the most ridiculous things always happened among us old hermits and saints? Verily, my folly has grown tall in the mountains. Now I hear six old fools' legs clattering along in a row. But may Zarathustra be afraid of a shadow? Moreover, it seems to me that he has longer legs than I."

Thus spoke Zarathustra, laughing with his eyes and entrails; he stopped quickly and turned around—and behold, he almost threw his follower and shadow to the ground: so close was the shadow by then, and so weak too. And when Zarathustra examined him with his eyes, he was startled as by a sudden ghost: so thin, swarthy, hollow, and outlived did this follower look. "Who are you?" Zarathustra asked violently. "What are you doing here? And why do you call yourself my shadow? I do not like you."

"Forgive me," answered the shadow, "that it is I; and if you do not like me, well then, O Zarathustra, for that I praise you and your good taste. I am a wanderer who has already walked a great deal at your heels—always on my way, but without any goal, also without any home; so that I really lack little toward being the Eternal Jew, unless it be that I am not eternal, and not a Jew. How? Must I always be on my way? Whirled by every wind, restless, driven on? O earth, thou hast become too round for me!

"I have already sat on every surface; like weary dust, I have gone to sleep on mirrors and windowpanes: everything takes away from me, nothing gives, I become thin—I am almost like a shadow. But after you, O Zarathustra, I flew and blew the longest; and even when I hid from you I was still your best shadow: wherever you sat, I sat too.

"With you I haunted the remotest, coldest worlds like a ghost that runs voluntarily over wintery roofs and snow. With you I strove to penetrate everything that is forbidden, worst, remotest; and if there is anything in me that is virtue, it is that I had no fear of any for-biddance. With you I broke whatever my heart revered; I overthrew all boundary stones and images; I pursued the most dangerous wishes: verily, over every crime I have passed once. With you I unlearned faith in words and values and great names. When the devil sheds his skin, does not his name fall off too? For that too is skin. The devil himself is perhaps—skin.

" 'Nothing is true, all is permitted': thus I spoke to myself. Into the coldest waters I plunged, with head and heart. Alas, how often have I stood there afterward, naked as a red crab! Alas, where has all that is good gone from me—and all shame, and all faith in those who are good? Alas, where is that mendacious inno-cence that I once possessed, the innocence of the good and their noble lies?

"Too often, verily, did I follow close on the heels of truth: so she kicked me in the face. Sometimes I thought I was lying, and behold, only then did I hit the truth. Too much has become clear to me: now it no longer concerns me. Nothing is alive any more that I love; how should I still love myself? 'To live as it pleases me, or not to live at all': that is what I want, that is what the saintliest want too. But alas, how could anything please me any more? Do I have a goal any more? A haven toward which my sail is set? A good wind? Alas, only he who knows where he is sailing also knows which wind is good and the right wind for him. What is left to me now? A heart, weary and impudent, a restless will, flutter-wings, a broken backbone. Trying thus to find *my* home—O Zarathustra, do you know it?—trying this was *my* trial; it consumes me. 'Where is—my home?' I ask and search and have searched for it, but I have not found it. O eternal everywhere, O eternal nowhere, O eternal—in vain!"

Thus spoke the shadow, and Zarathustra's face grew long as he listened. "You are my shadow," he finally said sadly. "Your danger is no small one, you free spirit and wanderer. You have had a bad day; see to it that you do not have a still worse evening. To those who are as restless as you, even a jail will at last seem bliss. Have you ever seen how imprisoned criminals sleep? They sleep calmly, enjoying their new security. Beware lest a narrow faith imprison you in the end—some harsh and severe illusion. For whatever is narrow and solid seduces and tempts you now.

"You have lost your goal; alas, how will you digest and jest over this loss? With this you have also lost your way. You poor roaming enthusiast, you weary butterfly! Would you have a rest and home this evening? Then go up to my cave. Up there goes the path to my cave.

"And now let me quickly run away from you again. Even now a shadow seems to lie over me. I want to run alone so that it may become bright around me again. For that, I shall still have to stay merrily on my legs a long time. In the evening, however, there will be dancing in my cave."

Thus spoke Zarathustra.

AT NOON

And Zarathustra ran and ran and did not find anybody any more, and he was alone and found himself again and again, and he enjoyed and quaffed his solitude and thought of good things for hours. But around the hour of noon, when the sun stood straight over Zarathustra's head, he came to an old crooked and knotty tree that was embraced, and hidden from itself, by the rich love of a grapevine; and yellow

grapes hung from it in abundance, inviting the wanderer. Then he felt the desire to quench a slight thirst
and to break off a grape; but even as he was stretching out his arm to do so, he felt a still greater desire for
something else: namely, to lie down beside the tree at
the perfect noon hour, and to sleep.

This Zarathustra did; and as soon as he lay on the
ground in the stillness and secrecy of the many-hued
grass, he forgot his slight thirst and fell asleep. For, as
Zarathustra's proverb says, one thing is more necessary
than another. Only his eyes remained open: for they
did not tire of seeing and praising the tree and the
love of the grapevine. Falling asleep, however, Zarathustra spoke thus to his heart:

Still! Still! Did not the world become perfect just
now? What is happening to me? As a delicate wind
dances unseen on an inlaid sea, light, feather-light,
thus sleep dances on me. My eyes he does not close,
my soul he leaves awake. Light he is, verily, feather-
light. He persuades me, I know not how. He touches
me inwardly with caressing hands, he conquers me. Yes,
he conquers me and makes my soul stretch out: how
she is becoming long and tired, my strange soul! Did
the eve of a seventh day come to her at noon? Has she
already roamed happily among good and ripe things
too long? She stretches out long, long—longer. She
lies still, my strange soul. Too much that is good has
she tasted; this golden sadness oppresses her, she makes
a wry mouth.

Like a ship that has sailed into its stillest cove—now
it leans against the earth, tired of the long voyages
and the uncertain seas. Is not the earth more faithful?
The way such a ship lies close to, and nestles to, the
land—it is enough if a spider spins its thread to it from
the land: no stronger ropes are needed now. Like such

a tired ship in the stillest cove, I too rest now near the earth, faithful, trusting, waiting, tied to it with the softest threads.

O happiness! O happiness! Would you sing, O my soul? You are lying in the grass. But this is the secret solemn hour when no shepherd plays his pipe. Refrain! Hot noon sleeps on the meadows. Do not sing! Still! The world is perfect. Do not sing, you winged one in the grass, O my soul—do not even whisper! Behold—still!—the old noon sleeps, his mouth moves: is he not just now drinking a drop of happiness, an old brown drop of golden happiness, golden wine? It slips over him, his happiness laughs. Thus laughs a god. Still!

"O happiness, how little is sufficient for happiness!" Thus I spoke once and seemed clever to myself. But it was a blasphemy: *that* I have learned now. Clever fools speak better. Precisely the least, the softest, lightest, a lizard's rustling, a breath, a breeze, a moment's glance—it is *little* that makes the *best* happiness. Still!

What happened to me? Listen! Did time perhaps fly away? Do I not fall? Did I not fall—listen!—into the well of eternity? What is happening to me? Still! I have been stung, alas—in the heart? In the heart! Oh break, break, heart, after such happiness, after such a sting. How? Did not the world become perfect just now? Round and ripe? Oh, the golden round ring—where may it fly? Shall I run after it? Quick! Still! (And here Zarathustra stretched and felt that he was asleep.)

"Up!" he said to himself; "you sleeper! You noon napper! Well, get up, old legs! It is time and overtime; many a good stretch of road still lies ahead of you. Now you have slept out—how long? Half an eternity! Well! Up with you now, my old heart! After such a sleep, how long will it take you to—wake it off?" (But then he fell asleep again, and his soul spoke against him and resisted and lay down again.) "Leave me alone! Still! Did not the world become perfect just now? Oh, the golden round ball!"

"Get up!" said Zarathustra, "you little thief, you lazy little thief of time! What? Still stretching, yawning, sighing, falling into deep wells? Who are you? O my soul!" (At this point he was startled, for a sunbeam fell from the sky onto his face.) "O heaven over me!" he said, sighing, and sat up. "You are looking on? You are listening to my strange soul? When will you drink this drop of dew which has fallen upon all earthly things? When will you drink this strange soul? When, well of eternity? Cheerful, dreadful abyss of noon! When will you drink my soul back into yourself?"

Thus spoke Zarathustra, and he got up from his resting place at the tree as from a strange drunkenness; and behold, the sun still stood straight over his head. But from this one might justly conclude that Zarathustra had not slept long.

THE WELCOME

It was only late in the afternoon that Zarathustra, after much vain searching and roaming, returned to his cave again. But when he was opposite it, not twenty paces away, that which he now least expected came about: again he heard the great *cry of distress*. And—amazing!—this time it came from his own cave. But it was a long-drawn-out, manifold, strange cry, and Zarathustra could clearly discern that it was composed of many voices, though if heard from a distance it might sound like a cry from a single mouth.

Then Zarathustra leaped toward his cave, and behold, what a sight awaited him after this sound! For all the men whom he had passed by during the day were sitting there together: the king at the right and the king at the left, the old magician, the pope, the voluntary beggar, the shadow, the conscientious in spirit, the sad soothsayer, and the ass; and the ugliest man had put on a crown and adorned himself with two crimson belts, for like all who are ugly he loved to disguise himself and pretend that he was beautiful. But in the middle of this melancholy party stood Zarathustra's eagle, bristling and restless, for he had been asked too many questions for which his pride had no answer; and the wise serpent hung around his neck.

Zarathustra beheld all this with great amazement; then he examined every one of his guests with friendly curiosity, read their souls, and was amazed again. Meanwhile all those gathered had risen from their seats and were waiting respectfully for Zarathustra to speak. But Zarathustra spoke thus:

"You who despair! You who are strange! So it was *your* cry of distress that I heard? And now I also know where to find him whom I sought in vain today: *the higher man*. He sits in my own cave, the higher man. But why should I be amazed? Have I not lured him to myself with honey sacrifices and the cunning siren calls of my happiness?

"Yet it seems to me that you are poor company; you who utter cries of distress upset each other's hearts as you sit here together. First someone must come—someone to make you laugh again, a good gay clown, a dancer and wind and wildcat, some old fool. What do you think?

"Forgive me, you who despair, that I speak to you with such little words, unworthy, verily, of such guests. But you do not guess *what* makes me so prankish: it is you yourselves who do it, and the sight of you; forgive me! For everyone becomes brave when he observes one who despairs. To encourage one who despairs—for that everyone feels strong enough. Even to me you gave this strength: a good gift, my honored guests! A proper present to ensure hospitality! Well then, do not be angry if I also offer you something of what is mine.

"This is my realm and my dominion; but whatever is mine shall be yours for this evening and this night. My animals shall serve you, my cave shall be your place of rest. In my home and house nobody shall despair; in my region I protect everybody from his wild animals. And this is the first thing I offer you: security. The second thing, however, is my little finger. And once you have *that*, by all means take the whole hand; well, and my heart too! Be welcome here, welcome, my guests!"

Thus spoke Zarathustra, and he laughed from love and malice. After this welcome his guests bowed again and were respectfully silent; but the king at the right hand answered him in their name: "From the manner, O Zarathustra, in which you offered us hand and welcome, we recognize you as Zarathustra. You humbled yourself before us; you almost wounded our reverence. But who would know as you do, how to humble himself with such pride? *That* in itself uplifts us; it is refreshing for our eyes and hearts. Merely to see this one thing, we would gladly climb mountains higher than this one. For we came, eager to see; we wanted to behold what makes dim eyes bright. And behold, even now we are done with all our cries of distress. Even now our minds and hearts are opened up and delighted. Little is lacking, and our spirits will become sportive.

"Nothing more delightful grows on earth, O Zarathustra, than a lofty, strong will: that is the earth's most beautiful plant. A whole landscape is refreshed by one

such tree. Whoever grows up high like you, O Zarathustra, I compare to the pine: long, silent, hard, alone,
of the best and most resilient wood, magnificent—and
in the end reaching out with strong green branches for
his *own* dominion, questioning wind and weather and
whatever else is at home on the heights with forceful
questions, and answering yet more forcefully, a commander, triumphant: oh, who would not climb high
mountains to see such plants? Your tree here, O Zarathustra, refreshes even the gloomy ones, the failures;
your sight reassures and heals the heart even of the
restless. And verily, toward your mountain and tree
many eyes are directed today; a great longing has arisen,
and many have learned to ask, 'Who is Zarathustra?'

"And those into whose ears you have once dripped
your song and your honey, all the hidden, the lonesome,
the twosome, have all at once said to their hearts, 'Does
Zarathustra still live? Life is no longer worth while, all
is the same, all is in vain, or—we must live with Zarathustra.'

" 'Why does he not come who has so long announced
himself?' ask many. 'Has solitude swallowed him up? Or
are we perhaps supposed to come to him?'

"Now it happens that solitude itself grows weary
and breaks, like a tomb that breaks and can no longer
hold its dead. Everywhere one sees the resurrected.
Now the waves are climbing and climbing around your
mountain, O Zarathustra. And however high your height
may be, many must come up to you: your bark shall not
be stranded much longer. And that we who were despairing have now come to your cave and no longer
despair—that is but a sign and symbol that those better
than we are on their way to you; for this is what is on
its way to you: the last remnant of God among men—
that is, all the men of great longing, of great nausea,

of great disgust, all who do not want to live unless they learn to *hope* again, unless they learn from you, O Zarathustra, the *great* hope."

Thus spoke the king at the right, and he seized Zarathustra's hand to kiss it; but Zarathustra resisted his veneration and stepped back, startled, silent, and as if he were suddenly fleeing into remote distances. But after a little while he was back with his guests again, looking at them with bright, examining eyes, and he said: "My guests, you higher men, let me speak to you in plain and clear German. It was not for *you* that I waited in these mountains."

("Plain and clear German? Good God!" the king at the left said at this point, in an aside. "One can see that he does not know our dear Germans, this wise man from the East! But what he means is 'coarse German'; well, these days that is not the worst of tastes.")

"You may indeed all be higher men," continued Zarathustra, "but for me you are not high and strong enough. For me—that means, for the inexorable in me that is silent but will not always remain silent. And if you do belong to me, it is not as my right arm. For whoever stands on sick and weak legs himself, as you do, wants *consideration* above all, whether he knows it or hides it from himself. To my arms and my legs, however, I show no consideration; *I show my warriors no consideration:* how then could you be fit for *my* war? With you I should spoil my every victory. And some among you would collapse as soon as they heard the loud roll of my drums.

"Nor are you beautiful and wellborn enough for me. I need clean, smooth mirrors for my doctrines; on your surface even my own image is distorted. Many a burden, many a reminiscence press on your shoulders; many a wicked dwarf crouches in your nooks. There is hidden mob in you too. And even though you may be high and of a higher kind, much in you is crooked and misshapen. There is no smith in the world who could hammer you right and straight for me.

"You are mere bridges: may men higher than you stride over you. You signify steps: therefore do not be angry with him who climbs over you to *his* height. A genuine son and perfect heir may yet grow from your seed, even for me: but that is distant. You yourselves are not those to whom my heritage and name belong.

"It is not for you that I wait in these mountains; it is not with you that I am to go down for the last time. Only as signs have you come to me, that those higher than you are even now on their way to me: *not* the men of great longing, of great nausea, of great disgust, and that which you called the remnant of God; no, no, three times no! It is for others that I wait here in these mountains, and I will not lift my feet from here without them; it is for those who are higher, stronger, more triumphant, and more cheerful, such as are built perpendicular in body and soul: *laughing lions* must come!

"O my strange guests! Have you not yet heard anything of my children? And that they are on their way to me? Speak to me of my gardens, of my blessed isles, of my new beauty—why do you not speak to me of that? This present I beseech from your love, that you speak to me of my children. For this I am rich, for this I grew poor; what did I not give, what would I not give to have one thing: these children, this living plantation, these life-trees of my will and my highest hope!"

Thus spoke Zarathustra, and suddenly he stopped in his speech, for a longing came over him, and he closed his eyes and mouth as his heart was moved. And all his guests too fell silent and stood still in dismay; only the old soothsayer made signs and gestures with his hands.

THE LAST SUPPER

For it was at this point that the soothsayer interrupted the welcome, pushed forward like one who has no time to lose, seized Zarathustra's hand, and shouted: "But Zarathustra! One thing is more necessary than another: thus you say yourself. Well then, one thing is more necessary to *me* now than anything else. A word at the right time: did you not invite me to *supper?* And here are many who have come a long way. Surely, you would not feed us speeches alone? Also, all of you have thought far too much, for my taste, of freezing, drowning, suffocating, and other physical distress; but nobody has thought of *my* distress, namely, starving—"

(Thus spoke the soothsayer; but when Zarathustra's animals heard these words they ran away in fright. For they saw that whatever they had brought home during the day would not be enough to fill this one soothsayer.)

"Including dying of thirst," continued the soothsayer. "And although I hear water splashing nearby like speeches of wisdom—that is, abundantly and tirelessly —I want *wine.* Not everybody is a born water drinker like Zarathustra. Nor is water fit for the weary and wilted: *we* deserve wine. *That* alone gives sudden convalescence and immediate health."

On this occasion, as the soothsayer asked for wine, it happened that the king at the left, the taciturn one, got a word in too, for once. "For wine," he said, "*we* have taken care—I together with my brother, the king at the right; we have wine enough—a whole ass-load. So nothing is lacking but bread."

"Bread?" countered Zarathustra, and he laughed. "Bread is the one thing hermits do not have. But man does not live by bread alone, but also of the meat of good lambs, of which I have two. *These* should be slaughtered quickly and prepared tastily with sage: I love it that way. Nor is there a lack of roots and fruit, good enough even for gourmets and gourmands, nor of nuts and other riddles to be cracked. Thus we shall have a good meal in a short while. But whoever would join in the eating must also help in the preparation, even the kings. For at Zarathustra's even a king may be cook."

This suggestion appealed to the hearts of all; only the voluntary beggar objected to meat and wine and spices. "Now listen to this glutton Zarathustra!" he said jokingly; "is that why one goes into caves and high mountain ranges, to prepare such meals? Now indeed I understand what he once taught us: 'Praised be a little poverty!' And why he wants to abolish beggars."

"Be of good cheer," Zarathustra answered him, "as I am. Stick to your custom, my excellent friend, crush your grains, drink your water, praise your fare; as long as it makes you gay!

"I am a law only for my kind, I am no law for all. But whoever belongs with me must have strong bones and light feet, be eager for war and festivals, not gloomy, no dreamer, as ready for what is most difficult as for his festival, healthy and wholesome. The best belongs to my kind and to me; and when one does not give it to us, we take it: the best food, the purest sky, the strongest thoughts, the most beautiful women."

Thus spoke Zarathustra; but the king at the right retorted: "Strange! Has one ever heard such clever things out of the mouth of a sage? And verily, he is the strangest sage who is also clever and no ass."

Thus spoke the king at the right, and he was amazed; but the ass commented on his speech with evil intent:

Yeah-Yuh. But this was the beginning of that long-drawn-out meal which the chronicles call "the last supper." And in the course of it, nothing else was discussed but *the higher man*.

ON THE HIGHER MAN

1

The first time I came to men I committed the folly of hermits, the great folly: I stood in the market place. And as I spoke to all, I spoke to none. But in the evening, tightrope walkers and corpses were my companions; and I myself was almost a corpse. But with the new morning a new truth came to me: I learned to say, "Of what concern to me are market and mob and mob noise and long mob ears?"

You higher men, learn this from me: in the market place nobody believes in higher men. And if you want to speak there, very well! But the mob blinks: "We are all equal."

"You higher men"—thus blinks the mob—"there are no higher men, we are all equal, man is man; before God we are all equal."

Before God! But now this god has died. And before the mob we do not want to be equal. You higher men, go away from the market place!

2

Before God! But now this god has died. You higher men, this god was your greatest danger. It is only since he lies in his tomb that you have been resurrected. Only now the great noon comes; only now the higher man becomes—lord.

Have you understood this word, O my brothers? You are startled? Do your hearts become giddy? Does the abyss yawn before you? Does the hellhound howl at you? Well then, you higher men! Only now is the mountain of man's future in labor. God died: now *we* want the overman to live.

3

The most concerned ask today: "How is man to be preserved?" But Zarathustra is the first and only one to ask: "How is man to be overcome?"

I have the overman at heart, *that* is my first and only concern—and *not* man: not the neighbor, not the poorest, not the most ailing, not the best.

O my brothers, what I can love in man is that he is an overture and a going under. And in you too there is much that lets me love and hope. That you despise, you higher men, that lets me hope. For the great despisers are the great reverers. That you have despaired, in that there is much to revere. For you did not learn how to surrender, you did not learn petty prudences. For today the little people lord it: they all preach surrender and resignation and prudence and industry and consideration and the long etcetera of the small virtues.

What is womanish, what derives from the servile, and especially the mob hodgepodge: *that* would now become master of all human destiny. O nausea! Nausea! Nausea! *That* asks and asks and never grows weary: "How is man to be preserved best, longest, most agreeably?" With that—they are the masters of today.

Overcome these masters of today, O my brothers— these small people, *they* are the overman's greatest danger.

You higher men, overcome the small virtues, the small prudences, the grain-of-sand consideration, the ants' riff-raff, the wretched contentment, the "happiness of the greatest number"! And rather despair than surrender. And verily, I love you for not knowing how to live today, you higher men! For thus *you* live best.

4

Do you have courage, O my brothers? Are you brave? *Not* courage before witnesses but the courage of hermits and eagles, which is no longer watched even by a god.

Cold souls, mules, the blind, and the drunken I do not call brave. Brave is he who knows fear but *conquers* fear, who sees the abyss, but with *pride*.

Who sees the abyss but with the eyes of an eagle; who grasps the abyss with the talons of an eagle—that man has courage.

5

"Man is evil"—thus said all the wisest to comfort me. Alas, if only it were still true today! For evil is man's best strength.

"Man must become better and more evil"—thus *I* teach. The greatest evil is necessary for the overman's best. It may have been good for that preacher of the little people that he suffered and tried to bear man's sin. But I rejoice over great sin as my great consolation.

But this is not said for long ears. Not every word belongs in every mouth. These are delicate distant matters: they should not be reached for by sheeps' hoofs.

6

You higher men, do you suppose I have come to set right what you have set wrong? Or that I have come to you that suffer to bed you more comfortably? Or to you that are restless, have gone astray or climbed astray, to show you new and easier paths?

No! No! Three times no! Ever more, ever better ones

of your kind shall perish—for it shall be ever worse and harder for you. Thus alone—thus alone, man grows to the height where lightning strikes and breaks him: lofty enough for lightning.

My mind and my longing are directed toward the few, the long, the distant; what are your many small short miseries to me? You do not yet suffer enough to suit me! For you suffer from yourselves, you have not yet suffered *from man.* You would lie if you claimed otherwise! You all do not suffer from what *I* have suffered.

7

It is not enough for me that lightning no longer does any harm. I do not wish to conduct it away: it shall learn to work for me.

My wisdom has long gathered like a cloud; it is becoming stiller and darker. Thus does every wisdom that is yet to give birth to lightning bolts.

For these men of today I do not wish to be *light,* or to be called light. *These* I wish to blind. Lightning of my wisdom! put out their eyes!

8

Will nothing beyond your capacity: there is a wicked falseness among those who will beyond their capacity. Especially if they will great things! For they arouse mistrust against great things, these subtle counterfeiters and actors—until finally they are false before themselves, squinters, whited worm-eaten decay, cloaked with strong words, with display-virtues, with splendid false deeds.

Take good care there, you higher men! For nothing today is more precious to me and rarer than honesty.

Is this today not the mob's? But the mob does not

know what is great, what is small, what is straight and honest: it is innocently crooked, it always lies.

9

Have a good mistrust today, you higher men, you stouthearted ones, you openhearted ones! And keep your reasons secret! For this today is the mob's.

What the mob once learned to believe without reasons —who could overthrow that with reasons?

And in the market place one convinces with gestures. But reasons make the mob mistrustful.

And if truth was victorious for once, then ask yourself with good mistrust: "What strong error fought for it?"

Beware of the scholars! They hate you, for they are sterile. They have cold, dried-up eyes; before them every bird lies unplumed.

Such men boast that they do not lie: but the inability to lie is far from the love of truth. Beware!

Freedom from fever is not yet knowledge by any means! I do not believe chilled spirits. Whoever is unable to lie does not know what truth is.

10

If you would go high, use your own legs. Do not let yourselves be *carried* up; do not sit on the backs and heads of others. But you mounted a horse? You are now riding quickly up to your goal? All right, my friend! But your lame foot is sitting on the horse too. When you reach your goal, when you jump off your horse—on your very *height*, you higher man, you will stumble.

11

You creators, you higher men! One is pregnant only with one's own child. Do not let yourselves be gulled and beguiled! Who, after all, is *your* neighbor? And even if you act "for the neighbor"—you still do not create for him.

Unlearn this "for," you creators! Your very virtue wants that you do nothing "for" and "in order" and "because." You shall plug up your ears against these false little words. "For the neighbor" is only the virtue of the little people: there one says "birds of a feather" and "one hand washes the other." They have neither the right nor the strength for *your* egoism. In your egoism, you creators, is the caution and providence of the pregnant. What no one has yet laid eyes on, the fruit: that your whole love shelters and saves and nourishes. Where your whole love is, with your child, there is also your whole virtue. Your work, your will, that is *your* "neighbor": do not let yourselves be gulled with false values!

12

You creators, you higher men! Whoever has to give birth is sick; but whoever has given birth is unclean. Ask women: one does not give birth because it is fun. Pain makes hens and poets cackle.

You creators, there is much that is unclean in you. That is because you had to be mothers.

A new child: oh, how much new filth has also come into the world! Go aside! And whoever has given birth should wash his soul clean.

13

Do not be virtuous beyond your strength! And do not desire anything of yourselves against probability.

Walk in the footprints where your fathers' virtue walked before you. How would you climb high if your fathers' will does not climb with you?

But whoever would be a firstling should beware lest

he also become a lastling. And wherever the vices of your fathers are, there you should not want to represent saints. If your fathers consorted with women, strong wines, and wild boars, what would it be if you wanted chastity of yourself? It would be folly! Verily, it seems much to me if such a man is the husband of one or two or three women. And if he founded monasteries and wrote over the door, "The way to sainthood," I should yet say, What for? It is another folly. He founded a reformatory and refuge for himself: may it do him good! But I do not believe in it.

In solitude, whatever one has brought into it grows— also the inner beast. Therefore solitude is inadvisable for many. Has there been anything filthier on earth so far than desert saints? Around them not only was the devil loose, but also the swine.

14

Shy, ashamed, awkward, like a tiger whose leap has failed: thus I have often seen you slink aside, you higher men. A throw had failed you. But, you dice-throwers, what does it matter? You have not learned to gamble and jest as one must gamble and jest. Do we not always sit at a big jesting-and-gaming table? And if something great has failed you, does it follow that you yourselves are failures? And if you yourselves are failures, does it follow that *man* is a failure? But if man is a failure—well then!

15

The higher its type, the more rarely a thing succeeds. You higher men here, have you not all failed?

Be of good cheer, what does it matter? How much is still possible! Learn to laugh at yourselves as one must laugh!

Is it any wonder that you failed and only half succeeded, being half broken? Is not something thronging and pushing in you—man's *future*? Man's greatest distance and depth and what in him is lofty to the stars, his tremendous strength—are not all these frothing against each other in your pot? Is it any wonder that many a pot breaks? Learn to laugh at yourselves as one must laugh! You higher men, how much is still possible!

And verily, how much has already succeeded! How rich is the earth in little good perfect things, in what has turned out well!

Place little good perfect things around you, O higher men! Their golden ripeness heals the heart. What is perfect teaches hope.

16

What has so far been the greatest sin here on earth? Was it not the word of him who said, "Woe unto those who laugh here"? Did he himself find no reasons on earth for laughing? Then he searched very badly. Even a child could find reasons here. He did not love enough: else he would also have loved us who laugh. But he hated and mocked us: howling and gnashing of teeth he promised us.

Does one have to curse right away, where one does not love? That seems bad taste to me. But thus he acted, being unconditional. He came from the mob. And he himself simply did not love enough: else he would not have been so wroth that one did not love him. All great love does not *want* love: it wants more.

Avoid all such unconditional people! They are a poor sick sort, a sort of mob: they look sourly at this life, they have the evil eye for this earth. Avoid all such unconditional people! They have heavy feet and sultry hearts: they do not know how to dance. How should the earth be light for them?

17

All good things approach their goal crookedly. Like cats, they arch their backs, they purr inwardly over their approaching happiness: all good things laugh.

A man's stride betrays whether he has found his own way: behold me walking! But whoever approaches his goal dances. And verily, I have not become a statue: I do not yet stand there, stiff, stupid, stony, a column; I love to run swiftly. And though there are swamps and thick melancholy on earth, whoever has light feet runs even over mud and dances as on swept ice.

Lift up your hearts, my brothers, high, higher! And do not forget your legs either. Lift up your legs too, you good dancers; and better yet, stand on your heads!

18

This crown of him who laughs, this rose-wreath crown: I myself have put on this crown, I myself have pronounced my laughter holy. Nobody else have I found strong enough for this today.

Zarathustra the dancer, Zarathustra the light, waves with his wings, ready for flight, waving at all birds, ready and heady, happily lightheaded; Zarathustra the soothsayer, Zarathustra the sooth-laugher, not impatient, not unconditional, one who loves leaps and side-leaps: I myself have put on this crown!

19

Lift up your hearts, my brothers, high, higher! And do not forget your legs either. Lift up your legs too, you good dancers; and better yet, stand on your heads!

In happiness too there are heavy animals; there are

pondrous-pedes through and through. Curiously they labor, like an elephant laboring to stand on its head. But it is still better to be foolish from happiness than foolish from unhappiness; better to dance ponderously than to walk lamely. That you would learn my wisdom from me: even the worst thing has two good reverse sides—even the worst thing has good dancing legs; that you would learn, you higher men, to put yourselves on your right legs! That you would unlearn nursing melancholy and all mob-sadness! Oh, how sad even the mob's clowns seem to me today! But this today is the mob's.

20

Be like the wind rushing out of his mountain caves: he wishes to dance to his own pipe; the seas tremble and leap under his feet.

What gives asses wings, what milks lionesses—praised be this good intractable spirit that comes like a cyclone to all today and to all the mob. What is averse to thistle-heads and casuists' heads and to all wilted leaves and weeds—praised be this wild, good, free storm spirit that dances on swamps and on melancholy as on meadows. What hates the mob's blether cocks and all the bungled gloomy brood—praised be this spirit of all free spirits, the laughing gale that blows dust into the eyes of all the black-sighted, sore-blighted.

You higher men, the worst about you is that all of you have not learned to dance as one must dance—dancing away over yourselves! What does it matter that you are failures? How much is still possible! So *learn* to laugh away over yourselves! Lift up your hearts, you good dancers, high, higher! And do not forget good laughter. This crown of him who laughs, this rose-wreath crown: to you, my brothers, I throw this crown. Laughter I have pronounced holy; you higher men, *learn* to laugh!

1

While Zarathustra delivered these discourses he stood near the entrance of his cave; but with the last words he slipped away from his guests and fled into the open for a short while.

"O pure smells about me!" he cried out. "O happy silence about me! But where are my animals? Come here, come here, my eagle and my serpent! Tell me, my animals: these higher men, all of them—do they perhaps *smell* bad? O pure smells about me! Only now I know and feel how much I love you, my animals."

And Zarathustra spoke once more: "I love you, my animals." But the eagle and the serpent pressed close to him as he spoke these words, and looked up to him. In this way the three of them were together silently, and they sniffed and sipped the good air together. For the air out here was better than among the higher men.

2

But Zarathustra had scarcely left his cave when the old magician got up, looked around cunningly, and said: "He has gone out! And immediately, you higher men— if I may tickle you with this laudatory, flattering name, as he did—immediately my wicked spirit of deception and magic seizes me, my melancholy devil, who is through and through an adversary of this Zarathustra— forgive him! Now he *wants* to show you his magic; he has *his* hour right now; in vain do I wrestle with this evil spirit. Of all of you, whatever honors you may confer on yourselves with words, whether you call your- selves 'free spirits' or 'truthful' or 'ascetics of the spirit or 'the unbound' or 'the great longers'—of all of you who, like me, are suffering of *the great nausea,* for whom the old god has died and for whom no new god lies as yet in cradles and swaddling clothes—of all of you my evil spirit and magic devil is fond.

"I know you, you higher men; I know him; I also know this monster whom I love against my will, this Zarathustra: he himself sometimes seems to me like a beautiful mask of a saint, like a new strange masquerade in which my evil spirit, the melancholy devil, enjoys himself. I love Zarathustra, it often seems to me, for the sake of my evil spirit.

"But even now he attacks me and forces me, this spirit of melancholy, this devil of the dusk; and verily, you higher men, he has the desire—you may well open your eyes wide!—he has the desire to come *naked;* whether male or female I do not know yet—but he is coming, he is forcing me; alas, open up your senses! The day is fading away, evening is now coming to all things, even to the best things: hear then and see, you higher men, what kind of devil, whether man or woman, this spirit of evening melancholy is!"

Thus spoke the old magician, looked around cunningly, and then reached for his harp.

3

In dim, de-lighted air
When the dew's comfort is beginning
To well down to the earth,
Unseen, unheard—
For tender is the footwear of
The comforter dew, as of all that gently comfort—
Do you remember then, remember, hot heart,
How you thirsted once
For heavenly tears and dripping dew,

Thirsting, scorched and weary,
While on yellow paths in the grass
The glances of the evening sun were running
Maliciously around you through black trees—
Blinding, glowing glances of the sun, mocking your
  pain?

"Suitor of truth?" they mocked me; "you?
No! Only poet!
An animal, cunning, preying, prowling,
That must lie,
That must knowingly, willingly lie:
Lusting for prey,
Colorfully masked,
A mask for itself,
Prey for itself—
This, the suitor of truth?
No! Only fool! Only poet!
Only speaking colorfully,
Only screaming colorfully out of fools' masks,
Climbing around on mendacious word bridges,
On colorful rainbows,
Between false heavens
And false earths,
Roaming, hovering—
Only fool! *Only* poet!

This—the suitor of truth?
Not still, stiff, smooth, cold,
Become a statue,
A pillar of God,
Not placed before temples,
A god's gate guard—
No! an enemy of all such truth statues,
More at home in any desert than before temples,

Full of cats' prankishness,
Leaping through every window—
Swish! into every chance,
Sniffing for every jungle,
Eagerly, longingly sniffing:
That in jungles
Among colorfully speckled beasts of prey
You might roam, sinfully sound and colorful, beautiful
With lusting lips,
Blissfully mocking, blissfully hellish, blissfully blood-
    thirsty—
Preying, prowling, peering—

Or like the eagle that gazes long,
Long with fixed eyes into abysses,
His *own* abysses—
Oh, how they wind downward,
Lower and lower
And into ever deeper depths!—
Then,
Suddenly, straight as sight
In brandished flight,
Pounce on *lambs*,
Abruptly down, hot-hungry,
Lusting for lambs,
Hating all lamb souls,
Grimly hating whatever looks
Sheepish, lamb-eyed, curly-wooled,
Gray, with lambs' and sheeps' goodwill.

Thus
Eagle-like, panther-like,
Are the poet's longings,
Are *your* longings under a thousand masks,
You fool! You poet!

You that have seen man
As god and sheep:
Tearing to pieces the god in man
No less than the sheep in man,
And *laughing* while tearing—

This, this is your bliss!
A panther's and eagle's bliss!
A poet's and fool's bliss!"

In dim, de-lighted air
When the moon's sickle is beginning
To creep, green between crimson
Reds, enviously—
Hating the day,
Secretly step for step
Scything at sloping rose meads
Till they sink and, ashen,
Drown in night—

Thus I myself once sank
Out of my truth-madness,
Out of my day-longings,
Weary of day, sick from the light—
Sank downward, eveningward, shadowward,
Burned by one truth,
And thirsty:
Do you remember still, remember, hot heart,
How you thirsted?
That I be banished
From all truth,
Only fool!
Only poet!

Thus sang the magician; and all who were gathered there went unwittingly as birds into the net of his cunning and melancholy lust. Only the conscientious in spirit was not caught: quickly he took the harp away from the magician and cried: "Air! Let in good air! Let in Zarathustra! You are making this cave sultry and poisonous, you wicked old magician. You are seducing us, you false and subtle one, to unknown desires and wildernesses. And beware when such as you start making speeches and fuss about *truth!* Woe unto all free spirits who do not watch out against such magicians! Then it is over with their freedom: you teach us and lure us back into prisons. You old melancholy devil: out of your lament a bird call lures us; you are like those whose praise of chastity secretly invites to voluptuous delights."

Thus spoke the conscientious man; but the old magician looked around, enjoyed his triumph, and for its sake swallowed the annoyance caused him by the conscientious man. "Be still!" he said in a modest voice; "good songs want to resound well; after good songs one should long keep still. Thus do all these higher men. But perhaps you have understood very little of my song? In you there is little of a magic spirit."

"You praise me by distinguishing me from yourself," retorted the conscientious man. "Well then! But you others, what do I see? You are all still sitting there with lusting eyes: you free souls, where is your freedom gone? You are almost like men, it seems to me, who have long watched wicked, dancing, naked girls: your souls are dancing too. In you, you higher men, there must be more of what the magician calls his evil spirit of magic and deception: we must be different.

"And verily, we talked and thought together enough before Zarathustra returned home to his cave for me to know that we *are* different. We also seek different things up here, you and I. For I seek more *security,* that is why I came to Zarathustra. For he is the firmest tower and will today, when everything is tottering and all the earth is quaking. But you—when I see the eyes you make, it almost seems to me that you are seeking *more insecurity:* more thrills, more danger, more earthquakes. You desire, I should almost presume—forgive my presumption, you higher men—you desire the most wicked, most dangerous life, of which *I* am most afraid: the life of wild animals, woods, caves, steep mountains, and labyrinthian gorges. And it is not the leaders *out* of danger who appeal to you most, but those who induce you to leave all ways, the seducers. But even if such desire in you is real, it still seems impossible to me.

"For fear is the original and basic feeling of man; from fear everything is explicable, original sin and original virtue. From fear my own virture too has grown, and it is called: science. For the fear of wild animals, that was bred in man longest of all—including the animal he harbors inside himself and fears: Zarathustra calls it 'the inner beast.' Such long old fear, finally refined, spiritualized, spiritual—today, it seems to me, this is called *science.*"

Thus spoke the conscientious man; but Zarathustra, who was just coming back into his cave and had heard and guessed this last speech, threw a handful of roses at the conscientious man and laughed at his "truths." "What?" he cried. "What did I hear just now? Verily, it seems to me that you are a fool, or that I am one myself; and your 'truth' I simply reverse. For *fear*—that is our exception. But courage and adventure and pleasure in the uncertain, in the undared—*courage* seems to me man's whole prehistory. He envied the wildest, most courageous animals and robbed all their virtues: only thus did he become man. *This* courage, finally refined, spiritualized, spiritual, this human courage with eagles' wings and serpents' wisdom—*that*, it seems to me, is today called—"

"*Zarathustra!*" all who were sitting together cried as with one mouth, and they raised a great laughter that rose above them like a heavy cloud. The magician too laughed and said cleverly: "Well then, he is gone, my evil spirit. And have I myself not warned you of him when I said that he was a deceiver, a spirit of lies and deceptions? Especially when he appears naked. But am *I* responsible for his wiles? Did *I* create him and the world? Well then, let us make up again and make merry! And although Zarathustra looks angry—look at him, he bears me a grudge—before night falls he will learn again to love me and laud me; he cannot live long without committing such follies. He loves his enemies; this art he understands best of all whom I have ever seen. But he takes revenge for this on his friends."

Thus spoke the old magician, and the higher men applauded him; so Zarathustra walked around and shook his friends' hands with malice and love—like one who has to make up for something and apologize. But when he reached the door of his cave, behold, he again felt a desire for the good air outside and for his animals—and he wanted to slip out.

AMONG DAUGHTERS OF THE WILDERNESS

1

"Do not go away!" said the wanderer who called himself Zarathustra's shadow. "Stay with us. Else our old musty depression might seize us again. Even now that old magician has given us a sample of his worst; and behold, that good pious pope there has tears in his eyes and has again embarked on the sea of melancholy. These kings may still put up a bold front, for of all of us here today they have learned this best. But if they had no witness, I wager that for them too the evil routine would resume—the evil routine of drifting clouds, of moist melancholy, of overcast skies, of stolen suns, of howling autumn winds—the evil routine of our own howling and cries of distress. Stay with us, O Zarathustra! There is much hidden misery here that desires to speak, much evening, much cloud, much musty air. You have nourished us with strong virile food and forceful maxims: do not let the feeble feminine spirits seize us again after dinner! You alone make the air around you strong and clear. Have I ever found such good air anywhere on earth as here in your cave? Many countries have I seen; my nose has learned to test and estimate many kinds of air: but in your cave my nostrils are tasting their greatest pleasure.

"Unless it were—unless it were—oh, forgive an old reminiscence! Forgive me an old afterdinner song that I once composed among daughters of the wilderness: for near them the air was equally good, bright, and oriental; never was I farther away from cloudy, moist, melancholy old Europe. In those days I loved such Oriental girls and other blue skies over which no clouds and thoughts hang. You would not believe how nicely they sat there when they were not dancing, deep but without thoughts, like little secrets, like beribboned riddles, like afterdinner nuts—colorful and strange, to be sure, but without clouds; riddles that let themselves be guessed: for such girls I then thought out an afterdinner psalm."

Thus spoke the wanderer and shadow; and before anyone answered him he had already seized the harp of the old magician, crossed his legs, and looked around, composed and wise. But with his nostrils he drew in the air slowly and questioningly, as one tastes the new foreign air in a new country. Then he began to sing with a kind of roar.

2

Wilderness grows: woe unto him that harbors wildernesses!

Hah! Solemn!
Indeed solemn!
A worthy beginning.
African solemnity.
Worthy of a lion
Or of a moral howling monkey—
But nothing for you,
My most charming friends
At whose feet I,
As the first
European under palm trees,
Am allowed to sit. Selah.

Wonderful surely!
There I sit now,
Near the wilderness and already
So far from the wilderness again,

And in no way wild or wanton—
Merely swallowed
By this smallest oasis:
It just opened, yawning,
Its lovely orifice,
The most fragrant of all little mouths—
And I fell in
And down and through—among you,
My most charming friends. Selah.

Hail, hail to that whale
If he let his guest be that
Well off! You do understand
My scholarly allusion?
Hail to his belly
If it was as
Lovely an oasis belly
As this—which, however, I should certainly doubt;
After all, I come from Europe
Which is more doubt-addicted than all
Elderly married women.
May God improve it!
Amen.

There I sit now,
In this smallest oasis,
Just like a date,
Brown, sweet through, oozing gold, lusting
For the round mouth of a girl,
But even more for girlish,
Ice-cold, snow-white, cutting
Incisors: for after these
Pants the heart of all hot dates. Selah.

Similar, all-too-similar

To the aforementioned fruit,
I lie here, sniffed at
And played about
By little winged bugs—
Also by still smaller,
More foolish, more sinful
Wishes and notions—
Enveloped by you,
Silent and foreboding
Girl-cats,
Dudu and Suleika—
Ensphinxed, to crowd many
Feelings into one word
(May God forgive me
This linguistic sin!)—
I sit here, sniffing the best air,
Verily, paradise air,
Bright, light air, golden-striped,
As good air as ever
Fell down from the moon—
Whether by chance
Or did it happen from prankishness?
As the old poets relate.
I, being a doubter, however, should
Doubt it; after all, I come
From Europe
Which is more doubt-addicted than all
Elderly married women.
May God improve it!
Amen.

Drinking this most beautiful air,
My nostrils distended like cups,
Without future, without reminiscences,
Thus I sit here, O

My most charming friends,
And am watching the palm tree
As, like a dancer, she curves
And swerves and sways above her hips—
One does it too, if one watches long.
Like a dancer who, as it would seem to me,
Has stood too long, dangerously long
Always, always only on one little leg.
She has forgotten, it would seem to me,
The other leg.
In vain, at least,
I looked for the missed
Twin jewel—
Namely, the other leg—
In the holy proximity
Of her most lovely, most delicate
Flimsy little fan-, flutter-, and tinsel-skirt.
Yes, if you would, my beautiful friends,
Believe me wholly:
She has lost it!
It is gone!
Forever gone!
The other leg!
What a shame about that lovely other leg!
Where may it be staying and mourning, forsaken?
The lonely leg?
Perhaps afraid of a
Grim, blond, curly
Lion monster? Or even now
Gnawed away, nibbled away—
Misery, alas! alas! Nibbled away! Selah.

Oh do not weep,
Soft hearts!
Do not weep, you

Date hearts! Milk bosoms!
You little licorice
Heart-sacs!
Weep no more,
Pale Dudu!
Be a man, Suleika! Courage! Courage!
Or should
Something invigorating, heart-invigorating
Be appropriate here?
An unctuous maxim?
A solemn exhortation?

Hah! Come up, dignity!
Virtuous dignity! European dignity!
Blow, blow again,
Bellows of virtue!
Hah!
Once more roar,
Roar morally!
As a moral lion
Roar before the daughters of the wilderness!
For virtuous howling,
My most charming girls,
Is more than anything else
European fervor, European ravenous hunger.
And there I stand even now
As a European;
I cannot do else; God help me!
Amen.

Wilderness grows: woe unto him that harbors wilder-
nesses!

THE AWAKENING

1

After the song of the wanderer and shadow, the cave all at once became full of noise and laughter; and since all of the assembled guests talked at the same time and even the ass, thus encouraged, would no longer remain silent, Zarathustra was overcome by a slight aversion and by scorn for his company, although he enjoyed their gaiety. For this seemed to him a sign of convalescence. So he slipped out into the open and talked to his animals.

"Where is their distress now?" he said, and immediately he felt relief from his own little annoyance. "Up here with me, it seems, they have unlearned crying in distress. Although unfortunately not yet crying in general." And Zarathustra covered up his ears, for just then the Yeah-Yuh of the ass was strangely blended with the jubilating noise of these higher men.

"They are merry," he began again, "and, who knows? perhaps at their host's expense. And if they learned to laugh from me, it still is not *my* laughter that they have learned. But what does it matter? They are old people, convalescing in their own way, laughing in their own way; my ears have suffered worse things without becoming grumpy. This day represents a triumph: he is even now retreating, he is fleeing, *the spirit of gravity,* my old archenemy. How happily this day wants to end after beginning so badly and gravely. And it *wants* to end. Even now evening is approaching: he is riding over the sea, this good rider. How the blessed one, returning home, sways in his crimson saddle! The sky looks clear, the world lies deep: O all you strange visitors, living with me is well worth while!"

Thus spoke Zarathustra. And again the clamor and laughter of the higher men came to him from the cave, so he began again: "They are biting, my bait is working: from them too their enemy retreats, the spirit of gravity. Even now they have learned to laugh at themselves: do I hear right? My virile nourishment, the savor and strength of my words, are taking effect; and verily, I did not feed them bloating vegetables, but warriors' nourishment, conquerors' nourishment: I wakened new desires. New hopes throb in their arms and legs; their hearts stretch out. They are finding new words, soon their spirit will breathe prankishness. Such nourishment, to be sure, may not be suitable for children or for nostalgic old and young little females. Their entrails are persuaded in a different way; I am not their physician and teacher.

"Nausea is retreating from these higher men. Well then! That is my triumph. In my realm they feel safe, all stupid shame runs away, they unburden themselves. They unburden their hearts, good hours come back to them, they celebrate and chew the cud: they become grateful. *This* I take to be the best sign: they become grateful. Not much longer, and they will think up festivals and put up monuments to their old friends. They are convalescing!" Thus spoke Zarathustra gaily to his heart, and he looked out; but his animals pressed close to him and respected his happiness and his silence.

2

Suddenly, however, Zarathustra's ears were startled; for the cave which had so far been full of noise and laughter suddenly became deathly still, while his nose perceived a pleasant smoke and incense, as of burning pine cones. "What is going on? What are they doing?"

he asked himself, and he stole to the entrance to watch his guests, unnoticed. But, wonder upon wonder! What did he have to see with his own eyes?

"They have all become pious again, they are praying, they are mad!" he said, and he was amazed beyond measure. And indeed, all these higher men, the two kings, the retired pope, the wicked magician, the voluntary beggar, the wanderer and shadow, the old soothsayer, the conscientious in spirit, and the ugliest man— they were all kneeling like children and devout little old women and adoring the ass. And just then the ugliest man began to gurgle and snort as if something inexpressible wanted to get out of him; but when he really found words, behold, it was a pious, strange litany to glorify the adored and censed ass. And this litany went thus:

Amen! And praise and honor and wisdom and thanks and glory and strength be to our god, from everlasting to everlasting!

But the ass brayed: Yea-Yuh.

He carries our burden, he took upon himself the form of a servant, he is patient of heart and never says No; and whoever loves his God, chastises him.

But the ass brayed: Yea-Yuh.

He does not speak, except he always says Yea to the world he created: thus he praises his world. It is his cleverness that does not speak: thus he is rarely found to be wrong.

But the ass brayed: Yea-Yuh.

Plain-looking, he walks through the world. Gray is the body color in which he shrouds his virtue. If he has spirit, he hides it; but everybody believes in his long ears.

But the ass brayed: Yea-Yuh

What hidden wisdom it is that he has long ears and only says Yea and never No! Has he not created the world in his own image, namely, as stupid as possible?

But the ass brayed: Yea-Yuh.

You walk on straight and crooked paths; it matters little to you what seems straight or crooked to us men. Beyond good and evil is your kingdom. It is your innocence not to know what innocence is.

But the ass brayed: Yea-Yuh.

Behold how you push none away from you, not the beggars nor the kings. Little children you let come unto you, and when sinners entice you, you simply say Yea-Yuh.

But the ass brayed: Yea-Yuh.

You love she-asses and fresh figs; you do not despise food. A thistle tickles your heart if you happen to be hungry. In this lies the wisdom of a god.

But the ass brayed: Yea-Yuh.

THE ASS FESTIVAL

1

At this point of the litany Zarathustra could no longer control himself and himself shouted Yea-Yuh, even louder than the ass, and he jumped right into the middle of his guests, who had gone mad. "But what are you doing there, children of men?" he cried as he pulled the praying men up from the floor. "Alas, if someone other than Zarathustra had watched you! Everyone would judge that with your new faith you were the worst blasphemers or the most foolish of all little old women.

"And you too, old pope, how do you reconcile this with yourself that you adore an ass in this way as a god?"

"O Zarathustra," replied the pope, "forgive me, but

in what pertains to God I am even more enlightened than you. And that is proper. Better to adore God in this form than in no form at all! Think about this maxim, my noble friend: you will quickly see that there is wisdom in such a maxim.

"He who said, 'God is a spirit,' took the biggest step and leap to disbelief that anybody has yet taken on earth: such a saying can hardly be redressed on earth. My old heart leaps and jumps that there is still something on earth to adore. Forgive, O Zarathustra, an old pious pope's heart!"

"And you," Zarathustra said to the wanderer and shadow, "you call and consider yourself a free spirit? And you go in for such idolatry and popery? You are behaving even more wickedly, verily, than with your wicked brown girls, you wicked new believer."

"Wickedly enough," replied the wanderer and shadow; "you are right: but is it my fault? The old god lives again, Zarathustra, you may say what you will. It is all the fault of the ugliest man: he has awakened him again. And when he says that he once killed him—in the case of gods *death* is always a mere prejudice."

"And you," said Zarathustra, "you wicked old magician, what have you done? Who should henceforth believe in you in this free age, if *you* believe in such theo-asininities? It was a stupidity that you committed; how could you, you clever one, commit such a stupidity?"

"O Zarathustra," replied the clever magician, "you are right, it was a stupidity; and it was hard enough for me too."

"And you of all people," said Zarathustra to the conscientious in spirit, "consider with a finger alongside your nose: doesn't anything here go against your conscience? Is your spirit not too clean for such praying and the haze of these canters?"

"There is something in this," replied the conscientious man, placing a finger alongside his nose; "there is something in this spectacle that even pleases my conscience. Perhaps I may not believe in God; but it is certain that God seems relatively most credible to me in this form. God is supposed to be eternal, according to the witness of the most pious: whoever has that much time, takes his time. As slowly and as stupidly as possible: in *this* way, one like that can still get very far.

"And whoever has too much spirit might well grow foolishly fond of stupidity and folly itself. Think about yourself, O Zarathustra! You yourself—verily, over-abundance and wisdom could easily turn you too into an ass. Is not the perfect sage fond of walking on the most crooked ways? The evidence shows this, O Zarathustra—and *you* are the evidence."

"And you yourself, finally," said Zarathustra, turning to the ugliest man, who still lay on the ground, and raising his arm toward the ass (for he was offering him wine to drink). "Speak, you inexpressible one, what have you done? You seem changed to me, your eyes are glowing, the cloak of the sublime lies over your ugliness: *what* have you done? Is it true what they say, that you have wakened him again? And why? Had he not been killed and finished for a reason? You yourself seem awakened to me: what have you done? Why did *you* revert? Why did *you* convert yourself? Speak, you inexpressible one!"

"O Zarathustra," replied the ugliest man, "you are a rogue! Whether that one *still* lives or lives again or is thoroughly dead—which of the two of us knows that best? I ask you. But one thing I do know; it was from you yourself that I learned it once, O Zarathustra: whoever would kill most thoroughly, *laughs*.

" 'Not by wrath does one kill, but by laughter'—thus

you once spoke. O Zarathustra, you hidden one, you annihilator without wrath, you dangerous saint—you are a rogue!"

2

But then it happened that Zarathustra, amazed at all these roguish answers, jumped back toward the door of his cave and, turning against all his guests, cried out with a strong voice:

"O you roguish fools, all of you, you jesters! Why do you dissemble and hide before me? How all your hearts wriggled with pleasure and malice that at last you had become again as little children, that is, pious; that at last you did again what children do, namely, prayed, folded your hands, and said, 'Dear God!' But now leave *this* nursery, my own cave, where all childishness is at home today! Cool your hot children's prankishness and the noise of your hearts out there!

"To be sure: except ye become as little children, ye shall not enter into *that* kingdom of heaven. (And Zarathustra pointed upward with his hands.) But we have no wish whatever to enter into the kingdom of heaven: we have become men—*so we want the earth.*"

3

And yet once more Zarathustra began to speak. "O my new friends," he said, "you strange higher men, how well I like you now since you have become gay again. Verily, you have all blossomed; it seems to me such flowers as you are require *new festivals*, a little brave nonsense, some divine service and ass festival, some old gay fool of a Zarathustra, a roaring wind that blows your souls bright.

"Do not forget this night and this ass festival, you higher men. *This* you invented when you were with me and I take that for a good sign: such things are invented only by convalescents.

"And when you celebrate it again, this ass festival, do it for your own sakes, and also do it for my sake. And in remembrance of *me*."

Thus spoke Zarathustra.

THE DRUNKEN SONG

1

Meanwhile one after the other had stepped out into the open and into the cool reflective night; but Zarathustra himself led the ugliest man by the hand to show him his night-world and the big round moon and the silvery waterfalls near his cave. There they stood together at last in silence, old people all of them, but with comforted brave hearts and secretly amazed at feeling so well on this earth; but the secrecy of the night came closer and closer to their hearts. And again Zarathustra thought to himself: "How well I like them now, these higher men!" But he did not say it out loud, for he respected their happiness and their silence.

But then that happened which, on that whole long amazing day, was the most amazing thing of all: the ugliest man began once more and for the last time to gurgle and snort, and when he found words, behold, a question jumped out of his mouth, round and clean, a good, deep, clear question, which moved the hearts of all who were listening to him.

"My friends, all of you," said the ugliest man, "what do you think? For the sake of this day, *I* am for the first time satisfied that I have lived my whole life. And that I attest so much is still not enough for me. Living on earth is worth while: one day, one festival with Zarathustra, taught me to love the earth.

" 'Was *that* life?' I want to say to death. 'Well then! Once more!'

"My friends, what do you think? Do you not want to say to death as I do: Was *that* life? For Zarathustra's sake! Well then! Once more!"

Thus spoke the ugliest man; but it was not long before midnight. And what do you suppose happened then? As soon as the higher men had heard his question they all at once became conscious of how they had changed and convalesced and to whom they owed this: then they jumped toward Zarathustra to thank, revere, caress him, and kiss his hands, each according to his own manner; and some were laughing and some were crying. But the old soothsayer was dancing with joy; and even if, as some of the chroniclers think, he was full of sweet wine, he was certainly still fuller of the sweetness of life and he had renounced all weariness. There are even some who relate that the ass danced too, and that it had not been for nothing that the ugliest man had given him wine to drink before. Now it may have been so or otherwise; and if the ass really did not dance that night, yet greater and stranger wonders occurred than the dancing of an ass would have been. In short, as the proverb of Zarathustra says: "What does it matter?"

2

But when this happened to the ugliest man, Zarathustra stood there like a drunkard: his eyes grew dim, his tongue failed, his feet stumbled. And who could guess what thoughts were then running over Zarathustra's soul? But his spirit fled visibly and flew ahead and was in remote distances and, as it were, "on a high ridge," as it is written, "between two seas, wandering like a heavy cloud between past and future." But as the higher men held him in their arms, he gradually recovered his senses to some extent and with his hands warded off the throng of the revering and worried; yet he did not speak. All at once, however, he turned his head quickly, for he seemed to be hearing something. Then he put one finger to his mouth and said, "*Come!*"

And presently it became quiet and secret around; but from the depth the sound of a bell came up slowly. Zarathustra and the higher men listened for it; but then he put one finger to his mouth another time and said again, "*Come! Come! Midnight approaches.*" And his voice had changed. But still he did not stir from his place. Then it grew still more quiet and secret, and everything listened, even the ass and Zarathustra's animals of honor, the eagle and the serpent, as well as Zarathustra's cave and the big cool moon and the night itself. But Zarathustra put his hand to his mouth, for the third time and said, "*Come! Come! Let us wander now! The hour has come: let us wander into the night!*"

3

You higher men, midnight approaches: I want to whisper something to you as that old bell whispers it into my ears—as secretly, as terribly, as cordially as that midnight bell, which has experienced more than any man, says it to me. It has counted the beats even of your fathers' hearts and smarts. Alas! Alas! How it sighs! How it laughs in a dream! Old deep, deep midnight!

Still! Still! Here things are heard that by day may not become loud; but now in the cool air, when all the noise of your hearts too has become still—now it speaks, now it is heard, now it steals into nocturnal, overawake souls. Alas! Alas! How it sighs! How it laughs in a dream!

Do you not hear how it speaks secretly, terribly, cordially to *you*—the old deep, deep midnight?

O man, take care!

4

Woe unto me! Where is time gone? Have I not sunk into deep wells? The world sleeps. Alas! Alas! The dog howls, the moon shines. Sooner would I die, die rather than tell you what my midnight heart thinks now.

Now I have died. It is gone. Spider, what do you spin around me? Do you want blood? Alas! Alas! The dew falls, the hour approaches—the hour when I shiver and freeze, which asks and asks and asks, "Who has heart enough for it? Who shall be the lord of the earth? Who will say: thus shall you run, you big and little rivers!" The hour approaches: O man, you higher man, take care! This speech is for delicate ears, for your ears: *What does the deep midnight declare?*

5

I am carried away, my soul dances. Day's work! Day's work! Who shall be the lord of the earth?

The moon is cool, the wind is silent. Alas! Alas! Have you flown high enough yet? You have danced: but a leg is no wing. You good dancers, now all pleasure is gone: wine has become lees, every cup has become brittle, the tombs stammer. You did not fly high enough: now the tombs stammer, "Redeem the dead! Why does the night last so long? Does not the moon make us drunken?"

You higher men, redeem the tombs, awaken the corpses! Alas, why does the worm still burrow? The hour approaches, approaches; the bell hums, the heart still rattles, the deathwatch, the heart-worm still burrows. Alas! Alas! *The world is deep.*

6

Sweet lyre! Sweet lyre! I love your sound, your drunken ranunculus' croaking. From how long ago, from how far away your sound comes to me, from the distant ponds of love! You old bell, you sweet lyre! Every pain has torn into your heart, father-pain, fathers' pain, fore-fathers' pain; your speech grew ripe—ripe as golden autumn and afternoon, as my hermit's heart; now you say: the world itself has grown ripe, the grape is turning brown, now it would die, die of happiness. You higher men, do you not smell it? A smell is secretly welling up, a fragrance and smell of eternity, a rose-blessed, brown gold-wine fragrance of old happiness, of the drunken happiness of dying at midnight, that sings: the world is deep, *deeper than day had been aware.*

7

Leave me! Leave me! I am too pure for you. Do not touch me! Did not my world become perfect just now? My skin is too pure for your hands. Leave me, you stupid, boorish, dumb day! Is not the midnight brighter? The purest shall be the lords of the earth—the most un-known, the strongest, the midnight souls who are brighter and deeper than any day.

O day, you grope for me? You seek my happiness? I seem rich to you, lonely, a treasure pit, a gold-chamber? O world, you want me? Am I worldly to you? Am I spiritual to you? Am I godlike to you? But day and world, you are too ponderous; have cleverer hands, reach for deeper happiness, for deeper unhappiness, reach for any god, do not reach for me: my unhappiness, my happiness is deep, you strange day, but I am yet no god, no god's hell: *deep is its woe.*

8

God's woe is deeper, you strange world! Reach for God's woe, not for me! What am I? a drunken sweet lyre—a midnight lyre, an ominous bell-frog that nobody understands but that *must* speak, before the deaf, you higher men. For you do not understand me!

Gone! Gone! O youth! O noon! O afternoon! Now evening has come and night and midnight—the dog howls, the wind: is not the wind a dog? It whines, it yelps, it howls. Alas! Alas! How the midnight sighs! How it laughs, how it rattles and wheezes!

How she speaks soberly now, this drunken poetess! Perhaps she overdrank her drunkenness? She became overawake? She ruminates? Her woe she ruminates in a dream, the old deep midnight, and even more her joy. For joy, even if woe is deep, *joy is deeper yet than agony.*

9

You vine! Why do you praise me? Did I not cut you? I am cruel, you bleed; what does your praise of my drunken cruelty mean?

"What has become perfect, all that is ripe—wants to die"—thus you speak. Blessed, blessed be the vintager's knife! But all that is unripe wants to live: woe!

Woe entreats: Go! Away, woe! But all that suffers wants to live, that it may become ripe and joyous and longing—longing for what is farther, higher, brighter. "I want heirs"—thus speaks all that suffers; "I want children, I do not want *myself*."

Joy, however, does not want heirs, or children—joy wants itself, wants eternity, wants recurrence, wants everything eternally the same.

Woe says, "Break, bleed, heart! Wander, leg! Wing,

fly! Get on! Up! Pain!" Well then, old heart: *Woe implores, "Go!"*

10

You higher men, what do you think? Am I a soothsayer? A dreamer? A drunkard? An interpreter of dreams? A midnight bell? A drop of dew? A haze and fragrance of eternity? Do you not hear it? Do you not smell it? Just now my world became perfect; midnight too is noon; pain too is a joy; curses too are a blessing; night too is a sun—go away or you will learn: a sage too is a fool.

Have you ever said Yes to a single joy? O my friends, then you said Yes too to *all* woe. All things are entangled, ensnared, enamored; if ever you wanted one thing twice, if ever you said, "You please me, happiness! Abide, moment!" then you wanted *all* back. All anew, all eternally, all entangled, ensnared, enamored—oh, then you *loved* the world. Eternal ones, love it eternally and evermore; and to woe too, you say: go, but return! *For all joy wants—eternity.*

11

All joy wants the eternity of all things, wants honey, wants lees, wants drunken midnight, wants tombs, wants tomb-tears' comfort, wants gilded evening glow.

What does joy not want? It is thirstier, more cordial, hungrier, more terrible, more secret than all woe; it wants *itself*, it bites into *itself*, the ring's will strives in it; it wants love, it wants hatred, it is overrich, gives, throws away, begs that one might take it, thanks the taker, it would like to be hated; so rich is joy that it thirsts for woe, for hell, for hatred, for disgrace, for the cripple, for *world*—this world, oh, you know it!

You higher men, for you it longs, joy, the intractable

blessed one—for your woe, you failures. All eternal joy longs for failures. For all joy wants itself, hence it also wants agony. O happiness, O pain! Oh, break, heart! You higher men, do learn this, joy wants eternity. Joy wants the eternity of *all* things, *wants deep, wants deep eternity.*

12

Have you now learned my song? Have you guessed its intent? Well then, you higher men, sing me now my round. Now you yourselves sing me the song whose name is "Once More" and whose meaning is "into all eternity"—sing, you higher men, Zarathustra's round!

> O man, take care!
> What does the deep midnight declare?
> "I was asleep—
> From a deep dream I woke and swear:
> The world is deep,
> Deeper than day had been aware.
> Deep is its woe;
> Joy—deeper yet than agony:
> Woe implores: Go!
> But all joy wants eternity—
> Wants deep, wants deep eternity."

THE SIGN

In the morning after this night, Zarathustra jumped up from his resting place, girded his loins, and came out of his cave glowing and strong as a morning sun that comes out of dark mountains.

"You great star," he said as he had said once before, "you deep eye of happiness, what would your happiness be had you not those for whom you shine? And if they stayed in their chambers even after you had awakened and come and given and distributed, how angry would your proud shame be!

"Well then, they still sleep, these higher men, while *I* am awake: *these* are not my proper companions. It is not for them that I wait here in my mountains. I want to go to my work, to my day: but they do not understand the signs of my morning; my stride is for them no summons to awaken. They still sleep in my cave, their dream still drinks of my drunken songs. The ear that listens for *me*, the *heedful* ear is lacking in their limbs."

Thus had Zarathustra spoken to his heart when the sun rose; then he looked questioning into the height, for he heard the sharp cry of his eagle above him. "Well then!" he cried back; "thus it pleases and suits me. My animals are awake, for I am awake. My eagle is awake and honors the sun as I do. With eagle talons he grasps for the new light. You are the right animals for me; I love you. But I still lack the right men."

Thus spoke Zarathustra. But then it happened that he suddenly heard himself surrounded as by innumerable swarming and fluttering birds: but the whirring of so many wings and the thronging about his head were so great that he closed his eyes. And verily, like a cloud it came over him, like a cloud of arrows that empties itself over a new enemy. But behold, here it was a cloud of love, and over a new friend.

"What is happening to me?" thought Zarathustra in his surprised heart, and slowly he sat down on the big stone that lay near the exit of his cave. But as he reached out with his hands around and over and under himself, warding off the affectionate birds, behold, something stranger yet happened to him: for unwittingly he reached into a thick warm mane; and at the same time he heard a roar in front of him—a soft, long lion roar.

"The sign is at hand," said Zarathustra, and a change came over his heart. And indeed, as it became light before him, a mighty yellow animal lay at his feet and pressed its head against his knees and out of love did not want to let go of him, and acted like a dog that finds its old master again. But the doves were no less eager in their love than the lion; and whenever a dove slipped over the lion's nose, the lion shook its head and was amazed and laughed.

About all this Zarathustra spoke but a single sentence: *"My children are near, my children."* Then he became entirely silent. But his heart was loosed, and tears dropped from his eyes and fell on his hands. And he no longer heeded anything and sat there motionless, without warding off the animals any more. Then the doves flew about and sat on his shoulders and caressed his white hair and did not weary of tenderness and jubilation. But the strong lion kept licking up the tears that fell on Zarathustra's hands and roared and growled bashfully. Thus acted these animals.

All this lasted a long time, or a short time: for properly speaking, there is *no* time on earth for such things. But meanwhile the higher men in Zarathustra's cave had awakened and arranged themselves in a procession to meet Zarathustra and bid him good morning; for they had found when they awakened that he was no longer among them. But when they reached the door of the cave and the sound of their steps ran ahead of them, the lion started violently, turned away from Zarathustra suddenly, and jumped toward the cave, roaring savagely. But when the higher men heard it roar, they all cried out as with a single mouth, and they fled back and disappeared in a flash.

Zarathustra himself, however, dazed and strange, rose from his seat, looked around, stood there amazed, questioned his heart, reflected, and was alone. "What did I hear?" he finally said slowly; "what happened to me just now?" And presently memory came to him and with a single glance he grasped everything that had happened between yesterday and today. "Here is the stone," he said, stroking his beard, "where I sat yesterday morning; and here the soothsayer came to me, and here I first heard the cry which I heard just now, the great cry of distress.

"O you higher men, it was *your* distress that this old soothsayer prophesied to me yesterday morning; to your distress he wanted to seduce and tempt me. O Zarathustra, he said to me, I come to seduce you to your final sin.

"To my final sin?" shouted Zarathustra, and he laughed angrily at his own words; "*what* was it that was saved up for me as my final sin?"

And once more Zarathustra became absorbed in himself, and he sat down again on the big stone and reflected. Suddenly he jumped up. "Pity! Pity for the higher man!" he cried out, and his face changed to bronze. "Well then, *that* has had its time! My suffering and my pity for suffering—what does it matter? Am I concerned with *happiness?* I am concerned with my *work*.

"Well then! The lion came, my children are near, Zarathustra has ripened, my hour has come: this is *my* morning, *my* day is breaking: *rise now, rise, thou great noon!*"

Thus spoke Zarathustra, and he left his cave, glowing and strong as a morning sun that comes out of dark mountains.